Boston Theater Marathon XXII:
Special Zoom Edition Anthology

Boston Theater Marathon XXII: Special Zoom Edition Anthology

Edited by Kate Snodgrass

Kate Snodgrass, Artistic Director

A Smith and Kraus Book
P.O. Box 564, Hanover, NH 03755
Editorial 603.643.6431 To Order 1.877.668.8680
www.smithandkraus.com

Manufactured in the United States of America

ISBN: 978-1-57525-952-9

Typesetting and layout by: Darren Evans
Cover by: K. Alexa Mavromatis

For information about custom editions, special sales, education and corporate purchases, please contact Smith and Kraus at 603.643.6431

TABLE OF CONTENTS

INTRODUCTION

Dear Reader:

Welcome to the largest ten-minute play festival in the world—the Boston Theater Marathon. We began the BTM in 1999, and we celebrated our 22nd play marathon in April/May of 2020. We hope to continue stumping for new work and introducing playwrights to producers until all the theatres go dark, and, as you will see, even that didn't stop us this year!

I don't know what the future holds for the BTM, but I can tell you what happened *this* year, and I'll let the ten-minute plays you encounter in this volume speak for themselves.

Every year the BTM celebrates 50 New England playwrights and their plays, each work supported by a different New England theatre company. Five plays are performed each hour for 10 hours on one day in April—usually the day before the annual Boston footrace (the Boston Marathon). Our audiences come and go all day long—meeting friends for lunch or dinner but always returning to see their favorite writers, actors, directors, companies. Then at 10 p.m. sharp, we celebrate our hard work with food and drink and congratulations all around.

In this 22nd year of production, our pre-arranged date was Sunday, April 19—the day before Patriot's Day here in Boston when the traditional Boston Marathon is run. We planned to meet at Boston Playwrights' Theatre on Commonwealth Avenue in Boston and spend the day coming and going, watching five plays per hour, and lauding all of our favorite New England writers (yes, 50 of them).

This year, it was…different. Due to the escalating coronavirus pandemic, we were all quarantined in our homes, all the theatres were dark, and we were reminded viscerally of Shakespeare facing the plague(s) that savaged the population of London and closed all the ale houses, the bear-baitings, and the theatres (not so different from this Quarantine of 2020, minus the bears).

We decided immediately that, at the very least, our playwrights deserved publication—after all, if we couldn't come together to see the plays, reading them (and imagining them) was the next best thing. So here we are!

BUT…

What makes this Anthology so special is that we actually performed these plays on another platform—on the now ever-present video conferencing tool Zoom. Companies brought their playwrights and casts each day at noon to "read" and discuss their plays with the audience via chat. This happened every day (weekends included!) for almost seven weeks—one play per day—and it was addictive. Plus, not only could families all across the nation watch their Boston friends perform, but friends watched from all over the world!

What we lost in ticket sales, we made up for in donations to the charity the BTM supports—the Theatre Community Benevolent Fund, a non-profit organization helping to fund theatre artists and companies in need. The TCBF tells us that we helped to raise over $56,000 for our community. You see, everyone in the BTM benefits from the TCBF, and just by its existence, it gives us all hope for our futures.

It's *my* hope that you enjoy reading these wonderful ten-minute plays as much as we enjoyed bringing them to you (both on Zoom and in this anthology). They run the gamut of theatricality, from drama to comedy, from satire to social commentary, and all of them are from New England-area playwrights—the best in the business. Enjoy!

With warmest regards,

Kate Snodgrass

Kate Snodgrass, Artistic Director
Boston Theater Marathon

P. S. None of the above would have been possible without the generosity of the Boston University Center for the Humanities which has supported this event since 1999. Our deepest thanks to the BUCH!

TURBULENCE: A MONOLOGUE

by Rosanna Yamagiwa Alfaro

Rosanna Yamagiwa Alfaro has been produced by many theaters, including Huntington Theatre Company, Pan Asian Repertory, East West Players, Magic Theater, La MaMa, and the Edinburgh Fringe. She wrote and narrated the documentary *Japanese American Women: a Sense of Place*, directed by Leita Luchetti, for the Smithsonian Institution and PBS Seattle. She was a Huntington Playwriting Fellow (2010) and MCC Artist Fellow in Playwriting (2011). Her shorter plays have been produced in festivals like the Boston Theater Marathon and anthologized by Baker's Plays, Heinemann, Meriwether, PlaySource, Smith and Kraus, in vivo Ink, and Charta Books. A member of the Asian American Playwright Collective and MUTT: A Pack of Playwrights, she was just named to the inaugural group of 20 Cambridge Cultural Visionaries by the Cambridge Community Foundation. **Contact: alfaros@comcast.net**

Turbulence was sponsored by **Umbrella Stage Company**, Greater Boston's newest professional theater with a commitment to producing Bold, Daring, and Innovative work. Since 2008, The Umbrella has received over 125 award nominations including its back-to-back wins for Best Musical for *Big Fish* (2017) and *Parade* (2018). Its 2019-2020 season was staged in The Umbrella's newly constructed, multi-theater Performing Arts facility at 40 Stow Street, Concord. **TheUmbrellaStage.org**

Turbulence was presented on April 9, 2020, with the following creative team:

Directed by Danny Gidron
TRISH: Bobbie Steinbach
STAGE DIRECTIONS: Michelle Aguillon

(The ambient sound of an airplane in flight, punctuated by the wailing of a baby. The aisle of an airplane. Two rows, three seats on either side. TRISH (58) stands, drink in hand, regaling her fellow passengers.)

TRISH: The Metropole normally goes for 400 a night, but I got it on the internet for 300. 300 dollars, not pounds. That's unbelievable for London in the summer. Where is it? On Edgware Road, surrounded by little Arab cafes and men smoking their hookahs. Women too. Who said feminism isn't coming to that part of the world?

(The plane gives a shudder. Trish spills a little wine as she grabs on to the back of a seat.)

Sorry! Did I get that on your shirt? Lucky it's white wine, not red. Tell me, why is it, there's always turbulence when they're close to landing or when they're about to serve dinner? What was I saying? Oh yes. The Metropole. I loved it. The lobby was absolutely fantastic. Arabs and Americans and Russian hit men. No really. Last week they caught one staying at another Hilton. I said to Ralph, "Watch out! Your coffee might be spiked with radioactive polonium."

Anyway, there was so much life in that lobby: The Arab women, wrapped in black from top to toe, surrounded by their little children. The American families wandering through in their shorts, their hair dripping wet, fresh from the swimming pool. The large men sitting at the bar smoking and drinking—talking shady multi-million dollar deals, global politics, whatever. You couldn't tell whether they were Americans or Russians.

(The plane gives another jolt, but she manages to keep her wine from spilling.)

Ha! Didn't get you that time. *(//)* Anyway, our room at the Hilton? It was high up on the 25th floor, and even the elevator ride there was magical—you weren't aware it was moving, it was that fast and quiet. The Holiday Inn we stayed in a couple of years ago was just the opposite. It was p.c.—they only changed your towels if you left them on the floor. Well, the Hilton gave us stacks of towels of all shapes and sizes and changed them every day. The room was huge, and the bed was the biggest I've ever seen. I swear, Ralph and I could be at the opposite ends of the huge room and still be in the same bed. Not exactly like the cozy little beds of our misspent youth.

(She turns to speak to the flight attendant.) No, I'm not going to sit down. I don't want to sit in a seat that isn't mine. I have to get back to my own seat. My husband's probably missing me. *(to the passengers)* Well, not really. He's passed out. He hasn't slept a minute in the last three nights. He needs his rest. *(She casts a backward glance at the retreating flight attendant.)* I guess that showed her. In this world you have to give yourself importance because no one else does, believe me. *(indicating the flight attendant)* It's people like that who make you never want to travel.

Our week at the Hilton was one of those out of time/out of space experiences. We knew our vacation was over the moment the taxi pulled up to drive us to the airport. An Arab family was taking too long to load their stuff into a limo so our driver leaned on the horn and shouted out the window, "Scum! Animals! You don't belong here! Bloody eejits! Go back home and kill yourselves!" I was about to say that except for his accent he sounded just like an American, but Ralph gave me a little kick. Our luggage was in the trunk. We had a plane to catch. *(to flight attendant)* Are you back again? What? No, I told you before. I will not sit down!

(She swings her pocketbook at the flight attendant, and several small bottles of shampoo and cakes of soap fall to the floor. She gets on her hands and knees to pick them up.)

Now look what you made me do! *(to the passengers)* My precious little soaps from the Hilton. I have a collection of hotel soaps. *(to the flight attendant)* Would you stop standing there like an idiot and help me pick them up? Would you please let go of my arm?

(She is forcibly pulled to her feet. She climbs over two chairs to get to the window seat.)

(to the passenger) Sorry about that. I nearly landed in your lap. *(to the flight*

attendant) Yes, I will buckle myself in, but don't hold me accountable for my husband's actions when he wakes up and doesn't find me by his side. *(to the passenger)* Thank God, she's moved on! Have you ever seen such rudeness? *(/)* At least it wasn't as bad as the time we were flying back from Japan, and the necklace Ralph gave me snapped and the pearls rolled everywhere. Mikimoto pearls. That was 25 years ago. Back then we had no money, but Ralph bought me anything my little heart desired.

These days Ralph's got a lot on his mind. When he's not sleeping he's on red alert. He had a dream last night in that huge bed at the Hilton. He dreamt the FBI boarded the plane when we landed at Logan and took him away in handcuffs. Something like that actually happened to someone last week when we landed at Gatwick. The plane had come to a stop, but they told everyone to remain seated. Three men in suits got on board and firmly and quietly told this poor man to stand up. *(/)* No, he seemed very ordinary—he didn't look like a bomb thrower in a turban or anything. He could have peed in his pants, he was so scared. They surrounded him, two men in back of him and one in front, and escorted him off the plane.

I should be sitting with my husband. Suppose something happens... I wonder what they do with the wife in a case like that? Would they let me go with him? Would I feel someone's hand on my head as I got into the car?

Those large men sitting at the bar every night at the Hilton—you know, the ones that could have been Americans or Russians? Well, one of them was my husband. Last night he was so drunk he actually wanted to tell me what they had been talking about—that's a first in all the years we've been together. And you know what I said? I said, "Don't tell me now. I've waited all these years for you to talk to me and tell me what you were up to, and you wouldn't say anything. Don't tell me now. Please don't implicate me now."

I can't believe what got into me. I felt awful. *(/)* Life goes by so fast. How old are you? Twenty-two? Wait till you've been married thirty years. Honey, no matter how smart you are, you have no idea what life's got in store for you.

(She turns away to collect herself, then looks out the window.)

Just look at that view! It's a little like seeing the world from the 25th floor of the Hilton. I used to like the aisle seat so I could get to the toilet without having to climb over someone. But these days I prefer the window seat. Boston landings are spectacular—the way they swoop over the coastline, the way they tilt back and forth so you see the water first through the windows on one side of the plane, then the other.

Everything's fine until they lower the landing gear. Your ears pop, your stomach rises to your throat, then, bang, the plane hits the tarmac, just when you were half hoping it was going to belly flop in the water and sink down, down, down, like a stone, straight to the bottom of the sea.

(end of play)

UNAPOLOGETIC

by Andrea Aptecker

Andrea Aptecker, a playwright from Cambridge, Massachusetts, serves on the Board of Directors of Playwrights' Platform and is a member of the Dramatists Guild of America. Her plays and monologues have been performed across the United States and in Europe. Recent plays by Andrea include *You Can Bake!* (Taphouse Theatre, Shelter In Place, A Quarantined New Play Festival 2020), *Vendetta* (Playwrights' Platform Festival 2020), *PDA* (Kibo Productions Amplify Showcase of New Work by Women Artists, Theatro Technis, London 2019), and *Beyond Our Desires* (Fresh Ink Theatre Mad Dash 24-Hour Play Festival, the Lyric Stage, Boston 2019). Her new short film is a documentary (In The Darkroom, 2020). You can read her plays on the New Play Exchange: **newplayexchange.org/users/42328/andrea-aptecker** and contact her at: **aptecker@yahoo.com**

Unapologetic was sponsored by **The Lyric Stage Company of Boston** (with Matt Chapuran/Executive Director; Courtney O'Connor/Artistic Director), which produces and presents live theatre in Greater Boston with an intimate approach that promotes inclusivity and connection. The Lyric Stage leads an effort to integrate live theater and theater education into the lives of all residents of greater Boston. Established in 1974, and in residence at 140 Clarendon Street since 1991, the Lyric Stage is Boston's oldest resident theatre company, producing a seven-show season which ranges in theatrical genres including classic Broadway-style musicals, new plays, and established classics. The Lyric Stage is the recipient of 41 Elliot Norton Awards and 69 Independent Reviewers of New England (IRNE) Awards. In 2019, the Lyric Stage consolidated with City Stage Co. and now reaches over 65,000 students and families each year with its educational performances and workshops, including over 800 annual performances at the Children's Museum of Boston, and its work in the Boston Public Schools. **www.lyricstage.com**

Unapologetic was presented on April 8, 2020, with the following creative team:

Directed by Courtney O'Connor
BRYNN: Kat Murphy O'Connor
MARIAN: Katherine C. Shaver
STAGE DIRECTIONS: Matt Chapuran

CHARACTERS:

BRYNN (f) Self-assured. (She speaks the French words in italics with flourish). 35 or older.

MARIAN (f) A baker. A sweet, delightful person. 25 or older.

A slash in dialogue (/) indicates when the next person begins speaking.

(The dining room or kitchen of an apartment. BRYNN is seated at a table with a spoon and small bowl of chocolate mousse before her. Another bowl of mousse

and spoon also rests on the table, along with two tea towels. MARIAN stands beside the table, looking on in anticipation.)

BRYNN: Here goes nothing.

MARIAN *(smiles sweetly)*: Yes.

(BRYNN lifts the bowl and sniffs.)

I didn't poison it.

(MARIAN laughs shyly and awkwardly.)

(BRYNN takes a taste. Beat. She places her spoon down.)

BRYNN: Well. *(beat)* It is quite a rich chocolate mousse.

MARIAN *(hopeful)*: Yes. *(beat)* I'm so glad you could come by. I've been looking forward to it.

BRYNN: Anything for a neighbor, I always say. You're a step up from the last girl. Men coming and going at all hours. She wasn't alluring. Quite garish. Some boys like that.

(beat)

MARIAN: Would you like a cup of tea?

BRYNN: Marian dear, about your mousse—what brand chocolate did you use?

MARIAN: Oh! I meant to use Valrhona chocolate, but couldn't find it, so I settled on Ghiradelli—chocolate, two eggs, two egg yolks…

BRYNN: Butter?

MARIAN: No. Heavy cream.

BRYNN: Julia Child used butter.

MARIAN: Oh yes, / but it's …

BRYNN: And the sugar…?

MARIAN: Light brown sugar.

BRYNN: Not white?

MARIAN: Brown sugar has a delicate, subtle sweetness.

BRYNN: No flavoring?

MARIAN: Grand Marnier. I should have used more. I didn't want it to be boozy…

BRYNN: Orange zest?

MARIAN: I'm afraid not.

BRYNN: But surely...well...*(beat)* Zest would be infinitely better. Would give it pizazz. You know what I mean?

MARIAN: Yes, yes of course. I'm a fool. I thought it would overpower it if I used zest AND Grand Marnier. I wanted the chocolate to come through.

BRYNN: Nothing comes through. What recipe is it?

MARIAN: I started with the back of *Cook's Country* magazine, and then discovered a recipe from an old issue of *Gourmet*, and combined it with a Fanny Farmer recipe, circa 1979...

BRYNN: How industrious.

MARIAN: I made mousse every night for a month, with different flavors, extracts, alcohol, fruit compotes, whipped cream, egg yolks, egg whites, mascarpone—my co-workers love me. *(smiles shyly)* They've been my taste testers.

BRYNN: Marian—it's lifeless.

MARIAN: Ah. *(MARIAN sits, shaken.)* I had so hoped...

BRYNN: Listen to me. I studied in Paris. Larry and I went to every *patisserie* and tasted every *Crème Brulee* and *macaron* in every *arrondissement* in Paris. Do you know how many arrondissements there are? Twenty. That's right.

MARIAN: Oh, wow. That's impressive.

BRYNN: It's a miracle I have the waistline I do. Larry says I can eat like a horse and still retain my girlish figure. *(beat)* Have you been to France?

MARIAN: Gosh, no. It would be a dream.

BRYNN: Never?? What about Europe? Been to Europe?

MARIAN: No.

BRYNN: The Balkans?

MARIAN: Balkans? *(trails off uncertainly)* Do people go to...?

BRYNN: Not even the Balkans. Well.

MARIAN: I was in Canada once. My mother had family there.

BRYNN: Who's from *Canada*? Nobody's from Canada these days.

(BRYNN inspects the mousse.) Perhaps it's your technique. How did you incorporate the cream with the chocolate?

MARIAN: I whipped the eggs and yolks with the sugar and folded the / cream....

BRYNN: No, no, no. I know mousse. This is not French mousse.

MARIAN: It's American mousse. It's better!

BRYNN: *C'est sacrilege*!

MARIAN: I just thought it would / be...

BRYNN: That's your problem, dear. Stop thinking. No disrespect, but if a Parisian ate this, they would *(hesitates)*...vomit. It's the unvarnished truth. They would vomit all over your Target tea towels.

MARIAN: My mother made these towels. Not Target.

BRYNN: Oops, sorry. The pattern looks...I thought it was mass produced.

(MARIAN picks up a tea towel and looks at it.)

It is airy, your mousse. I give you that. You've whipped it decently. It has proper texture.

MARIAN: Thank you.

BRYNN: But still, texture won't save it. Well. I have to be going.

MARIAN: So soon? Would you like coffee or an aperitif?

BRYNN: Not if it's anything like your mousse. I don't want diarrhea. (*beat*) I don't mean to offend. I studied food and wine in Paris for six months. I became immersed in every aspect of culture. I know a *magnifique* dessert when I see one. Your dessert is pedestrian—*inferieur* if you will.

(BRYNN begins to exit to the door. Marian follows.)

MARIAN (*gets up her gumption*): I think you're wrong.

BRYNN: Come again?

MARIAN: Taste it. Go ahead.

BRYNN: Thank you. I already have.

MARIAN: I said taste it. You're mistaken.

BRYNN: My palate is impeccable. Look. I came here as a friend. I'm sorry if you're upset.

MARIAN: No, you're not.

(BRYNN gives her a look.)

BRYNN: I get paid to write restaurant reviews. It's what I do, sweetheart.

MARIAN: They don't pay you. You do it for free.

BRYNN *(bristles)*: They pay my meals. All my expenses. You know what. I tried to do something nice and this is the thanks I get.

MARIAN: I see. I understand.

BRYNN: I'm glad you understand. *(to herself)* Never do a favor for a friend. No good deed…

MARIAN: Thank you for coming.

BRYNN: Food isn't your calling. Try something else. Maybe cleaning—that's all the rage now. Teaching slobs how to declutter. Or office work. It's easy. But not cooking, not dessert, and definitely not mousse. I'm truly sorry, but it was a travesty. I'm relieved I didn't keel over from food poisoning.

MARIAN: Me too.

BRYNN: I can only do me. When I'm asked for my expertise, I speak the UNAPOLOGETIC truth. You should try it sometime. Stop being wishy washy and grow some balls. *(beat)* I must run. *Au Revoir.*

(BRYNN starts for the door and then stops abruptly.)

Oh no, I've been an absolute beast. I forgot all about your mother. She passed away recently, didn't she? *(MARIAN nods.)* My deepest condolences. You must feel like hell. It's not easy to lose a mother, especially when there's no one else…your mother's tea towels are very pretty. Really, they are. You poor thing.

(BRYNN impulsively goes to hug MARIAN. It's an awkward hug. MARIAN doesn't know how to respond at first—and then her arms circle around BRYNN—she applies pressure until she's pressing BRYNN too hard. BRYNN struggles, MARIAN's hands go around BRYNN's neck. Muffled noises escape BRYNN. After what seems like a long time with the two women clenched together in silent battle, BRYNN finally crumbles to the floor, dead. MARIAN looks down at her friend, stunned for a moment.)

(pause)

MARIAN: You must try the mousse. I'm certain you'll have a change of heart.

(MARIAN takes the bowl of mousse and bends down to BRYNN. She brings the mousse to BRYNN's lifeless lips and feeds her.)

Oh, look at you. You've made a mess of yourself.

(MARIAN takes her mother's tea towel and wipes BRYNN's lips.)

There now. Much better.

(MARIAN rises.)

This has been a productive evening. *(to BRYNN's lifeless body.)* You're right as always. It's better to be unapologetic.

(end of play)

The orange chocolate mousse recipe used for this play can be found at Cook's Country: **www.cookscountry.com**

A CALL TO MOM

by Taylor Badoyen

Originally from Las Vegas, Nevada, **Taylor Badoyen** is fairly new to the Boston theater scene. She graduated from Boston College in 2019 with a BA in both Theatre and English. She considers herself a jack-of-all-trades theatre artist, with experience in multiple design fields, stage management, carpentry, electrics work, puppetry, and of course, playwriting. In 2018, Taylor had her one-act play *The Things We Do* produced at Boston College as part of their theatre season. *A Call to Mom* is the first of Taylor's ten-minute plays to be produced, and she is grateful to have had this opportunity. **Contact: taylor.badoyen@gmail.com**

A Call to Mom was sponsored by **Playwrights' Platform** (with Greg Hovanesian, President), one of the country's oldest continuously operating cooperatives of playwrights, directors, and resident actors, now in its 48th year. With membership available to New England playwrights wherever they are in their careers, the Platform helps develop new plays by providing readings with actors throughout the year and producing an annual Festival of New Plays. Visit **playwrightsplatform.org** or find us on Facebook, Instagram and Twitter to learn more about upcoming Platform readings and events.

A Call to Mom was presented on April 7, 2020, with the following creative team:

Directed by Katie Suchyta
JO: Adjovi A. Koene
BELLA: Tiffany Santiago

CHARACTERS.

JO—Female, Age 21, should be portrayed by an African American or mixed race woman

BELLA—Female, Age 21, should be portrayed by a woman of East Asian descent

(JO and BELLA's apartment. BELLA stands in the middle of the room with her phone in her hand. Her other arm is wrapped around her stomach. The look on her face is impossible to make out. The door opens and slams as JO enters carrying a bag of groceries.)

JO: They didn't have the tortilla chips you like but I got the ones that are shaped like little bowls. Thought it'd be a good substitute, and besides, if you don't eat 'em, I will… I also picked up some of that salsa that Señora Cruz makes. Thought I'd give a try. You remember Señora Cruz?

BELLA: Yeah.

JO: Sometimes, I still have nightmares about her pop quizzes—"Pluscua-mperfecto, clase!" But you gotta admit, the fact that I can still conjugate in the subjunctive is all thanks to her— *(JO notices that BELLA has not moved since JO entered.)* Hola?… Hello? Earth to Jo!

BELLA: What?

JO: You okay, dude?

BELLA: Um, not really.

JO: You wanna talk about it?

BELLA: I got a call today.

JO: What was it? Weird telemarketer?

BELLA: No. No it wasn't.

JO: Was it the guys at the lab? Did you get the position?

BELLA: No.

JO: You didn't get the position?

BELLA: No, I haven't even had the interview yet.

JO: So, it wasn't the lab?

BELLA: No.

JO: Was it…your doctor? Your dentist? Your vet?

BELLA: No it wasn't anything like that.

JO: Rich? Sheila? Dan? Krish? Your dad? Your mom?

BELLA: Jesus, no. Just—not them.

JO: So, what? Are you going to keep making me guess?

BELLA: No. I just—don't know how to talk about this.

JO: Well, start with the obvious. Did you know the person?

BELLA: No.

JO: Okay. And it wasn't a telemarketer or like some spam call?

BELLA: I told you that it wasn't.

JO: Right. Right. Well, you're going to have to help me out here.

BELLA: It was some girl.

JO: Oh, don't tell me it was Trinity. Bells, I told you to block her—

BELLA: No it wasn't Trinity. I wouldn't care if— No. It wasn't Trinity. It was just some girl. Some girl. She sounded young.

JO: Like our-age young or like five-year old young?

BELLA: Like maybe thirteen? Fourteen? I don't know.

JO: What'd she say then?

BELLA: She wanted her mom.

JO: What kind of thirteen year old wants their mom? When I was thirteen I was running around the mall with—

BELLA: Jo, I'm being serious. She must've called the wrong number because she kept saying "Mom, mom, mom," and— What if— Oh my god—

JO: Jesus. Bella, you okay?

BELLA: I just need to— I need to sit down.

JO: You need water or something? Hold on—*(JO goes to get BELLA a glass of water. She returns and gives the glass to BELLA.)* There. So this girl... Was she in trouble or something, Bella? *(BELLA nods.)* Bella, what'd she say?

BELLA: It was hard to tell at first. There was a bunch of static or white noise or something. Just noise. I was going to hang up but— But then I heard her crying.

JO: God. What did you say?

BELLA: I just said, "Hello?" And she must've heard because she started crying a little louder and— She was crying so much, Jo. I could hardly tell what she was saying but—

JO: Bella?

BELLA: "Mom, please help." She kept repeating that. "Mom, please help."

JO: Jeez. This is serious.

BELLA: I didn't need to tell you this, Jo. I'm sorry.

JO: No, no, this is okay. I mean us talking is okay— I don't mean— What happened?

BELLA: I don't want to bother you with this, really—

JO: Bella. Just tell me.

BELLA: She kept crying, but she—but then she said, "Mom. Please. I'm in the back of a van. I don't know where they're taking me. Mom, please."

(beat)

JO: What did you say?

BELLA: Nothing. I mean I tried to ask her name but it was too late—

JO: What? What happened to her?

BELLA: I don't know. The call got cut off there.

JO: Holy crap—please tell me you—

BELLA: I called the police.

JO: Thank god.

BELLA: But they were no help.

JO: But you told them everything, right?

BELLA: Yeah, but all I could give them was the phone number, what the girl said, and anything I could discern from the call.

JO: So what did the police say?

BELLA: They were like, "There's not much we can do." They said they'd try to ping the number or something but it didn't sound like they were too convinced they'd find anything.

JO: Did you try calling her?

BELLA: What?

JO: Like calling her back?

BELLA: I thought about it, but—

JO: But what?

BELLA: But what if she—whoever took her probably didn't know she had her phone right? So if I called her, what if that gave away her only chance at freedom? What if, by trying to be some type of savior, I actually doomed her?

JO: Fuck, you're right. Don't call her back.

BELLA: I did think about it though. I mean, I've spent the last two hours thinking about it.

JO: Well… I think you did the right thing. Calling the police, I mean.

BELLA: I could've done more for her.

JO: No, don't do this to yourself.

BELLA: No really.

JO: Bella, you said it yourself, the phone call got cut off.

BELLA: But before that, I had plenty of time to let her know I was listening. That someone was there for her. Can you imagine what she must have been thinking? She thought— She kept calling me— She said—

JO: Mom.

BELLA: Yeah. I just keep thinking, like, what if she isn't okay? What if she— What if she's dead now, Jo? What if that was the last chance she had to talk to anyone? What if the last time she heard her mom's voice wasn't actually her mom? It was just some college girl who thought she had shitty signal and the only thing she could think of to say was "Hello."

JO: Bells.

BELLA: Jo, she thought I was her mom.

JO: And you were.

BELLA: Shut up. Be serious.

JO: No, really. You were. For that brief moment, Bella, you were her mom. She needed someone to be there, to listen, to hear her and you did. You let her know that someone was listening. And then? You did the best thing you could do. You called the police and let them know that this girl was in trouble.

BELLA: Jo–

JO: On top of all of that, if she—and let us hope not—but if she is in extreme danger, then that one word from you is enough. That is confirmation enough that someone heard her cry for help. Be it from her mom or just some college girl— If anything, it might be like some small glimmer of hope that someone might come to her rescue. I don't know.

BELLA: You know, I'm normally real optimistic about this kind of stuff, but—hearing her like that, she was so scared. She sounded so young, Jo.

JO: Bella, there's nothing more you could've done.

BELLA: Sure.

JO: …My cousin, Kiana, used to call her Kiki, she was kidnapped when she was five. I was like seven or something.

BELLA: Jo, you never told me—

JO: Because I didn't need to. But now I do.

BELLA: What happened?

JO: They found her a couple of weeks later floating in the lake.

BELLA: No...

JO: They say she didn't suffer long. They think that she was probably dead within a week of being taken.

BELLA: I don't want to think about that—

JO: But you're already thinking about it. Despite what you're telling me, I know for a fact that you're blaming yourself for this. There is nothing more to be done.

BELLA: But I could have! I could have said something else!

JO: What would you have told her?

BELLA: That everything would be okay. That I would help her.

JO: And?

BELLA: And what?

JO: And how would that change anything?

BELLA: I don't know. She might have— I could— Ugh, I don't know. What's your point?

JO: That there's nothing else you can do. You just need to let go.

BELLA: How can you say that? How do you know that for sure?

JO: Because I was with Kiki when she was taken.

BELLA: Jo...

JO: We were in the front yard. Everyone else was in the backyard. Our dads were barbecuing together. I remember the smoke was bugging our eyes so we went inside. But then we got bored so she and I went out to the front yard. I remember our aunties were hanging out near the front door. Kiki and I went outside and started playing in the grass. We were talking and making up stories and then Kiki wanted to pick some dandelions. So we started picking dandelions. It became like a competition. We had nearly cleared the whole yard of those weeds, and then Kiki spotted a small cluster of them near the curb. That's where they got her. They just pulled up and took her. No one had a chance to do anything. No one even noticed until they heard me screaming for her.

BELLA: Jo...

JO: And I know that this might not be what you wanted to hear, but

I need you to know that sometimes things happen. Sometimes terrible things happen to those who don't deserve it. You can even be standing right next to someone and you can't do anything to stop it from happening… How do you imagine Jackie Kennedy felt?

BELLA: That's terrible, Jo.

JO: But seriously, she was right by his side. Right next to him when he got shot.

BELLA: I get it—

JO: You can't stop a bullet, Bells. And when you're seven, you can't stop a grown man. Bella, I know how torn up you are right now, trust me, but I need you to tell yourself that there is nothing more you could've done. You are maybe the most removed from this situation as you can be. You weren't near her in person, you don't know where she was taken from, you don't even know her name.

BELLA: But I'm the closest person to her right now, right? I'm probably the last person she was able to talk to or the last person to know that she was alive.

JO: Yes.

BELLA: So I'm not *removed*, okay? I am— This is very close to me, right now, Jo.

JO: Okay. I'm sorry I said that. You're not removed.

BELLA: Besides, you're the one who just told me that I was basically some type of pseudo-mom to her now. By letting her know I was there, I took on the role of mom. And are you going to tell me that a mom would just accept that there was nothing that she could've done?

JO: No, I'm not saying that.

BELLA: Oh man, I just thought—

JO: What?

BELLA: Do you think her mom knows?

JO: You don't know her name or where she's from—

BELLA: Her mom probably doesn't even know yet.

JO: Bella—

BELLA: She probably thinks her daughter is safe somewhere, or that she's just late coming home or something. Maybe she's pissed at her daughter for being late, but she doesn't know. She can't have known. She's mad for no reason when really she should be—

JO: Bella, stop.

BELLA: I can't know.

JO: Right.

BELLA: For all I know, this could have been a prank call.

JO: See, now that's just denial.

BELLA: But it makes it easier to think about.

JO: I know.

BELLA: When they found Kiki, what happened? I mean—how did you deal with that?

JO: I mean, like they say, grief manifests in different ways. Her parents had been convinced she would come back safely and to hear she had been dead for a few weeks—that just broke them. My parents were also torn up over the whole thing. They loved Kiki. Everyone did. I didn't really know how to imagine someone being dead. Like the concept of someone just no longer being there didn't connect. It took almost another year for me to fully acknowledge Kiki was dead. And then, as I got older, I began to realize how lucky I was and how easily things could have been the other way around I started to blame myself and I thought of all of the ways I might have been able to save her. But eventually, I realized that there was nothing I could have done. Once she was in that car— There was nothing I could've said or done to change her fate.

BELLA: My dad says that everyone gets dealt a hand in life. Your fate is dealt to you and you've gotta stick with it till the end.

JO: Some people get dealt bad hands.

BELLA: That's real fucked, Jo.

JO: But it's true right?

BELLA: I guess… Listen, thank you for telling me about Kiki. I really needed to hear that. And I'm sorry—

JO: Don't apologize—

BELLA: I hope this girl will be okay.

JO: Me too… You want some salsa?

BELLA: No. I'm okay.

JO: Okay. Let's save it for a happier occasion.

BELLA: Yeah.

JO: Are you hungry at all?

BELLA: Kind of.

JO: Tell you what, I'll go pick up some sushi down the street. My treat. Yamamoto's or Arigato Sushi?

BELLA: Yamamoto's. I got sick from the sashimi at Arigato.

JO: Yamamoto's it is. Anything else you want while I'm out?

BELLA: No. No, thank you.

JO: Okay. I'll be back soon alright?

BELLA: Stay safe.

JO: Will do.

(JO goes to leave but stops short of the door. JO turns around and pulls BELLA into a hug. They stay there a moment.)

BELLA: Thanks, Jo.

JO: I needed that too. Alright, be back soon. Don't eat the salsa while I'm gone.

(JO exits.)

(BELLA remains still for a moment before she picks up her phone. She stares at the screen. She dials a number or two before putting the phone back down. Another moment. BELLA picks up the phone again and dials a number. She puts the phone to her ear and waits.)

BELLA: Hello?… Hi!… Hey mom… Yes, I'm— I'm fine… No I don't need another care package— No, mom— Mom, I'm fine. I just wanted to talk with you. Missed you, that's all.

(end of play)

GLISSADE

by Richard Ballon

Glissade is **Richard Ballon**'s third work to be performed in the Boston Theater Marathon. Richard is a poet and playwright, who lives in Florence, MA. He has been a recipient of several grants from the Massachusetts Arts Council for his six-part miniseries, *Zephyr*, which aired on access television and garnered several awards. He was commissioned by Easthampton High School to create two dramatic works for LGBT youth. Richard's work has been performed in many cities, including NYC, Boston, Minneapolis, Baltimore, Chicago, Denver, Provincetown, Iowa City, Toronto, Calgary, and Montreal as well as further afield (London and Manchester UK). Richard is a member of the Dramatists Guild and has an MFA in Playwriting and Screenwriting from Lesley University. His collection of short plays, poems, and stories, *Enough of a Little to Know the All*, is available through Amazon and Leveller's Press. More can be found at **richardballon.com** or contact Richard at: **P. O. Box 1017, Amherst MA 01004-1017**

Glissade was sponsored by **Hub Theatre Company of Boston**. Now in its eighth season, Hub is the area's only theatre company with a "Pay-What-You-Can" ticket policy for every seat, every show, every time! Our goal is to cultivate a diverse audience spanning all ages, cultures, races, and socioeconomic levels by removing monetary barriers between our audiences and our art. Join us this this fall at First Church Boston for *The Waiting Room* by Lisa Loomer, directed by Bryn Boice (Friday, November 6th-Saturday, November 21st). To find out more, like us on Facebook, follow us on Twitter (**@HubTheatreBos**), and Instagram (**@hubtheatreboston**) or sign up for our mailing list at **www.hubtheatreboston.org**

Glissade was presented on April 6, 2020, with the following creative team:

Directed by Lauren Elias
BARBARA: Maureen Keiller
MEREDITH: Karen MacDonald

CHARACTERS:

BARBARA: Ballet instructor, 40 years old. Hair streaked with blonde highlights, full makeup in ballet shoes, leg warmers and a diaphanous top. While standing, she often takes fifth position unconsciously. She speaks as precisely as a pirouette.

MEREDITH: Successful realtor in casual business wear, slacks and matching jacket. She holds in her hand her cellphone as if to signal she's way too busy to be in just one place.

(Small "office" the kind you find tucked in a hallway next to a dilapidated couch at a community Ballet School with a couple of chairs and a desk. There's the lonely sound of solo piano accompanying a ballet class with an occasional adult voice counting. Time is the present. BARBARA is gathering papers from a desk and turns as MEREDITH enters.)

BARBARA: It's good of you to come in. I know how busy you are.

MEREDITH: Always good to have an excuse to take a break from the office.

BARBARA: Your market seems to be booming! That whole new development on King Street.

MEREDITH: That's at a standstill.

BARBARA: Again?

MEREDITH: Lawyers love to create conflict. It's what keeps them employed and meanwhile the people depending on the condos have sold their homes and are scrambling to find a place to live. The lawyers probably set up the whole delay.

BARBARA: My husband's a lawyer.

MEREDITH: Oh.

BARBARA: Divorce lawyer. I don't think he intentionally obstructs marriages.

MEREDITH: Point noted. *(beat)* So?

BARBARA: I'd like to talk to you about Sara?

MEREDITH: Cripes! I was at the school yesterday morning about this! She can't be on her cell phone in ballet class!

BARBARA: No. No. I have a bucket of water by the ballet bar that I tell them I'll use if I see a cell phone in the studio. Does the trick.

MEREDITH: Good. Nice to know there's one place she can focus.

BARBARA: She's spot on. I'd like her to take the lead in Swan Lake.

MEREDITH: Twelve doesn't seem a bit too young?

BARBARA: The older girls would probably throw out the Prince's back.

MEREDITH: Oh that's wonderful! You must have noticed she's been a little down since her cat died. This will be just the thing to give her a boost!

> *(MEREDITH's phone buzzes. She turns it on and quickly reads a text. Glances up, shrugs and holds it still on against her leg.)*

BARBARA: There's just a tiny problem.

MEREDITH: Those words don't usually fit in the same sentence. "Tiny. Problem."

BARBARA: A small thing, really. I'm sure you've noticed.

MEREDITH: Oh. Yes. Her acne. I think I can make an exception in this case and allow her to wear make up on stage at least.

BARBARA: I didn't know that may have been an issue.

MEREDITH: Those make up companies make a waste dump of our skin.

BARBARA: *(with a light laugh)* Then I must have died long ago.

MEREDITH: Some would say so. *(beat)* It was a joke, Barbara. I mean, you know, Ballet is so old world. It certainly isn't break dancing.

BARBARA: Break dancing went out decades ago.

MEREDITH: Guess I'm dating myself.

BARBARA: Because no one else will? *(beat)* A joke, Meredith. A joke.

MEREDITH: Okay. You have my permission for Sara to be the prima donna. Have you told her?

BARBARA: Not yet. Three of them have been rehearsing the role, I didn't want any of them to lose interest, just in case.

MEREDITH: In case what?

BARBARA: You must have noticed that in the last couple months she has gained some weight.

MEREDITH: I know, looks good on her, filling her out like a young woman. That wonderful transition, of course at the time it feels all awkward, but the ballet has given her the grace, the poise.

BARBARA: The poise looks wobbly when you're overweight.

MEREDITH: She looks great!

BARBARA: She shouldn't jiggle.

MEREDITH: What are Sports bras for? These kids burn off calories faster than we collect them.

BARBARA: She's six pounds overweight.

MEREDITH: We don't even own a bathroom scale! How do you know?

BARBARA: I weigh my students before class.

MEREDITH: Is that even legal?

BARBARA: My husband knew someone would ask that question.

MEREDITH: Of course, he would.

BARBARA: It's voluntary.

MEREDITH: Oh, is it?

BARBARA: I ask them to step on the scale. It's their choice.

MEREDITH: I hardly think an eleven or twelve-year-old realizes she has an option.

BARBARA: If you want Sara to have the role-

MEREDITH: Didn't you imply she was best for the role?

BARBARA: She needs to lose nine pounds.

MEREDITH: I'm sorry, didn't you just say *six*? She's thin as a piece of paper.

BARBARA: She may seem that way—

MEREDITH: I spend more time with her than you do!

BARBARA: With that busy job? I hardly think so. Nine pounds would be ideal, that way she has some wiggle room to maintain her ideal weight.

MEREDITH: So she can look like she just walked out of Auschwitz!

BARBARA: The reason ballet girls look so thin is because of the obesity epidemic in this country.

MEREDITH: You expect her to lose nine pounds in what? Two weeks?

BARBARA: Actually, one week would be ideal. There are safe ways to do so and other ways which are less so. I thought I would bring it to your attention. As we said before, it's all about choice. In my day, some of the girls had discovered less conventional ways to rid themselves of the creeping fat. Of course you may inspire her by losing some yourself and perhaps be a role model! There is a dietician I know who is reasonable and has worked with some film actors.

MEREDITH: I bet she cost a pretty penny.

BARBARA: You said business was booming! This is an incredible opportunity for your daughter.

MEREDITH: I knew it! I knew this school was a mistake! I should have followed my gut.

BARBARA: *(looking her over)* Looks like you are. *(beat)* But I can tell you've had some training, it's in your carriage. The ones who schlump are destined for kitchens but the poise forces people to at least open doors for us.

MEREDITH: It may teach us to walk, but it's hardly natural.

BARBARA: Why should it be? That is what makes it an art.

MEREDITH: I only brought her to this studio because she was so shy, and oddly those mirrors seem to help her, coax her out of herself. But I don't want her damaging her body.

BARBARA: Listen, I danced most of my life and when I took off my pointe shoes they were often filled with blood. Almost every toe has been broken, but that is the sacrifice. That is what carried me to my heights. But I do not teach pointe or choreograph with pointe, even in Swan Lake. I don't care that the critics call me Madame Flatfoot. I won't do that to my girls! And I also won't have them fluttering around a fat girl who has the talent but not the discipline to lose a few pounds.

MEREDITH: Beef up the boy, send him to the gym.

BARBARA: Sara is the best choice! She has been practicing the role along with two others, but you should see her! She glows! You can't want your daughter to look like a pigeon among butterflies. I need your commitment. Now. We have two weeks.

MEREDITH: This is ridiculous! I don't want to set her on a course toward an eating disorder! I can pull her out.

(MEREDITH's phone rings and continues to ring to the tune of Yankee Doodle Dandy.)

BARBARA: This may be the boost Sara needs to break that dreadful depression. At least she has stopped the cutting.

MEREDITH: What? What did you just say?

BARBARA: Cutting. *(MEREDITH turns her phone off and sits down.)* Oh. I thought you knew! But of course, you don't see her in tights. Her thighs, crisscrossed. But when I moved her into the main role it seems to have stopped.

MEREDITH: I had no idea.

BARBARA: That job of yours, of course, has been keeping you at all hours. Of course, it is your choice whether your child is happy or not. *(beat)* Let her dance the role of a lifetime, a memory she can return to for the rest of her life, without blood in her shoes. Here. Sit for a minute. I do need to know by today. What course to take. Here. Have a snickers bar. They are your favorite, aren't they?

(slow fade to blackout)

CAIN

by Alan Brody

Alan Brody is Professor Emeritus of Theater Arts at Massachusetts Institute of Technology. His play *Invention For Fathers and Sons* was the first winner of the annual Rosenthal Award at the Cincinnati Playhouse in the Park in 1989. It was subsequently produced at the American Jewish Theater in New York. *The Company of Angels* was the recipient of the 1990 Eisner Award from the Streisand Center for Jewish Culture in Los Angeles. It had its world premiere at the New Repertory Theater in Massachusetts in the spring of 1993. *The Housewives of Mannheim* premiered at the New Jersey Repertory and then went on to be produced at 59E59 in New York City. Three of his plays, *Five Scenes From Life*, *Greytop in Love*, and *One-on-One* were developed at the Missouri Repertory Theatre. Two of them were fully produced there. *Greytop in Love* was later produced at the Walnut Street Theatre starring Kim Hunter. *Operation Epsilon* had its world premiere at Central Square Theater in Cambridge. It was nominated for three Eliot Norton Awards and won the Independent Reviewers of New England Award for best play. **Contact: www.alanbrodyworks.com**

Cain was sponsored by **Underground Railway at Central Square Theater**, which creates live performance in the activist and collaborative spirit of its namesake, inspiring an expanded image of the possible. Through interdisciplinary inquiry and partnership, URT creates accessible theater of great beauty and social content–theater that challenges and delights, informs and celebrates. Through its productions and a constellation of education/outreach programs and special initiatives (including a model science/theater partnership - Catalyst Collaborative@MIT), URT activates commitments to cultivating local artists of all ages and to creating new work. Founded in Oberlin, Ohio, one of the stops on the Underground Railroad, URT toured nationally for thirty years before building Central Square Theater with The Nora. Current Projects: *Arts is Our Activism Online Series* (Summer/Fall 2020), *Ada and the Engine* by Lauren Gunderson and directed by Debra Wise (Jan. 2021, part of CST's Women & Science Festival), and *Angels in America (Millennium Approaches and Perestroika)* by Tony Kushner, a collaboration with Bedlam and directed by Eric Tucker (March-May, 2021). An ebook of the history of URT's first 25 years will come out in the summer of 2020: *Underground Railway Theater: Engine of Delight and Social Change.* **www.centralsquaretheater.org**

Cain was presented on April 22, 2020, with the following creative team:

Directed by Adam Zahler
Stage Manager: Catherine Giorgetti
CAIN: Adrian Peguero
ABEL: Daniel Rios

CHARACTERS:

ABEL—A shepherd in his thirties.

CAIN—A farmer, a few years older

> *(An empty space with just a suggestion that it is really a rocky sacrificial place. ABEL is kneeling in prayer next to large, smoking platter. CAIN appears with a platter filled with vegetables.)*

CAIN: You're here already *(ABEL signals him to be quiet while he prays.)* Sorry. *(He is silent but edgy. Finally...)* I got distracted. *(ABEL signals him again.)* Do I have to wait until the whole fucking lamb consumed? *(ABEL signals.)* Great crop this year. I was even able to put berries in my offering. I would offer you some, too, but I know you play by the rules. *(approaches to platter)* Fuck, that's going fast. Good breeze up here today. *(ABEL signals to be quiet.)* Turnips, radishes, potatoes, a lot of green stuff. I cleaned it off the best I could. Hard to get the dirt off some of these mothers. You know what I did before I brought them up here?

ABEL: Amen.

CAIN: All gone? *(ABEL shows him the empty platter.)* So you want to know?

ABEL: Know what?

CAIN: What I did before I came up here.

ABEL: You did something?

CAIN: I said.

ABEL: I was praying.

CAIN: I was looking at all this shit in the sacrificial platter and I realized it would look better if I arranged the turnips different. Actually made a ring of them around the potatoes and all this green stuff. And that made the whole thing looked more balanced. And then I realized that the sun was already a ways down in the sky so there were these great shadows all over the arrangement and that looked fucking great. I wished I had a stone and some kind of slab so that I could copy the arrangement, 'cause it looked so perfect. But I didn't. I couldn't find a slab. Or a stone. But you can see the real thing. Look at it. It's perfect.

ABEL: Only God is perfect.

CAIN: You always do that, Abel.

ABEL: What?

CAIN: *(imitating and mocking)* "Only God is perfect." Simp, simp. Fuck that.

ABEL: Not funny.

CAIN: Just lay off the goody-good-good shit. Do you want to see this or not? Before I burn it all up.

ABEL: I'm going to rest a bit.

CAIN: Just look at it, asshole!

ABEL: *(ABEL looks at the platter.)* Are those the best greens?

CAIN: That's all you've got to say?

ABEL: They look a little faded.

CAIN: I was going to use the freshest. But after I did the arrangement I thought these would look more realistic.

ABEL: I sacrificed my fattest lamb.

CAIN: That's because you're a fucking ass-kisser. I want my sacrifice to look interesting and. . . *(searches for the word)*

ABEL: *(mocking)* Perfect?

CAIN: *(finds it)* Beautiful!

ABEL: Vegetables can't be beautiful. Women are beautiful. Our mother is beautiful.

CAIN: You think I should sacrifice one of them?

ABEL: God isn't interested in beauty. He wants to see that you've given up something important to you.

CAIN: This *is* important to me.

ABEL: How is he supposed to know that?

CAIN I'll tell him when I'm praying

ABEL: He won't believe you.

CAIN: Why not?

ABEL: It's not your best crop.

CAIN: You really think God has a stick up His ass about "the best"?

ABEL: It shows you're sincere.

CAIN: I'm sincere. This is my best.

ABEL: What did you do with the freshest greens?

CAIN: I saved them for mother.

ABEL: You're going to make God angry. He's going to see what you do and he's going to be very angry.

CAIN: Well, fuck Him then.

ABEL: Be careful.

CAIN: Are you worried about me? I'm the older one here. I can take care of myself. Everyone else takes care of you. You know why? Because they want to keep you a child.

ABEL: I'm not a child anymore.

CAIN: And they're going to make sure you stay that way.

ABEL: Why are you saying that?

CAIN: You can't see what's right in front of you. Ever since they moved here from where they were before they've had to farm the land and raise their own meat and then they had me and then you, and they've gotten more and more tired looking.

ABEL: So what does that have to do with keeping me a child?

CAIN: Schmuck! It's because if you grow up, they grow old. And die.

(ABEL considers this.)

ABEL: So what am I supposed to do about that?

CAIN: Stop being such a sanctimonious God-fearing prick. Look around you. Think. See what's there instead of what everyone tells you is there. Grow up in spite of them.

ABEL: God doesn't want me to stay a child.

CAIN: God wants us all to stay children.

ABEL: You're just jealous because I'm the favorite.

CAIN: And you'll stay that way if you keep kissing ass and showing the world what a good boy you are.

ABEL: You want me to be like you.

CAIN: No, you asshole. Like *you*, whoever that is. Just be a man.

ABEL: Why don't you offer up your sacrifice?

CAIN: 'Cause you're distracting me.

ABEL: I'm just lying here.

CAIN: All right, then.

(He goes about setting up the offering and lights it. He takes a praying position. ABEL watches him.)

ABEL: You're not really praying.

CAIN: How do you know?

ABEL: I can tell. You want to keep the beautiful arrangement for yourself. Leave it around so you can look at it whenever you want.

CAIN: *(still in his praying position)* I tried to share it with you.

ABEL: What would I do with it? Feed it to my sheep?

CAIN: You make me want to put my fist through your fucking mouth.

ABEL: God sees right through you.

(CAIN makes the same gesture to keep quiet that ABEL used when he was praying.)

God hates you. *(CAIN keeps praying.)* He knows you're faking it. *(CAIN keeps praying.)* He's not taking your sacrifice. Look at it. It's just a little charred at the edges. He's not consuming it at all. Just enough to spoil your beautiful arrangement.

(CAIN looks at his platter. Picks it up. Burns his hand, then finds something to cover his hand and picks it up again, to look at it.)

CAIN: It's gone.

ABEL: You're a loser, Cain.

CAIN: And you're a fucking cunt.

(He throws the platter at ABEL. ABEL ducks out of the way and lets it splatter to the ground.)

ABEL: God hates you. And He's taught me to hate you just like Him!

(He leaps at CAIN and tries to choke him. They fight.)

CAIN: *(as they fight)* I'll tear your smug face apart!

ABEL: I'm God's chosen! I'm father's chosen! I was mother's chosen before I was even born!

CAIN: And I have nothing! I'm free!

(CAIN picks up the platter and brings it down hard on ABEL.)

ABEL: Oh God! Avenge me!

(CAIN hits him again and ABEL crumples. CAIN retrieves the platter and looks at it.)

CAIN: It was so beautiful. *(looking up)* Was that all you could do. Destroy the beauty I made? Were you fucking jealous? Good. I hear You. But You can't touch me now. For an instant, when I saw my work on this platter, and saw that it was beautiful, I knew what it felt like to be You. But when You rejected it, I felt nothing but contempt. You didn't even see it for the act of love that it was. Then I knew you were blind to anything you hadn't made Yourself. And jealous. And then I knew I didn't need You. But I knew You needed me, because without belief like my brother's and without obedience like his from everyone, You're nothing. And as long as I'm able to live I'll keep making beauty out of everything I find, and sharing what I've made with whatever brothers like me that I find in the world away from here. Because I'm sure there are others like me. Out there. Somewhere. And I'll embrace them all.

(He stands looking up, waiting to see if there will be an answer and knowing that there won't be. Lights down slowly while he waits.)

(end)

LYING IN STATE

by Robert Brustein

Robert Brustein is an American theatrical critic, producer, playwright, writer, and educator. He founded both the Yale Repertory Theatre in New Haven, Connecticut, and the American Repertory Theatre in Cambridge, Massachusetts, where he remains a creative consultant. He was the theatre critic for The New Republic, and he comments on politics for the Huffington Post. Brustein is a senior research fellow at Harvard University and was a distinguished scholar in residence at Suffolk University in Boston. He was elected to the American Academy of Arts and Letters in 1999 and in 2002 was inducted into the American Theater Hall of Fame. In 2003, he served as a senior fellow with the National Arts Journalism Program at Columbia University and in 2004 and 2005 was a senior fellow at the National Endowment for the Arts' Arts Journalism Institute in Theatre and Musical Theatre at the University of Southern California. In 2010, he was awarded the National Medal of Arts by President Barack Obama. **Contact: brustein@fas.harvard.edu**

CHARACTERS:

TRUMP: The President Donald J. Trump

FUNERAL DIRECTOR: Male, 50s, Caucasian

(A funeral home, a coffin. FUNERAL DIRECTOR enters. He sees TRUMP lying in one of his coffins.)

FUNERAL DIRECTOR: President Trump. What an honor. But what are you doing in my funeral parlor?

TRUMP: I'm where?

FUNERAL DIRECTOR: Occupying a big casket in one of my funeral parlors.

TRUMP: What the hell am I doing there?

FUNERAL DIRECTOR: Beats me. Unless you're a corpse. I assume you're still breathing?

TRUMP: If you believe my last physical exam.

FUNERAL DIRECTOR: No problems whatsoever?

TRUMP: *(nodding 'No')* Only a few pectoral disorders.

FUNERAL DIRECTOR: Pecker disorders?

TRUMP: Pectoral. Chest cough.

(TRUMP coughs.)

FUNERAL DIRECTOR: Oh, that's a relief.

TRUMP: I don't have pecker disorders, as you might have learned from my first three wives....

FUNERAL DIRECTOR: Okay.

TRUMP: Not to mention all the other crotches I have grabbed in my time.

FUNERAL DIRECTOR: A few of which have already testified to that fact.

TRUMP: Bitchy tattletales....worse than the FBI.

FUNERAL DIRECTOR: You grab FBI crotches?

TRUMP: No, I mean the FBI is just as disgusting—a real squalid disease—along with the CIA.

FUNERAL DIRECTOR: The FBI and CIA are squalid diseases?

TRUMP: The most disgusting, unpatriotic, contagious, shithole pestilences in insect history.

FUNERAL DIRECTOR: But the FBI and CIA represent law and order, don't they?

TRUMP: Not to me, they don't.

FUNERAL DIRECTOR: Why not?

TRUMP: Because they don't like me.

FUNERAL DIRECTOR: How do you know that?

TRUMP: Have you read the Mueller report recently?

FUNERAL DIRECTOR: Too long for me. Have you?

TRUMP: I had one of my flunkies read it. He made it up to the first 1345 pages. But he wore himself out trying to sum it up.

FUNERAL DIRECTOR: Well, that's no reason for lying in a funeral parlor.

TRUMP: You're right. It's those other turds should be lying in a funeral parlor, not me.

FUNERAL DIRECTOR: You want them all silenced?

TRUMP: They want to silence me.

FUNERAL DIRECTOR: Who do you mean?

TRUMP: I mean all those left-wing Commie bastards who want me dead.

They haven't succeeded yet, have they?

(TRUMP feels himself all over.)

FUNERAL DIRECTOR: Not that I can tell. And I'm an expert on the subject.

TRUMP: That's a relief.

FUNERAL DIRECTOR: I'm glad.

TRUMP: Me, too. *(pause)* But if I'm not dead, why does everyone tell me I'm lying in state?

FUNERAL DIRECTOR: I think they may have something else in mind.

TRUMP: Like what, for instance?

FUNERAL DIRECTOR: Like, eh...

TRUMP: Go on.

FUNERAL DIRECTOR: You haven't by any chance told any of your bigger whoppers lately, have you?

TRUMP: *(proudly)* Fifteen thousand by recent count.

FUNERAL DIRECTOR: And you still hold an official position in this nation?

TRUMP: At present, at great personal sacrifice, I occupy the office of President of the United States...

FUNERAL DIRECTOR: Yes, you do.

TRUMP: The most prescient and preternatural President in existing presidential history, representing millions of Americans, of countless stripes and religions all over the world.

FUNERAL DIRECTOR: Then it's self-evident.

TRUMP: What is? That I preside preeminently over all the 48 states?

FUNERAL DIRECTOR: No, that all 50 states are united in representing opposition to your presiding presidentially over them.

TRUMP: So how did I ever get elected, tell me that?

FUNERAL DIRECTOR: That's a question a lot of people have been asking themselves lately.

TRUMP: Name a few hundred.

FUNERAL DIRECTOR: For one, it's rumored, your wife Melania.

TRUMP: You're not referring to that damned libel about her refusing to move into the White House?

FUNERAL DIRECTOR: Well, I do hear a few worries expressed about that.

TRUMP: She just hasn't found the right interior decorator yet. And she hates the cooking.

FUNERAL DIRECTOR: Oh, that explains it.

TRUMP: Also, you know, she can't stand the color white.

FUNERAL DIRECTOR: She wants to change the color of The White House?

TRUMP: Don't quote me, but it's a possibility. Her favorite color has always been ruby red.

FUNERAL DIRECTOR: The Ruby Red White House?

TRUMP: How does that sound?

FUNERAL DIRECTOR: A bit garish.

TRUMP: Garishness doesn't seem to have affected my popularity.

FUNERAL DIRECTOR: No, that seems pretty solid.

TRUMP: Maybe voters are united in gratitude over the way I have pumped up the stock market and built that Mexican wall to keep out illegal aliens.

FUNERAL DIRECTOR: Don't count on Wall Street. Not with the Corona virus on the loose.

TRUMP: Corona? So cigars are a virus now?

FUNERAL DIRECTOR: Only if you inhale them.

TRUMP: Sounds like I can count on the support of your coffins, too.

FUNERAL DIRECTOR: What do you think you're getting at this very moment?

TRUMP: How do you mean?

FUNERAL DIRECTOR: You're presently occupying one of my caskets, aren't you, lying in state?

TRUMP: And it is providing support for me, indeed. By God, you're right. Well, then, I want your promise to never close this coffin lid on me again.

FUNERAL DIRECTOR: Of course…

TRUMP: Unless I'm taking a nap.

FUNERAL DIRECTOR: I will, if you'll promise to cut back on some of your biggest whoppers.

TRUMP: I could reduce the published estimates attending my inauguration a bit.

FUNERAL DIRECTOR: Then you can keep sleeping. Or lying. Cozily. In state.

TRUMP: What's the alternative?

FUNERAL DIRECTOR: Lying shamelessly on your own two feet.

TRUMP: You gotta deal.

(They shake hands.)

(blackout)

BLACK JESUS

by Fabiola R. Decius

Fabiola R. Decius' plays include *Haiti Chérie*, *Final Verdict*, *In Sync*, *Ice Cream Bucket List*, *Date Night Surprise*, *Chicksmas*, *Draped in History*, *Free Before Eleven*, *Consent*, *Bus Stop*, *Man of the House*, and *Fighting Forgiveness*, which have been produced and/or developed at Bryn Mawr College, Lesley University, the Boston Public Library, Our Voices Festival, Fade to Black Festival, the Roxbury Repertory Theater, Controlled Kaos Productions, the Office of War Information (Bureau of Theater), the Boston Center for the Arts Plaza Theatres, and the Boston Neighborhood Network channel. Fabiola was a Creative City grant recipient through the New England Foundation for the Arts in 2018 and founded Teens WRITE (Writing, Reading, and Investigating Theater Everywhere), which is a program for teenagers to write, revise, cast, direct, and produce original plays culminating in a ten-minute play festival. Although writing is Fabiola's first passion, she often acts as well. She is currently a high school theater arts educator in the city of Boston. Fabiola graduated from Bryn Mawr College with a Bachelor of Arts and received a Master of Fine Arts in Creative Writing at Lesley University in Stage and Screen Writing. **newplayexchange.org/users/6305/fabiola-r-decius**

Black Jesus was sponsored by **Company One Theatre**, which builds community at the intersection of art and social change. Founded in 1998, Company One has situated itself as a home for social justice and artistic excellence by connecting Boston's diverse communities through live performance, the development of new plays and playwrights, arts education, and public engagement programming. By establishing a dedicated space for marginalized and alternative narratives to thrive and working with partners and collaborators across the city, Company One has become a local leader in the ongoing conversations that continue to define the era of social change in contemporary America. **www.companyone.org**

Black Jesus was presented on May 14, 2020, with the following creative team:

Directed by Elena Morris
WAYNE: Hubens 'Bobby' Cius
JESUS: Brandon G. Green
ANGEL: Rachel Cognata

CHARACTERS:

WAYNE—Black male, late teens

JESUS—Black male, thirty-three

ANGEL—Female voiceover

ANGEL (V.O.): "The hairs of his head were white, like white wool, like snow. His eyes were like a flame of fire, his feet were like burnished bronze, refined in a furnace, and his voice was like the roar of many waters."—Revelation 1:14-15

(WAYNE lies on the ground in a deep sleep. He is in a fetus position in front

of an entrance to a white gate, which leads to heaven. Seconds later, JESUS, dressed in a white robe, walks towards the gate. He sees WAYNE laying on the ground and sweeps his hands over WAYNE's body without actually touching him. WAYNE jolts up as if struck by electricity.)

WAYNE: What the-? Who are you?

JESUS: Who do they say I am?

WAYNE: Who does who-what? Where am I?

JESUS: You're at the gates of heaven.

(JESUS tries to help WAYNE up, but WAYNE backs away from him and gets up on his own.)

WAYNE: This is a joke, right?

JESUS: I wouldn't say that.

(pause)

WAYNE: Okay, so let me get this straight. If I'm at the gates of heaven, you are what, one of Jesus' disciples?

JESUS: Not quite.

WAYNE: So who are you?

JESUS: "I am who I am."

WAYNE: What is that supposed to be, a riddle?

JESUS: Son, you grew up in the church. You should be familiar with that scripture.

WAYNE: Well, I'm not.

JESUS: Okay Wayne, that's fine. Let's talk about why you're here.

WAYNE: Not just yet. First, you need to tell me who you— Wait, how do you know my name?

JESUS: "Do not fear, for I have redeemed you; I have summoned you by name; you are mine."

(pause)

WAYNE: Are you really who I think you are?

JESUS: "I am the way and the truth and the life. No one comes to—"

WAYNE: The Father except through me".

(silence)

WAYNE: Whoa. Jesus, is that really you?

(WAYNE tries to touch JESUS, and JESUS lets him.)

JESUS: If you believe.

WAYNE: I believe.

(pause)

I'm a little confused, but I believe.

JESUS: What are you confused about?

WAYNE: You're black?

JESUS: I am?

WAYNE: You didn't know? Are there no mirrors in heaven?

JESUS: Everything is in heaven.

(pause)

WAYNE: I always thought you were white.

JESUS: Is that how you pictured me?

WAYNE: That's how most of the world pictures you.

JESUS: What about you?

WAYNE: I always knew you were black.

JESUS: Well, there you have it.

(pause)

WAYNE: Wait, so you're black because I believed you were black.

JESUS: Exactly.

WAYNE: So if I believed you were white, you'd be white?

JESUS: I am whatever you believe I am.

WAYNE: So you could be an elephant if I believed that?

JESUS: Let's not get overboard, Wayne.

WAYNE *(chuckles)*: It's good to know you have a sense of humor, Jesus.

JESUS: I have to. If I didn't, you people would drive me crazy.

WAYNE: "You people". Can you say that?

JESUS: I'm black, remember?

WAYNE: Right.

(silence)

So what am I doing here? *(touching himself...)* Am I dead?

JESUS: Do you remember where you were or what you were doing right before you came here?

WAYNE: Not really.

JESUS: Do you need me to remind you?

(JESUS pulls a phone out of his robe pocket.)

WAYNE: Jesus, you have a smartphone?

JESUS: Wayne, my Father invented the smartphone.

(JESUS shows WAYNE a video.)

WAYNE: Hey, that's me!

JESUS: And what are you doing? *(pause)* Wayne, what are you doing here in this video?

WAYNE: Something I shouldn't be doing.

JESUS: So why are you doing it?

WAYNE: I don't know, peer pressure, I guess.

JESUS: And what would your mom say if she knew you were doing this?

WAYNE: She'd kill me.

JESUS: And where would you go if that were to happen?

WAYNE: Wait, did my mom kill me? Is that why I'm here? I'm dead? Oh my God! I'm too young to die. I have my whole life ahead of me, and I'm still a vir—

(WAYNE starts freaking out, but JESUS comforts him.)

JESUS: Wayne, relax. You're not dead.

WAYNE: Then why am I here?

JESUS: Because I love you and I want for you to be in paradise with me.

WAYNE: Right now?

JESUS: Not now. When the timing is right.

WAYNE: And when will that be?

JESUS: Like I'm going to tell you.

WAYNE: Okay, can you at least tell me this? Will I die a virgin?

JESUS: There's nothing wrong with dying a virgin?

WAYNE: Wait, were you a virgin when you— Nevermind. I'm sorry I brought that up.

JESUS: There's no need for you to apologize. I died willingly on that cross for you, your mom, your dad, your brother, and countless others.

WAYNE: Did you really know what you were doing?

JESUS: Yes.

WAYNE: And did you believe that you'd be brought back to life?

JESUS: I trust my Father.

(silence)

WAYNE: So if I'm not dead, what am I doing here?

JESUS: Let me show you.

(JESUS shows WAYNE something else on his phone.)

WAYNE: Who's that?

JESUS: It's you, can't you tell?

(pause)

WAYNE: What am I doing in the hospital, and why is my face and body bandaged up like that?

JESUS: You're in a coma. This video is a few hours after the first video I showed you.

WAYNE: What happened?

JESUS: Some people's idea of karma is what happened.

WAYNE: I was jumped by Hakim and his crew?

JESUS: You were hit by a car and almost ran over, and yes, by Hakim and his disciples.

WAYNE: What? How could you let that happen?

JESUS: I didn't let it happen, not fully at least.

(pause)

You see, you could've gotten run over by that car after it hit you, but one of my angels stepped in and grabbed you in the nick of time. And, that's the only reason why you're in the hospital in a coma instead of in a coffin dead.

WAYNE: So I'm currently in a coma?

JESUS: Yes.

WAYNE: So how am I standing here talking to you?

JESUS: Your physical body is in that coma, but your spiritual body is here with me.

(silence)

WAYNE: Is my spiritual body going to go back?

JESUS: I can't answer that question, Wayne. That's up to you.

WAYNE: I want it to. I mean, this looks real nice, the set up you have here. I hear people singing, and it smells good, but I'm not ready to be here yet. I have a lot I want to do.

JESUS: I agree. There's a lot I *need* you to do as well.

WAYNE: Like what?

JESUS: Stop being stupid for one.

WAYNE: Did you just call me stupid?

JESUS: If that's how you interpreted it.

WAYNE: Never mind how I interpreted it. I need you not to speak in parables and be straight up with me. What do I need to do?

JESUS: I need you to remember me.

WAYNE: That's it?

JESUS: That's it.

WAYNE: I can do that.

JESUS: Great, I guess I'll see you on the other side then.

WAYNE: On the other side of what?

JESUS: These gates?

WAYNE: Jesus wait, can I take a picture with you? I want to be able to remember this moment.

JESUS: You will.

WAYNE: I would still like a picture though.

JESUS: "Ask and it will be given to you; seek and you will find; knock and the door will be opened to you."

(JESUS and WAYNE pose for a selfie. As WAYNE takes the picture, the lights slowly dim into a blackout. Seconds later, the lights come back on to WAYNE still in the selfie pose, but JESUS and the gate are gone. WAYNE looks around, confused.)

WAYNE: Jesus? Jesus? Where did you go?

(pause)

It's a good thing I took the picture when I did.

(WAYNE looks at his phone, distressed.)

WAYNE: Wait, where's the picture? This can't be it, can it? *(pause)* Why isn't Jesus in it? *(pause)* Whoa, this is some crazy—

ANGEL (V.O.): "Don't fear, because I am with you; don't be afraid, for—

JESUS and ANGEL (V.O.): I am your God. I will strengthen you, I will surely help you; I will hold you with my righteous hand."

WAYNE: Okay, Black Jesus. I'm going to hold you to that.

(blackout)

(end of play)

SCATTERED

by Lisa Deily

Lisa Deily is the author of several plays including *Dinner with Marie*, *Scattered*, *Lucky You*, and *The Send-Off*. Born in Chicago, Lisa is a writer, filmmaker, and actor. She is currently working on a full-length play exploring followers of a famed dietary cult in Jacksonian America. Lisa recently produced the short film *Dark Room* for Detroit Street Films in Los Angeles, collaborating with Gareth Williams (*Mindhunter*, *True Detective*, *The Shield*). After spending several years in Los Angeles recently, Lisa Deily now resides full time in New England with her husband. In her spare time, she performs as the bass player in Lemonheads co-founder Ben Deily's pop/punk band VARSITY DRAG, with which she has toured domestically and overseas. **Contact: www.lisadeily.com**

Scattered was sponsored by **The Front Porch Arts Collective**, a new black theatre company committed to advancing racial equity in Boston through theater. Our namesake signifies a communal spirit, inspiring us to serve communities of color and produce art that is inclusive of all communities and welcoming to all audiences, to inspire a more tolerant and inclusive Boston. **www.frontporcharts.org**

Scattered was presented on April 14, 2020, with the following creative team:

Directed by Rosalind Bevan
CHRISSY: Elle Borders
DIANE: Shannon Lamb

CHARACTERS:

CHRISSY (25) wears sneakers, capri pants, t-shirt, gardening gloves and a wide-brimmed straw hat. She is a young stay-at-home mom with an 8-month-old baby napping inside. Chrissy herself is the baby of the family, she is the youngest of her two older sisters.

DIANE (40) is the eldest of the three sisters. She wears a dark, modest yet stylish dress, and her hair is swept up off her neck. She carries an expensive leather tote, and looks like a corporate kind of power mom. She has two kids and is efficient and controlling with her schedule.

(A quiet middle class neighborhood at a modest suburban home. The play takes place outside on a backyard patio that looks out onto the nicely manicured lawn. It's a beautiful sunny afternoon in May. Present day.

This neighborhood is located in one of Chicago's northwest suburbs, with a mixed population of blue- and white-collar families.

This neighborhood could be a suburb of any city. References to Chicago can be interchanged for any city with similar characteristics.

The backyard has just been renovated with everything new, from new outdoor chairs to the patio that was just put in. It is now set up for the beginning of summertime with some potted flowers placed onstage. A lilac tree is off to the side or back of the theater. This could be set up simply as a large container with artificial lilac branches placed inside.

Lights up on CHRISSY'S patio in the backyard. She's tidying up outside when her older sister DIANE shows up unexpectedly. Two outdoor chairs and potted flowers are on the patio. If audio is possible, the sounds of birds may be heard briefly: various twitters and cheeps.)

DIANE: *(enters patio, all business)* Hey. Joe let me in. He said you were out back.

(CHRISSY is surprised to see DIANE suddenly standing there in her yard.)

CHRISSY: Hi. What's going on? You haven't come by since...jeez...Christmas. Were we supposed to—?

DIANE: Everything looks nice out here. Pretty flowers.

CHRISSY: Thanks—

DIANE: Looks like Joe got the patio all done.

CHRISSY: Uh, yeah, him and his crew got it in yesterday...just in time for next weekend. I'm making lemon squares. Mom's recipe...your favorite. Think you and Steven and the kids can make it?

DIANE: Ah, that's right, time for the big Memorial Day cookout. *(a bit brusque)* No, we've already got plans for the weekend. So...mom. Speaking of plans...that's why I'm here. We gotta work out details, right? Where do you think she wants to go? I keep thinking someplace sunny...maybe the beach?

CHRISSY: Oh, I thought we were thinking, ya know, maybe later in the summer to make plans?

DIANE: *You* were thinking later. This has been put off way too long. We should figure it out. Today.

CHRISSY: Today?

DIANE: Yeah. Today.

CHRISSY: Ok. You know, *first* we should—

DIANE: Oh God. Now what? Don't tell me, you want to make a pendant out of her? Split her up into equal parts and turn her into a diamond so we can wear our mother on a necklace?

CHRISSY: Actually—

DIANE: What? You want a drone to scattter her ashes while you try to play that ukulele she bought off craigslist that she used twice? Or maybe you want to have our mother's cremains turned into ink and get a tattoo of her? No! No more crazy ideas, no more delays...we are scattering her ashes *today*. Cindy's off work today. We can pick her up and do this. So, go inside, *go get mom*, we'll pick up our sister and we'll all figure it out as we drive. *(Pause)* How about North Avenue beach? The lake at the park? Or how about that pretty field up in Caldwell Woods? Everything's blooming now, it's all butterflies and wildflowers. Remember those picnics? When we were little? We can say a few words and then—

CHRISSY: *(interrupts angrily)* That was you and Cindy. *I* never went there. By the time I was born, you guys were like, in high school. Mom and I did our own stuff. Different stuff.

DIANE: Ok, calm down! I just meant...it's pretty and she loved it there so...what's wrong with that?

CHRISSY: Diane, I don't know how to—

(DIANE sets down an expensive leather tote bag. A bouquet of flowers peeks out.)

DIANE: Chris, please, I know you don't want to do this, but you've had mom's ashes at your house since she died and it's been over two years now! We need to have a memorial or...or *something* at least. It's time to let her go and get closure. We can't just leave her on your fireplace mantle forever. *(pause)* Remember last Christmas? My youngest kid gift wrapped the box mom's ashes are in and put it under the tree with your name on it from "Santa"! That was fun, huh?

CHRISSY: *(scoffing)* I blame you! He got his sick sense of humor from his mother, obviously!

DIANE: More like from mom. *(chuckles)* That was just the kind of prank that she used to play with my boys. A little dark? *(laughing)* Sure, but admit it—she probably would have *loved* it.

CHRISSY: Fine. Have it your way. Be right back.

(CHRISSY turns and walks off, leaving the patio. DIANE gets out her cell. She calls CINDY.)

DIANE: Cind? All set, we'll pick you up in fifteen minutes. No, really! I don't know, but Chrissy's not fighting me this time! Ok, see you soon.

(DIANE hangs up. CHRISSY comes back with the box.)

CHRISSY: Here she is.

DIANE: Great. I've got room in my bag—

(DIANE reaches for the box, but CHRISSY holds on.)

CHRISSY: No. I can hold her while you drive.

DIANE: Chris. C'mon.

CHRISSY: No, *I* want to carry her—

DIANE: Oh my god, will you just give it to me?

(A quick tug of war ensues as CHRISSY refuses to let go and DIANE tries to wrestle it away from her.)

CHRISSY: Diane, let go.

DIANE: No, *you* let go.

(The box falls to the ground and breaks open. The plastic bag of ashes comes tumbling out, spilling the ashes on the ground. They both look down in disbelief.)

DIANE: I can't believe you. Look at this. This is...this is ridiculous!

CHRISSY: Don't move, I'll just—

DIANE: Yeah, you'll just fix this is what you're gonna do. Go get a broom and a...dustpan or something. God! Go! Ya better hurry up before a good strong wind comes along! Unless you want to have her scattered right here.

(CHRISSY turns and walks over to get a broom and pan that is nearby. She brings it back to sweep up the mess.)

DIANE:
This is just unbelievable. I can't believe we have to "sweep" up our mother. *(calls out loudly to the pile of ashes) Sorry Mom! This one's on Chrissy!*

(CHRISSY starts sweeping but not good enough for DIANE.)

CHRISSY: It's not *my* fault, you shouldn't be so grabby and controlling.

DIANE: Ok, look at this. Now you're just making a bigger mess. Give me the broom.

(CHRISSY fumes as DIANE grabs the broom from her. She squats down and carefully sweeps ashes into the pan. She pauses and looks thoughtful, staring at the ashes. DIANE takes a deep breath.)

DIANE: Chris?

CHRISSY: Yeah?

DIANE: What are we doing?

CHRISSY: What do you mean?

(Pause. DIANE looks down at the ashes and then back up at her.)

DIANE: This. This isn't mom is it?

CHRISSY: What? What are you talking about? Of *course* it's mom!

DIANE: Chris...come on. What...*is* this? This looks like sand..and that's definitely *not* the plastic bag her ashes came in. I know it was over two years ago, but I don't remember her ashes being in a Ziplock-brand-gallon-size-freezer-bag!

(CHRISSY sinks into one of the chairs.)

CHRISSY: Oh god. I-

DIANE: Well?

CHRISSY: I thought that if we ever did finally scatter her ashes, you guys wouldn't notice. You'd both be busy reading a poem or something—

DIANE: So what am I looking at? And *where*'s mom?!

CHRISSY: Well, it's some...sand...

DIANE: Unbelievable.

CHRISSY: And ash from our firepit and...well, then I mixed it all up with some ground up quinoa...

DIANE: Quinoa? You substituted *quinoa* for our mother?

CHRISSY: *(Her words come tumbling out.)* Yeah. I uh, I put it in the coffee grinder and then I mixed everything up and added some whole wheat flour and some regular white flour, I guess it's like...a fifty fifty blend? I was trying to get it to look right, like...ya know, bits and chunks of bone that should be in there—

DIANE: Chrissy! Bits and chunks?! Ugh! Stop!

CHRISSY: You wanted me to explain!

DIANE: Yeah, whatever, enough! Where are the ashes?

(CHRISSY looks up at her reluctantly.)

DIANE: What? In the kitchen counter next to the spice rack? Or maybe they're in the trunk of your car so you can drive around with her?

(Silence. CHRISSY looks down at the ground.)

DIANE: I'll tear your house apart and find the box myself—

CHRISSY: No! You don't have to do that. Mom's here. *(pause)* Right...here.

(DIANE looks at her confused. CHRISSY points down at the ground. DIANE looks down and around their feet at the ground. Realization hits her.)

DIANE: *(gasps)* You don't mean—

CHRISSY: Yeah.

DIANE: No.

CHRISSY: Uh-huh.

DIANE: Mom's under the patio?

CHRISSY: Yeah.

DIANE: Right here?

CHRISSY: *(awkward pause, but not too long)* Yep.

DIANE: You put mom under your patio. You've got to be kidding me!

CHRISSY: Nope.

DIANE: I wish you were.

CHRISSY: No, she's down there. Right...underneath us.

(DIANE looks at the patio area again below them. CHRISSY gets up and stands looking around at the area.)

CHRISSY: Yep. Pretty much this whole area.

DIANE: *(DIANE explodes.)* I can't BELIEVE you. WHY would you do that? Cindy is going to kill you! I'M going to KILL you! You know what? I'm gonna put YOU under this patio!

CHRISSY: Stop! I didn't...*plan* it! It just...happened, you know? I was out here yesterday when it was all dug up before the concrete went in. Joe and his crew left to go on a break before they poured the cement. It was so nice and quiet out here...the birds were singing, the flowers were blooming and I just suddenly had this idea that if she was in something solid... something that felt...permanent, then I wouldn't have to worry about her anymore. Next thing I knew I was standing here with the bag. So yeah, she's down there.

DIANE: Wow. I should get a jackhammer and blast this thing and get her out.

CHRISSY: Oh, there's no getting her out. I didn't just like...put the bag in there...I opened it up and ya know...spread her out. The guys came back from lunch to pour the concrete and it got all filled up right over her. It's - she's all mixed up. She's...part of the patio.

DIANE: She's part of the patio! Great. Just great. And you think *my* kid has a sick sense of humor? *(pause - looks at her)* Wait, what are you talking about, you wouldn't have to "worry" about her? *She's dead*, Chrissy! *Nobody* has to worry about her!

CHRISSY: I hated the thought of scattering her ashes outside somewhere because yeah, I'd worry about her. I know it probably sounds stupid to you, but if we just scatter her in a lake or in a field or something, then she'd just be blowing around and...lost out there. *I'd* feel lost if I was in pieces and floating around. *(pause)* Actually, I do feel...lost. I have since she's been gone. You were born in nineteen *seventy nine.* And Cindy a year later. You two were practically like twins and you grew up in the eighties. You guys ran around totally on your own. Me? I was born in ninety four! Ever since I was nine years old, I had a cellphone to text mom to pick me up and drop me off everywhere, we were in touch constantly. So, yeah... things were way different for me. Mom and I...we were like super close when I was a kid cause there was just one of me. It was just her...and me. You don't understand. You can't possibly understand.

(CHRISSY holds back tears and looks at her sister. DIANE shakes her head in defeat and reaches out for her. DIANE pulls CHRISSY in close for an exasperated hug.)

DIANE: I know. I miss her too. Me, you and Cindy, all three of us miss her. Every day.

(pause)

CHRISSY: You're not mad?

DIANE: Well, I wasn't expecting this, I'll tell you that. *(pause)* I guess now we'll know where she is. I mean, it is pretty goddamned...weird that you'll be standing over mom while you're grilling in the summer or when you're shoveling snow out here in the winter...

CHRISSY: It's not weird. I like knowing she's here. I thought she'd be spending summers outside here playing with my kids as they grew up but I missed that. Billy is only eight months old now, so she was already gone before he was even born. You...*both* you and Cindy and all your kids got to spend a lot of time with their Grandma because you guys were so much older than me. Your kids have memories of mom. Me and Billy, we're never gonna have that.

(DIANE takes a deep breath and blows it out in a huge sigh taking it all in. They sit on the two chairs.)

DIANE: *(deadpan/wryly)* You know, you're never moving...you're gonna have to own this house for the rest of your life.

CHRISSY: *(CHRISSY smiles just a bit.)* I know.

DIANE: *(DIANE smiles back at CHRISSY. DIANE looks around at the yard.)* Hey, the lilac is blooming.

CHRISSY: Yeah, it just opened up this morning. Mom got it for me. We planted it together after Joe and I bought this place. Lilacs were always her favorite. She used to say *"Oh, they smell so good! It's not a yard without a lilac!"*

DIANE: Mm. I remember her saying that.

(DIANE gets up and walks up through the space to where there is a big bunch lilacs. The lilacs could be in a vase or on a table in the theater. She plucks a branch off. She brings it back for CHRISSY to smell. DIANE sits back down on the chair.)

CHRISSY: *(CHRISSY inhales deeply.)* Mmmm.

DIANE: Love ya, mom.

CHRISSY: Yeah mom. I love you. Miss you.

(They scoot closer next to each other on the two chairs. DIANE puts her arm around CHRISSY. DIANE'S cell phone rings. She pulls her phone out.)

DIANE: Aaand that would be Cindy. Yep. It's her.

(DIANE tries to hand the phone to CHRISSY.)

DIANE: Answer it! *You* talk to her.

CHRISSY: No way! *You* answer it!

DIANE: *(DIANE can't help it, she starts laughing.)* Oh no! I'm not gonna explain this, *go on—take it!*

CHRISSY: Nooo!

(They start to really crack up, and keep trying to pass the phone off to one another. The sound of chirping birds is heard as we end.)

(blackout)

COMMON APP

by Martha Douglas-Osmundson

Martha Douglas-Osmundson is on the faculty of Lincoln School in Providence, RI. She is the 2013 recipient of the Charles M. Sullivan Award for Distinguished Service in the Arts *(*Pell Award*)* for her program, Shakespeare in the City. Martha has seen her work performed at Lemon Punch Theatre Lab Micro Play Festival, Coronavirus Play Festival, NYC, The Providence Fringe Festival, Culture*Park, WomensWork Theatre Collaborative, the St. Luke's Little Theatre, Acting Up *(*Orange Players Festival*)*, and AS220 *(*From Scratch works-in-progress*)*. Martha is thrilled to be part of Boston Theater Marathon XXII and sends love to her fellow members of The Blue Cow Group! **Contact: marthadougos@gmail.com**

Common App was sponsored by **ImprovBoston**, New England's home for comedy for over 35 years, with a regular performance selection of the area's best improv, sketch, and standup – as well as an acclaimed comedy training program. ImprovBoston seeks to create, cultivate, and explore comedy in all its forms at their current home in Central Square in Cambridge. ImprovBoston is a proud 501*(*c*)*3 and carries out its non-profit mission through initiatives in schools, local hospitals, and at our theater. **www.improvboston.com**

Common App was presented on April 26, 2020, with the following creative team:

Directed by Mike Carr
RENEE: Julianne Snyder
BELLA: Kayleigh Kane

CHARACTERS:

RENEE, woman in her 40s or 50s, attractive

BELLA, girl of 18, dresses very casually

(RENEE's kitchen. Table, chairs. At rise RENEE hurriedly wipes already clean counter, checks her hair (and her butt) in mirror. Doorbell rings. In a bit of a panic, RENEE looks again in the mirror, checks her hair, breath, then opens the door. BELLA stands outside, phone in hand, caught looking at phone.)

RENEE: Bella! *(good, sincere hug)*

BELLA: Hey, Renee.

RENEE: *(looking past BELLA)* Is your father coming in?

BELLA: No. He dropped me off.

RENEE: Oh....

BELLA: I thought this was just for me.

RENEE: Of course. Of course. *(another quick hug)* I am all yours. Sit. What would you like? Tea? Soda?

BELLA: Vodka?

RENEE: Bella. Come on.

BELLA: Tea, I guess. *(RENEE busies herself making tea as BELLA sets up camp at the table.)* I'm old enough to go to college. We don't have to pretend that I haven't gotten drunk.

RENEE: What is that? A prerequisite? "Must have intimate knowledge of the bottom of a red cup prior to admission"?

BELLA: Just sayin.

RENEE: You're never just sayin anything, sweetheart. *(pause)* Gosh, I've missed you. So. You're here to write the essay.

BELLA: Yeah. And you're here to get me into college.

RENEE: Um - that's *your* job.

BELLA: Not according to my dad.

RENEE: That's too much pressure. I can't work miracles.

BELLA: Thanks.

RENEE: I didn't mean -- I'm sure your essay will be great. You will be great. It's just that -- this is up to you.

BELLA: I know, I know. He knows it, too. He's just getting a little edgy. His baby is about to fly the coop

RENEE: Is he okay?

BELLA: He's fine. Why do you care, Renee? He was such a jerk to you.

RENEE: Bella, don't say that about your dad.

BELLA: It's true.

(The tea kettle whistles.)

RENEE: I made brownies.

BELLA: Shut. Up. Not the ones with the cheesecake filling. *(RENEE brings a plate to the table.)* Oh, my god! *(Eating)* You are the best cook! I could eat these every day.

RENEE: *(snarky)* Yes, you could have. *(catching herself)* Have -- another one. Have as many as you want.

BELLA: *(taking another brownie)* Oh, my god, these are so good. Mmmm…. *(eyes closed)* I close my eyes, and it's like no time has passed. *(RENEE laughs.)* I'm 13.

RENEE: What a great age to go back to.

BELLA: I'm in 8th grade. My parents just got divorced, and life couldn't possibly suck any more. But wait! My dad has this awesome new girlfriend! And she has us over for dinner --

RENEE: Chicken teriyaki --

BELLA: On the grill - I think I died and went to heaven - and then she serves these. *(opens eyes)* These brownies kept me alive, you know.

RENEE: Want another?

BELLA: I can't. I have—we're going somewhere for dinner.

RENEE: Oh. Pepino's?

BELLA: No.

RENEE: The Red Lion?

BELLA: No.

RENEE: I'm pretty sure the China House is closed on Sundays.

BELLA: His new girlfriend's.

RENEE: Oh.

BELLA: I swear she's younger than me. All she wants to do when it's my dad's weekend is *(girlfriend's voice)* "get a mani-pedi." Do I look like someone who gives a rat's ass about her nails? This is me dressed up. Shoes. And I brushed my teeth.

RENEE: Well, I guess we'd better get started. Let's look at those prompts. *(reads, erases)* Okay, first of all, it's not *collage.*

BELLA: Haha. I wrote that to make you laugh. *(erases)* Remember when I used to do it all the time in 8th grade?

RENEE: *(reads)* Yes. And you went to a collage prep school. Okay… *(reading)* "If you could have dinner with any Shakespearean character, who would it be, and what would you serve?" Hmmm! Let's hear what you wrote.

BELLA: *(reading)* "If I could have anyone that Shakespeare created to my house for dinner, I would hope my girl Lady Macbeth was free, and what we ate would depend on whether it was my dad's weekend or my mom's."

RENEE: Bella --

BELLA: Can I finish? "When my dad is in charge, there is exclusively meat on the menu—mostly bacon—and when it's my mom's weekend, it's take out. So if Lady M is a fan of pizza, she will eat well. Extra red sauce, of course. And bacon."

RENEE: Hmmm...okay, let's unpack that last bit.

BELLA: It's no good.

RENEE: No—it's just—read it again?

BELLA: Never mind. How about this one? "The poet, William Blake, uses imagery in the poem "The Tyger" *(She pronounces it "Tigger.")* to characterize the nature of the beast as cunning and everlasting and really smart and totally awesome...."

RENEE: Okay. Are there a lot of other prompts?

BELLA: It's terrible. They're all terrible.

RENEE: Not—terrible. Just—first drafts—let's see— When the reader encounters metaphysical poet John Donne, who compares..." see, that's not grammatically correct—John Donne isn't the one doing the comparing here....

BELLA: What?

RENEE: I'm sure you learned that. It's like this: you wouldn't say, "She hit the ball into my leg, which rolled into left field..."

BELLA: Why not?

RENEE: Her leg did not roll into left field!

BELLA: Pretty sure that's not what the writer meant.

RENEE: But that's what the writer wrote! Okay, and this one—"really smart" and "totally awesome" are not college essay expressions.

BELLA: *(becoming upset)* But that's how I want to come across: really smart and totally awesome! Like the smartest and most awesome in my demographic!

RENEE: Okay. Well, let's—

BELLA: My dad says that my application is just gonna be another girl trying to get into a liberal arts school in the Northeast! I have to stand out!

RENEE: Well, you want to stand out in the right way.

BELLA: What's the right way? Ugh. Can we just finish these?

RENEE: What's wrong?

BELLA: I'm just—I'm done.

RENEE: Okay. Take a tea break. *(They pour, stir.)*

(beat)

I know you were taught about misplaced modifiers. You had Mary Hadley for freshman comp—

BELLA: I don't even remember who that is—

RENEE: I know for a fact that Mary Hadley taught you that—

BELLA: Well, I didn't learn it!!!

RENEE: Bella!

BELLA: Don't *you* start, too! Teachers are always telling me I should know this or that. They can't just accept the fact that I am stupid!

RENEE: Bella—

BELLA: I am not college material! Why can't everyone just face that?

RENEE: Where is this coming from?

BELLA: Me, okay?

RENEE: But you are smart. And smart kids go to college.

BELLA: Not all of them.

RENEE: Well, no. Not every one. But you're a bright girl—you love language—you're funny—

BELLA: I flunked algebra three times.

RENEE: Well, math is just not your thing. You're a right brain thinker.

BELLA: Euphemism. Noun. From the Greek "eu" meaning "good" and "phem" meaning "speech.

RENEE: See? You can learn anything you set your mind to.

BELLA: It's only cuz you taught it to me. 8th grade English. The year my mom left—and my dad got a look at you.

RENEE: That was a nice time. *(looks through papers)* Okay. Let's try another prompt. "Discuss a parent or parental figure who sparked a period of personal growth and a new understanding of yourself or others."

BELLA: *(Reads; RENEE reacts throughout.)* "My mother was awol, and my sweet, funny dad had stopped being sweet and funny since they split. Gone were the practical jokes, the hand buzzers, the fake dog do on the kitchen floor. *(RENEE laughs.)* The snuggles on the couch watching Disney movies—the tickle wars—the Saturday morning diner breakfasts after swimming lessons at the Y when he let me play my favorite songs on the jukebox in our usual booth. We didn't do any of that anymore. I thought my life was over, and I was only 13. Then I stepped into my 8th grade English teacher's classroom, with its posters of Shakespeare—whose "high forehead" looked just like my dad's—and the clouds parted. I fell in love with words. And at the midterm parent-teacher conference, my dad fell in love with my English teacher. And he was sweet and funny again. Renee Daniels became my lifeline. She organized my planner, my dad's closets, and our lives. I told her things that my mother was obviously not interested in hearing. Renee was the only one who came to my swim meets, even as it became painfully obvious that I was never going to be good enough at that, like I was not good at so much of school. But I kept loving words, thanks to Renee. She signed me up for writing camps in the summer, and I met other wordy nerds, and Renee made us the most ridiculously delicious cheesecake brownies on earth. She tutored me to get me through 9th grade. And 10th grade. And if it weren't for Brenna Roberts posting a screenshot of the Snapchat of me and Renee and my dad in Greece - no one would have known that I was anything more than just a former student. The principal at my school had "a talk" with Renee, and bam! My dad was back to parenting by terse, biting commands, and Renee was transferred to a middle school across the city. Now I drive myself to the diner after swim practice, and I will drive myself to college if I even get in. *(BELLA is quietly crying.)* And I will miss my dad and Renee, but I'll get over it." *(RENEE is also crying and tries to hide the fact.)* Are you crying? *(RENEE rises, looks out the window. Beat.)* Do you think you would have broken up anyway? I do. He moved on like that! *(snaps fingers)*

RENEE: *(painfully)* I've come to realize it was just an excuse. It's moot, anyway.

BELLA: He's not good enough for you. *(RENEE checks her phone.)* Don't tell me you still have him on your phone.

(She grabs RENEE's phone.)

RENEE: Bella!

BELLA: Oh, my god—Renee—you texted him yesterday?!

RENEE: That is NONE of your business!

BELLA: He doesn't answer! Delete him!

RENEE: I can't.

BELLA: You go to Contacts—here—

RENEE: *(grabbing her phone)* I know how! I just can't!

BELLA: You deserve better.

RENEE: I know. Like I think you know you are college material.

BELLA: In my heart, I do. Like if I'm being honest.

RENEE: Then do it!

BELLA: If you delete my dad from your contacts—

RENEE: This is a very weird deal—

BELLA: My dad was just the way we met. He served his purpose. Like tonight. If you recall, I made these arrangements. He just gave me a ride.

RENEE: Oh. I thought this was his idea.

(BELLA grabs RENEE's phone, clicks a few times.)

Bella, give me my phone. I'll do it!

(RENEE takes her phone, clicks a few times; RENEE hands the phone to BELLA.)

Go ahead and look if you don't believe me.

(BELLA clicks a few times.)

What are you doing?

(There is a gentle fight over the phone. RENEE consults her phone.)

What's BrainySingles? *(swipe)* Wow! *(swipe)* Ooh!

BELLA: I'll just work on this essay while you—

RENEE: Okay. *(back to her phone)* I'll—help you—with your—essay. Are there other—apps like this?

BELLA: Oh, Renee, I have so much to teach you.

(curtain)

DON'T BE A SCROOGE

by James C. Ferguson

James C. Ferguson is an award-winning writer whose plays have been produced throughout the United States as well as in the UK and New Zealand. He has written two novels, numerous screenplays, and a number of projects for television and the web. James is also the co-writer and director of the well-reviewed feature length independent motion picture *Happy Holidays*, available through numerous digital platforms and on DVD through TLA Video. For additional info. go to his web site (**www. scalepluspoints.com**), or you can find him on Twitter **@scalepluspoints**. He is also on Instagram where he mostly posts pictures of his one-eyed cat. He's adorable (the cat, not the playwright). No, seriously. He also has two children (the playwright, not the cat), but they're not nearly as cute, so you won't see as many pictures of them.

Don't Be a Scrooge was sponsored by **Moonbox Productions**, a non-profit theater company based in Cambridge, Massachusetts. Our mission is to present top quality theater experiences using local talent, and to use our productions to promote the work of other non-profits doing important work in our community. **www.moonbox.org**

Don't Be a Scrooge was presented on April 2, 2020, with the following creative team:

Directed by Andrew Child
MARTHA CRATCHIT: Karina Wen
TINY TIM: Sara Kenney
MRS. EMILY CRATCHIT: Alyssa Germaine
EBENEZER SCROOGE: Liz Eacmen
PETER CRATCHIT: Gavin Damore
BOB CRATCHIT: Michael Eckenreiter

CHARACTERS:

SCROOGE: Male, 50s-70s

BOB CRATCHIT: Male, 30s-40s

MRS. EMILY CRATCHIT: Bob Cratchit's wife, female, 30s-40s

MARTHA CRATCHIT: the eldest daughter, female, 12-16ish

PETER CRACHIT: the heir, male, 11-14ish

TINY TIM: the youngest child, male, 8-10

(London. 1843. Summer. Day. Morning.

The Cratchits, the poor but resilient family made famous by Charles Dickens' timeless novel A Christmas Carol *(You know the one! … You've at least seen the movie, right?) populates their modest Victorian home, bustling about as they prepare for the day and breakfast. Everyone is chipper and energized, if a bit rushed. BOB CRATCHIT and TINY TIM are noticeably absent. It's several months after the well-trodden events of SCROOGE and the ghosts and Christmas and whatnot, on an unspecified date in July. The Cratchits are dressed in weather-appropriate (Victorian) summer clothing. BOB, the patriarch, enters, lugging a large suitcase, which he plops down in the middle of the floor, reaching for something to eat.)*

BOB CRATCHIT: *(calling out, as he enters, beaming)* Emily! *(then, quieter.)* We are officially all—packed!

MRS. CRATCHIT: *(gleeful)* Oh, Bob. Can you believe it? I cannot. I feel as light as a feather unencumbered by the burdensome heft of bones or beak. Or - giblets. I feel - alive. I love you, Bob Cratchit.

BOB CRATCHIT: And I you, Mrs. Cratchit.

(They kiss, briefly.)

BOB CRATCHIT: *(to the family)* The cab will be here in exactly one hour, children! Every one of us must be packed, fed and presentable!

THE CHILDREN: Yes, father.

BOB CRATCHIT: And remember— *(hushed)* Quiet as mice!

THE CHILDREN: *(quieter)* Yes, father.

MRS. CRATCHIT: Dead mice.

(silence)

MRS. CRATCHIT: *(whispering)* Perfect. *(to BOB)* I am going to miss our home, Bob.

BOB CRATCHIT: It is but a building, my love. Anything of importance we are taking with us!

MRS. CRATCHIT: *(with trepidation)* Did you tell…him?

BOB CRATCHIT: No... Never fear... As we agreed!

MRS. CRATCHIT: Good… I know you wanted to—

BOB CRATCHIT: I did. I did indeed. I do like deceiving him.

MRS. CRATCHIT: I know you don't. Of course, you don't! You are a good man with a good heart. But—You and I both know this—is the only—

BOB CRATCHIT: *(pointing outside, noticing something)*—window.

MRS. CRATCHIT: What?

BOB CRATCHIT: The window, my darling. The window is open.

(as BOB rushes to the window—)

MRS. CRATCHIT: It is a very warm day. The girls' undergarments were beginning to—stick. I thought—

BOB CRATCHIT: No... No, my darling... We must be vigilant! The curtains must remain pulled. The windows must remain closed. If he should pass— If he should hear us— Or see us— If he should realize that we are here—

MRS. CRATCHIT: Yes, but—Bob— You told *me* that you told him *that*— we were all dead.

BOB CRATCHIT: *(unsure)* I did, my love, but— Well—I'm not entirely sure he believed me.

MRS. CRATCHIT: Did you say it with conviction?

BOB CRATCHIT: Would that have helped?

(At that precise moment, who should appear at the open window - she really should have closed it - but SCROOGE; I know you know him. He looks like as he does at the very end of A Christmas Carol. *Manic, joyous, chuckling, and breathless.)*

SCROOGE: MERRRRRRY CHRISTMAS!!

MRS. CRATCHIT: Shit.

BOB CRATCHIT: *(hushed)* If we do not move, perhaps he will think that we are but—apparitions and—sally forth.

(SCROOGE knocks loudly at the door.)

SCROOGE: Helloooo??

MRS. CRATCHIT: He's not sallying, Bob.

BOB CRATCHIT: *(uncomfortable, very awkward)* Mr. Scrooge!... Why—hello, sir! What a - surprise.

(It's not a surprise at all.)

BOB CRATCHIT: What, uh— What can I do for you, sir?

SCROOGE: I'll be happy to tell you if you unlock your door, my good man.

BOB CRATCHIT: Oh... Is it locked? I didn't realize...

(Of course he did.)

BOB CRATCHIT: You can't be too careful these days, what with all the...

brigands and...bandits...and, um…

MRS. CRATCHIT: *(to BOB)* Tell him we're all vomiting!

BOB CRATCHIT: *(to his wife)* Oh, this is futile! He knows we're here, Emily. Let's just—get it over with...

MRS. CRATCHIT: Ugh. It's like our wedding night all over again!

(as BOB opens the door—)

BOB CRATCHIT: *(half-hearted)* Mr. Scrooge. Welcome. Please, come in.

(SCROOGE enters, holding a bag, and—)

SCROOGE: MERRRRRRY CHRISTMAS!!

MRS. CRATCHIT: It's the middle of July, you old goat!

SCROOGE: On paper, perhaps, Mrs. Cratchit. Emily... May I call you Emily?

MRS. CRATCHIT: No.

SCROOGE: But in our hearts—in our hearts, it is always Christmas!... Emily.

MRS. CRATCHIT: *(to BOB)* I'm going to hit him.

BOB CRATCHIT: Now now, dear... Let's not—exacerbate the situation...

SCROOGE: *(to EMILY, complimenting her, with lots of flourish)* I must say, Emily, you are looking quite lovely this morning. Like a bent spoon at a foal's birthday!

(awkward looks)

MARTHA CRATCHIT: *(to BOB, slightly panicked)* He's an insane person.

BOB CRATCHIT: Just go with it. *(to SCROOGE)* What, um— What can we do for you this morning, Mr. Scrooge?

SCROOGE: Why, I've brought you a gift, of course!

(SCROOGE pulls something out of his bag …)

SCROOGE: *(very grand)* It's—!

EVERYONE BUT SCROOGE: —a turkey.

(The Cratchits all say the word "turkey" with an air of exhaustion and dull frustration, as if this is entirely expected. It is not a large bird. One of the children starts to cry.)

SCROOGE: It's a little...smaller than I would have liked, but—...

MRS. CRATCHIT: Of course, it's a little smaller than you would have liked, you convalescent old nag! You've been bringing us a turkey every single day since Christmas! For months! They don't even sell turkey in a ten-mile radius, anymore, because you've driven everybody who *used* to sell turkey out of business! Anyone who *says* they're selling turkeys these days are just trying to get you buy a feather-laden *pudding*!

SCROOGE: I did have to go a bit far afield for this one...

MRS. CRATCHIT: We are sick to death of turkey! Turkey for breakfast, turkey for lunch, turkey for dinner, turkey soup, turkey sandwiches, turkey salads, turkey jam, turkey beer, turkey socks! I gave Tiny Tim a turkey pot pie a week and a half ago and he fell into a freakin' coma!!

(EMILY motions to the side, revealing TINY TIM, lying motionless in a nearby bed.)

SCROOGE: *(with a gasp)* Say it isn't so ...

MRS. CRATCHIT: I just said it was so, so— Arrggh!... My boy... My precious boy... And it's all your fault!

SCROOGE: Well... *(struggling to be optimistic)* At least he's not dead.

PETER CRATCHIT: You're a monster!

BOB CRATCHIT: Peter ...

MRS. CRATCHIT: *(breaking down)* Why do you insist on making us suffer so? Why can't you just leave us alone? Get a freakin' hobby!

MARTHA CRATCHIT: I practice taxidermy.

SCROOGE: I see. Um... Well ...This certainly hasn't turned out the way I expected... I was just trying to help. Atone for my sins!

MRS. CRATCHIT: Oh, I see, so, it's all about you, is it? Have you ever *once* given any consideration, at all, to how your actions effect others?

SCROOGE: I do believe that was sort of the point...

MRS. CRATCHIT: At the beginning, yes. One day. One time. But—every day—every single day—for months? We've tried to be polite, Mr. Scrooge, good Victorians and all that, but—come on. You've become obsessive. Needy. Irritating. Suffocating. You did your good deeds, you redeemed yourself, and you just kept right on going, as oblivious, and unaware, and as selfish as ever. Your like Christmas carolers. Once a year, delightful! Every freakin' day, kill me!

BOB CRATCHIT: Mr. Scrooge—

MRS. CRATCHIT: I wasn't finished!

(MRS. CRATCHIT thinks, then, realizing—)

MRS. CRATCHIT: No. Never mind. I'm done. Go on.

BOB CRATCHIT: Mr. Scrooge - There's - something I need to tell you ...

MRS. CRATCHIT: *(to SCROOGE)* You live in extremes! Oh. Sorry. I guess I wasn't done. I am now though. … Please continue ...

BOB CRATCHIT: You see – Well, the thing is - We've moving.

SCROOGE: Away?

MRS. CRATCHIT: *Farrrrrr away.*

SCROOGE: When?

BOB CRATCHIT: Today. Um—We were actually sort of hoping to—sneak off before you noticed.

SCROOGE: Where?

(BOB opens his mouth but—)

MRS. CRATCHIT: *Don't—you—dare*! If you tell him where we're going, he'll follow us, like one of those fish that stick to other fish and eat the algae off their backs. Or, or, um, uh—Hold on—I'll think of another one.

MARTHA CRATCHIT: I think mom's losing it.

PETER CRATCHIT: Is Mr. Scrooge coming with us, daddy?

MRS. CRATCHIT: *Ab-so-lute-ly not!*

PETER CRATCHIT: There's a spare room, isn't there?

MRS. CRATCHIT: No, there isn't. You're thinking of the roof. That—is not—a room.

PETER CRATCHIT: Why can't he have Tim's room, now that Tim's dead?

MRS. CRATCHIT: Tim isn't dead! He's just very very still.

SCROOGE: I must say—I'm a little, um—I had no idea... I feel so—betrayed.

MRS. CRATCHIT: *(irate) What*?!!

BOB CRATCHIT: My love, please, let me handle this. Mr. Scrooge—I am sorry but—

SCROOGE: What are you going to do for work?

BOB CRATCHIT: I got another job.

SCROOGE: Oh, so, you're abandoning me completely, are you? After all we've been through.

BOB CRATCHIT: Um …

SCROOGE: Well—That sort of leaves me up a creek, doesn't it, Bobby? What am I supposed to do without you, Bob? You do everything!

BOB CRATCHIT: Yes. I know. That's actually part of the problem, Mr. Scrooge. I do—do everything, while you run around in your nightshirt, buying poultry for every Tom, Dick and Helen from here to…there, putting half the population in England in a coma! I've done my best, sir. I have tried. I've worked hard. I've been loyal. But—You've—given everything you had—away. You're bankrupt, Mr. Scrooge. You're broke. You've spent so much of your time being—altruistic, you've let everything *you* have—every single thing—slip away from you, like, um—

MARTHA CRATCHIT: Undergarments!

BOB CRATCHIT: Your health and your livelihood will now be entirely dependent on the charity of others.

PETER CRATCHIT: Ironic.

BOB CRATCHIT: I'm sorry, but—I can't work for you anymore, Mr. Scrooge, because—you no longer have the resources to pay my wages.

SCROOGE: Are you trying to tell that my—charity has been my undoing?

BOB CRATCHIT: Your excessive charity, Mr. Scrooge. As I tell the children—

MARTHA CRATCHIT: Don't put the cat in the stove.

BOB CRATCHIT: No, not that one...

PETER CRATCHIT: Don't sit in your soup.

BOB CRATCHIT: No...

MARTHA CRATCHIT: No marrying family.

SCROOGE: Ooo, that's a good one.

MRS. CRATCHIT: "Everything in moderation!"

BOB CRATCHIT: That's the one. *(to EMILY)* Thank you, my darling. *(To SCROOGE)* A life that is built on extremes is a life that is doomed to failure.

PETER CRATCHIT: *(still quoting Cratchit aphorisms)* Don't give the goat a colonoscopy.

BOB CRATCHIT: Erm—That's—enough, Peter. Thank you. We've—moved on.

MARTHA CRATCHIT: *(under her breath)* Read the room.

SCROOGE: If only the spirits had told me not to be so nice. I blame them! Merry Christmas, indeed.

(beat)

SCROOGE: Well, this is all a bit of a downer. Not at all how I expected to start the day. What, precisely, am I supposed to do now? You can't just—abandon me, Bob. I saved your boy! Have you forgotten that because of me Tiny Tim lives!

MRS. CRATCHIT: Yes, and now, because of you, he is in a coma!

SCROOGE: *I'm* not the one that fed him all that turkey.

MRS. CRATCHIT: Do not pick nits with me Mr. Scrooge or I will strangle you with a corset!

SCROOGE: Sorry. Perhaps, in time, the boy will—revive. I have heard of a man who slept for a full week only wake one morning as if nothing was wrong. Unfortunately, the family had already buried him, so, in the end, it didn't actually work out all that well. But—as long as you don't bury the boy... Do you want me to give him a good shake?

BOB CRATCHIT: Mr. Scrooge—

(TINY TIM stirs. The children notice immediately.)

PETER CRATCHIT: Mother! Father! Look! Tiny Tim!

MARTHA CRATCHIT: He's stirring!

TINY TIM: *(groggy)* Uhhhh...

(The family rushes to his side.)

MRS. CRATCHIT: Tim! My boy! Oh! You're all right!

BOB CRATCHIT: Son...

SCROOGE: It's a Christmas miracle!

BOB CRATCHIT: How do you feel?

TINY TIM: I feel like I've been brined.

(The family laughs.)

SCROOGE: Well, that's that then.

MRS. CRATCHIT: Yes. Yes, it is. Goodbye, Mr. Scrooge. So long! Good day! Sayonara! *Toodaloo*!

SCROOGE: Goodbye.

MRS. CRATCHIT: Goodbye!

(beat)

PETER CRATCHIT: He's not leaving.

TINY TIM: I'm confused. What's going on? Why is Mr. Scrooge here? Is it Christmas?

SCROOGE: Every day is Christmas, my boy!

MRS. CRATCHIT: Oh, give it a rest, will you?

MARTHA CRATCHIT: Daddy?

BOB CRATCHIT: Yes, Martha?

MARTHA CRATCHIT: *(to BOB, hushed)* Didn't you say that once we settled into our new home you were going to hire a governess to help take care of us ...

BOB CRATCHIT: Yes...

MRS. CRATCHIT: *(knowing, disapproving)* No...

MARTHA CRATCHIT: Well... Why couldn't you hire—him?

MRS. CRATCHIT: No, no, NO!

BOB CRATCHIT: Humm. I suppose... It would be the charitable thing to do. He has given us much. Mr. Scrooge—

SCROOGE: *I accept!*

BOB CRATCHIT: Oh, good.

TINY TIM: God bless us, every one. Again.

MRS. CRATCHIT: *(sour)* I'll get the champagne.

(lights down)

SANTA'S DOLPHINS

by Patrick Gabridge

Patrick Gabridge's plays include *Mox Nox, Drift, Lab Rats, Blood on the Snow, Distant Neighbors, Chore Monkeys,* and *Blinders.* He's been a Playwriting Fellow with the Huntington Theatre Company and has received fellowships from the Boston Foundation/Brother Thomas Fund and the Massachusetts Cultural Council, and was the artist-in-residence at Mt. Auburn Cemetery from 2018-19 (the Cemetery will publish *The Mount Auburn Plays*, a book of the site-specific work that he created and produced while in residence). He's the author of four novels, most recently *The Secret of Spirit Lake.* He co-founded Boston's Rhombus playwright's group, the Playwrights' Submission Binge, and the New England New Play Alliance. He's currently the Eastern New England Regional Rep for the Dramatists Guild and is producing artistic director of Plays in Place, a company specializing in creating site-specific work for museums and historic sites. **Contact: www.gabridge.com**

Santa's Dolphins was sponsored by **Wheelock Family Theatre at Boston University** (WFT@BU), which brings the transformative power of live theatre within the reach of every child in the greater Boston area. Our unwavering commitment to diversity, affordability, access, and inclusion provides an artistic home for all families via our mainstage productions and education programs. Through imagination, collaboration, and empathy, WFT@BU empowers artists and audiences of all ages to go out and change their world. Wheelock Family Theatre was established in 1981 as an extension of Wheelock College's mission to improve the lives of children and families. With the merger between Wheelock College and Boston University (BU) in 2018, WFT joined the BU family and is proud to be a part of the College of Fine Arts. Upwards of 1.5 million people have experienced a WFT performance and we serve an average of 40,000 patrons per year. **www.wheelockfamilytheatre.org**

Santa's Dolphins was presented on May 13, 2020 with the following creative team:

Directed by Emily Ranii
Sound Design: Nick Vargas
BLIXEN: Nael Nacer
PRANCER: Lyndsay Allyn Cox
SPOUTY: Becca A. Lewis
LEAPER: Jacob Athyal

CHARACTERS:

BLIXEN: A reindeer.

PRANCER: A reindeer.

SPOUTY: A dolphin.

LEAPER: A dolphin.

The play is intentionally written to be open to casting actors of any gender, in any of the roles. Mix it up any way that works for you.

(Christmas eve on a beach. Two Reindeer, PRANCER and BLIXEN, sit in folding lawn chairs on the beach, drinking. There might be a cooler and scattered empties on the ground around them.)

PRANCER: Blixen.

BLIXEN: Dude.

PRANCER: Give me another.

BLIXEN: You've had enough, Prancer.

PRANCER: Santa's reindeer should not be celebrating Christmas Eve on a sunny beach! The world is ending. Give me another eggnog.

(BLIXEN hands PRANCER another drink.)

PRANCER: We could still do it. Put wheels on the sleigh and up we go.

BLIXEN: Without the ice caps there isn't a place for reindeer anymore. Now it's all about rebranding. I don't like it any more than you do. Santa's boat! Who ever heard of a flying boat?

PRANCER: I am still in my prime! I am meant to be freezing my tail off and pulling a sleigh full of toys, not stuck on a beach watching those idiots do it.

BLIXEN: I feel ya.

PRANCER: Whenever he starts them up it just sounds fishy, you know? "Now, Splashy! Now, Flashy! Now Spouty and Squeaky! On Leaper! On, Beeper! On Clicker and Whistler!"

BLIXEN: It does not roll off the tongue.

PRANCER: Flying dolphins, my ass.

BLIXEN: We had it good. And now.

PRANCER: They're just so smug about it.

BLIXEN: They do seem to love it.

PRANCER: Yeah, because they're bringing joy to children around the whole flippin' world. I don't want to be stuck doing logistics and navigation. That's elves' work. I am Prancer, I am a flying magic reindeer. And what's that get me now? Not all of us can be Rudolph, making fools of ourselves on *Dancing with the Stars.*

BLIXEN: Yeah. And Cupid and Vixen already did the memoir thing. I talked to an agent, but she said the market is already saturated with reindeer stories.

PRANCER: Fish-eating, splish-splashing blow holes.

(SPOUTY and LEAPER, two dolphins, enter.)

SPOUTY: Hey Reindeers!

PRANCER: There's no 'S' on the plural of reindeer.

LEAPER: Grammar! Glad to know you're good for something!

PRANCER: Don't push me, Leaper.

SPOUTY: We're just having some fun!

PRANCER: I've got antlers and I know how to use 'em.

LEAPER: Prancer, you are always good for a laugh!

PRANCER: Blixen?

BLIXEN: We've been working hard on flight paths all day. Just give us a break.

LEAPER: Yeah, take a break! You reindeers are good at that!

PRANCER: Maybe this year Santa's boat will have to be pulled by seven flying dolphins, because you're going to have my hoof up so far up your—

SPOUTY: We're kidding, we're just kidding!

LEAPER: The boss wants to talk to you, Prancer! About the flight path over Siberia!

PRANCER: We already went over it.

LEAPER: He thinks we'll get lost!

PRANCER: That's because you're dolphins.

LEAPER: Just do your job, fuzz face!

SPOUTY: The boss wants to talk to you!

PRANCER: Oh, I'll talk to him all right. Tell him that being pulled across the sky by fish is an embarrassment.

LEAPER: You did not just call us fish!

LEAPER AND PRANCER: SANTA!

(LEAPER and PRANCER storm off stage, leaving SPOUTY and BLIXEN. SPOUTY and BLIXEN are very still.)

BLIXEN: I thought they'd never leave.

SPOUTY: Oh, Blixen.

BLIXEN: Spouty.

SPOUTY: We can't do this.

BLIXEN: I can't stop thinking about you. Your skin is so smooth.

SPOUTY: Your fur is so soft.

BLIXEN: The sound of your squeak makes my heart race. When I see you splashing in the cove, it makes me want to dive into the waves.

SPOUTY: I can get lost in your eyes. Every current brings me back to you.

BLIXEN: I don't want to keep hiding.

SPOUTY: They'll never understand.

BLIXEN: The world has changed, Spouty. The fact that we're even here is proof of that. Yes, we should be pulling an actual sleigh, starting from the North Pole. But glaciers, blizzards, snowmen—that world is gone. It wasn't your fault and it wasn't mine. But we have to live with the consequences.

SPOUTY: So much suffering in the world. I know you reindeer think we don't see it because we're in the spotlight, but we feel it.

BLIXEN: I know you do. I don't know about the others. They way they splash and jump.

SPOUTY: That's just how we are!

BLIXEN: You're different.

SPOUTY: I'm a dolphin! I like to squeak and chirp and jump and swim. That's part of who I am.

BLIXEN: I love the way you are.

SPOUTY: I love what you are.

BLIXEN: Then let's tell everyone.

SPOUTY: The others will cut us off. We're both herd animals. We can't go it alone.

BLIXEN: We'll have each other.

(LEAPER and PRANCER enter. BLIXEN and SPOUTY quickly move apart.)

LEAPER: Prancer had it wrong!

PRANCER: It was an honest mistake.

LEAPER: That's what we get for putting ungulates in charge of calculations!

PRANCER: Oh, yeah, we'd be so much better off with fish making the maps.

LEAPER: We're mammals! With brains four times the size of yours!

PRANCER: Humans have big brains, and they wrecked the entire climate. If it wasn't for them, we'd still be pulling the sleigh. In the SNOW!

LEAPER: Yeah, well some of us can handle change!

PRANCER: At least I don't breathe out of the top of my head.

BLIXEN: We're in love.

(PRANCER and LEAPER stop in their tracks.)

LEAPER: Spouty! What did they just say!

BLIXEN: We're in love and I don't care who knows it.

PRANCER: That's the eggnog talking.

LEAPER: Tell me they're lying! They lie, they fabricate, they can't handle the truth! Spouty?

PRANCER: You wouldn't go there. Not the Blixen I know.

LEAPER: Answer me, Spouty!

PRANCER: We're reindeer, they're dolphins. It's not natural.

BLIXEN: I don't know how to explain it. I've never met anyone like Spouty. Beautiful and smart and kind.

PRANCER: And a dolphin. Look, we've come a long way from the tundra, because the herd sticks together, through thick and thin.

LEAPER: You want to go back to fleeing from great whites?

PRANCER: If you do this, you will not be allowed to join in any reindeer games.

LEAPER: There's a lot of sharp teeth in the ocean for a dolphin who goes rogue.

PRANCER: They're carnivores. You think you're ready for that?

LEAPER: They smell like moss!

PRANCER: Says the creature with constant fish breath.

LEAPER: Fish are delicious.

PRANCER: Disgusting.

LEAPER: *(to SPOUTY)* They're not very smart. Tell them they have it all wrong!

SPOUTY: It's true.

LEAPER: No!

PRANCER: Show some sense, dolphin.

SPOUTY: We live in a world that doesn't makes sense. We are riding a wave of global disaster. And you want us to stay separate? We are all in this together. Blixen and I have a connection, and it's deep. Like whale diving deep. We might not understand everything about each other, but we want to try.

PRANCER: I thought I knew you, reindeer.

BLIXEN: You do. Which is why you need to trust me.

LEAPER: What about you and Squeaky?

SPOUTY: That was never real.

LEAPER: And this is?

SPOUTY: I am one of Santa's Dolphins! Turning the impossible into reality is our specialty. That's the magic of Christmas. Joy, bringing people together, love for others. That's what we're supposed to be all about.

BLIXEN: Spouty understands why we're here. Don't you see?

PRANCER: Maybe. A little.

LEAPER: Oh, no. No, no, no, no, no! We are a highly intelligent evolved species. (*to PRANCER*) Surely even you can see that this is wrong.

PRANCER: It feels funky, but just look at 'em. I think they mean it.

LEAPER: SANTA!

(LEAPER rushes off in a huff.)

PRANCER: I don't quite get it, though the backflips are impressive. But the more happiness we can make in this crazy world, the better. It seems like you two might be right for each other.

SPOUTY: We are!

BLIXEN: Thanks.

PRANCER: I'd better see if I can put in a good word with the boss.

(PRANCER exits.)

BLIXEN: Are we ready for this?

SPOUTY: No. But I'm ready for you. Let's go for a swim.

BLIXEN: I do like to swim.

SPOUTY: Oh, just you wait.

(SPOUTY and BLIXEN exit, hand in hand/ hoof in flipper.)

(end of play)

ARE YOU ONE OF THOSE ROBOTS?

by Deirdre Girard

Deirdre Girard, who tells women's stories, received her Playwriting MFA at Boston University. She has had dozens of one-act plays produced both nationally and internationally; her full-length productions include *The Christina Experiment* at The Firehouse Center for the Arts and *Reconsidering Hanna(h)* at Boston Playwrights' Theatre. Deirdre was named a 2012/13 and returning 2013/14 Playwriting Fellow at New Repertory Theater, and was selected for both the Company One Play Labs and Central Square Theater's TWSS play development programs. She recently completed a commission from Peabody Essex Museum, won QC Theatre's Susan Glaspell National Playwriting Award for her one-act play *In the Buff*, won the 2019 Boston Playwright's Slam, and was selected for Boston Theater Marathon XXII and 2020 Barrington Stage's 10x10 festival. She is a playwriting instructor/ mentor for several organizations including Gloucester Stage, Boston University's Massachusetts Young Playwrights Project, and Northeastern University's Silver Masque Society, as well as an editor for StageSource's New Play Alliance Newsletter. **Contact: dagirard@comcast.net, newplayexchange.org/users/3280/deirdre-girard**

Are You One of Those Robots? was sponsored by **Open Theatre Project**, a professional theatre company from Jamaica Plain, MA, formed to transform lives and build thriving communities through high-quality theatrical experiences. We are dedicated to providing artistic opportunities which allow the expression of diverse ideas to traditional and non-traditional audiences. Our work is defined by the passion of individual artists in partnership with the culture of professionalism and collaboration we build around each of our creative endeavors. We welcome all backgrounds skill levels and perspectives in order to broaden voices in theater with a focus on developing opportunities at all levels for Women Artists of Color, LGBTQ+ members and the Elder Community. **www.TheOpenTheatre.com**

Are You One of Those Robots? was presented on May 8, 2020, with the following creative team:

Directed by Tom Grenon
RUTH: Karen Dervin
ANNE: Olivia Dumaine
VOICE 1: Dustin Bell
VOICE 2: Sarah Jacobs

CHARACTERS:

RUTH: Female, 50's-60's, traditional, buttoned up, exhausted by life.

ANNE: Female, mid 20's to late 30's, a young woman of simple, quiet dignity

VOICE 1: Any adult age, gender

VOICE 2: Any adult age, gender

NOTES:

1. At the director's option, offstage voices can be done as onstage roles, where each character simply walks on with a phone is his or her hand and directs dialogue to the audience.
2. / (backslash) indicates the next line should be said in overlap fashion. // (double backslash) indicates the overlap is over and the remaining part of that line should be said when the previous character is finished speaking.

(The home office of RUTH, *a TeleNurse, with computer;* ANNE'S *home. Both can be very simply suggested and both areas will be visible on stage at all times. The present, early evening.* ANNE *is in her home pacing, preoccupied. She reaches for her cell, dials, changes her mind. She tries to distract herself with a book but quickly puts it down, stares off. At the same time,* RUTH *is in her office wearing headphones, listening to a caller. She reads questions from her computer in a non-emotional, rote manner, and then types in answers.)*

RUTH: Have you noticed any redness or swelling?

VOICE 1: *(sounding in pain)* I already told you all that, plus about the puss!

RUTH: I need to go through the questions in the prescribed order. Have you noticed any redness or swelling?

VOICE 1: YES! And it hurts like hell! I need help here!

RUTH: I understand. How long have these symptoms persisted?

VOICE 1: *(moaning)* It's starting to burn now, like so bad! Are you a real person or one of those robots or something?

RUTH: How long have these symptoms persisted?

VOICE 1: Can you help me or not?

RUTH: If you answer my questions. How— (sound of disconnect)... Hello?

*(*RUTH *sighs and picks up a book to read, hoping for a few minutes to relax.* ANNE *takes a deep breath and finally dials. We hear a sound indicating a new call coming in for* RUTH. *She sighs again in exasperation, marks her book, and takes* ANNE'S *call.)*

Internet Health, Tele-Nurse Ruth speaking. May I have your membership number?

ANNE: 137934AA.

RUTH: *(entering on computer)* Thank you. Can you tell me in a few words why you are calling?

ANNE: I don't know really.

RUTH: Are you feeling ill?

ANNE: Uhm…not especially.

RUTH: Did you have questions about your membership?

ANNE: No.

RUTH: Perhaps you can call back when you're not feeling well.

ANNE: I don't feel great. I'm… I guess I'm just feeling sad and I'd like to talk to someone about it.

RUTH: *(suddenly coming to attention and rapidly typing into computer)* Oh. Okay then. I'm going to ask you a series of questions. *(reading from computer)* Have you already attempted or are you planning to attempt suicide today?

ANNE: What? No!

RUTH: Are you having thoughts of suicide?

ANNE: I'm just more like blue, down in the dumps.

RUTH: Are you having thoughts of suicide?

ANNE: I just said no!

RUTH: Thank you. I need specific answers before I can move on. How long have these symptoms persisted?

ANNE: Sadness? On and off my whole life. Mostly "on" when I was growing up, and mostly "off" since I've been on my own. Until now I guess.

RUTH: So would you say a week or more, a month or more or a—

ANNE: I just want to talk!

RUTH: I can refer you to our Tele-Therapist partner, but additional membership fees apply.

ANNE: No! I want you to help me.

RUTH: So would you say a week or—

ANNE: Stop! Not questions and answers, not you grilling me. I want to talk in my own way.

RUTH: I'm sorry but—

ANNE: Can you do that?Can you actually understand there is a human being on the other end of the line?

RUTH: As you know, calls may be monitored, and I'm required to—

ANNE: Are you a robot or a real—

RUTH: I'm a real person!

ANNE: Good to know. So stop with the list. I'm the customer, and I want to know what you as a human being think, not what some computer program tells you to think. *(beat)* So I've been kind of sad…

RUTH: Have you attempted or are you planning to attempt suicide—

ANNE: Only if you don't stop!

RUTH: Sorry. It's automatic. But try to understand. If someone really is that sad, they need help right away.

ANNE: I'm not that kind of sad.

RUTH: Okay.

ANNE: I just miss my mother.

RUTH: Oh. Uhm… Did she pass?

ANNE: No.

RUTH: Are you estranged?

ANNE: Yeah.

RUTH: *(hesitating, uncertain, but then decisive)* Call her. I mean it. Get on the phone right now. Because if too much time goes by…

ANNE: I don't think she wants to hear from me. She's very religious and she doesn't approve of what she calls my "lifestyle."

RUTH: *(after several moments, with dawning realization and emotion)* Anne? Is that you?

ANNE: So I left home right after high school—

RUTH: Oh my Gosh Annie, it really is you…

ANNE: …moved to Boston and—

RUTH: Boston? I would never have guessed Boston. It's so big…

ANNE: I love it here, this part of the country, nobody judges. I don't have to pretend I like boys or I'm just too busy to date.

RUTH: You, uhm…you changed your last name?

ANNE: Well, my family didn't want me so—

RUTH: That's not true!

ANNE: Not me me. You sent me to camp to pray the gay away!

RUTH: That was your step-father!

ANNE: I don't remember you trying to stop him.

RUTH: There were other programs there, crafts and archery…swimming! You always loved to swim.

ANNE: So you sent me for the sports?

RUTH: The church, all my friends…they were all so sure that if I just…it was hard for me to—

ANNE: It was hard for me! How do you think it feels to have a mother who doesn't love you, who wants you to be someone else, who—

RUTH: That's not true.

ANNE: *(sarcastically)* Great. So I guess I can come back home now and you can introduce me and my wife to all the church ladies.

RUTH: Wife? *(beat)* Oh goodness…

ANNE: Excuse me, did you mean to say "congratulations?"

RUTH: I'm just feeling a bit overwhelmed…

ANNE: Yeah. I figured. That's why I didn't invite you to the wedding. But at least the bakery didn't mind making us a cake.

RUTH: Why would anyone mind making a cake?

ANNE: Forget it.

RUTH: Was it like a wedding wedding or just…

ANNE: Yeah, we're allowed to have real weddings. They let us do it all—love each other, buy a wedding dress, hire a caterer, pick out flowers.

RUTH: I always thought I'd be there when you chose your wedding dress…

ANNE: Isn't it weird? I'm like a real person now.

RUTH: Of course you are.

ANNE: I'm not "less than." I'm not mixed up and confused. I'm not too ugly to get a man. I'm not—

RUTH: You're not ugly. You're beautiful.

ANNE: Patricia thinks so.

RUTH: Oh. *(beat)* Uhm…so…what are you doing for work?

ANNE: Did you want to ask about Patricia?

RUTH: What do you mean?

ANNE: I mean I just told you I'm married, that you have a daughter-in-law, that—

RUTH: Yes, I heard.

ANNE: Don't you want to know anything about your new daughter-in-law?

RUTH: My… are you sure? I mean, technically I don't think—

ANNE: Yeah, I'm sure.

RUTH: Okay then. That's something, isn't it?

ANNE: How will you ever explain it to your friends?

RUTH: It's none of their business!

ANNE: That's right. Just keep it a secret.

RUTH: /I didn't mean—

ANNE: You already have a daughter you never talk about. Now you have a daughter-in-law that you can't talk about either. And to complete the secret family, in six months you'll have a grandchild you'll be too embarrassed to mention. But you know what? I can't be sad about that anymore because it's all too wonderful. So this is it. It's me signing over and out forever because I will not expose my child to anything that is hateful and ugly. Not my beautiful baby. She deserves the world mom, she deserves to be loved and accepted. And you know what? I guess this is a great big relief for you too. You don't have to worry I'll pop up unexpectedly at home, walking hand in hand with my wife down Main Street, pushing our baby in a stroller. You don't even have to worry about anyone seeing my name, because we don't share that anymore. I officially release you from any connection, and I release myself too.

(ANNE bangs the phone down and wraps herself in a blanket, rocking in her chair, trying not to cry.)

RUTH: Anne? Annie? *(sound of a call coming in from RUTH'S work)* Damn it!

(She lets the phone buzz for a bit almost as if she won't answer, but then sighs in resignation and picks up the call, completely remote and disinterested now.)

Internet Health Tele-Nurse Ruth Speaking. How can I help you?

VOICE 2: There's something weird growing on my toe.

RUTH: Membership number?

VOICE 2: I gave it to the machine before the call came through. So this toe thing—

RUTH: Membership number?

VOICE 2: Are you a real human or one of them stupid robo voice things?

RUTH: *(after a few moments of seriously considering this)* I supposed I must be one of those automated things. *(beat)* I don't even know if I can think or feel anything that hasn't been programmed into me from the minute I was born.

VOICE 2: Huh?

RUTH: And that damn programming is getting pretty old and tired.

VOICE 2: Are you sure you're not a human?

RUTH: I'm sorry, but I have to disconnect you.

(She hangs up, checks the computer for the number and dials her daughter; ANNE tentatively picks up.)

ANNE: Hello?

RUTH: Hi. *(beat)* I'm calling because I need help.

ANNE: I don't understand…

RUTH: I'm feeling really sad and I'd like to talk to someone about it.

(ANNE gently smiles and puts her hand to her stomach.)

(lights down, end play)

JUST LISTEN

by Ken Green

Ken Green is a Chicagoan currently residing in Boston's Dorchester neighborhood. A former news reporter, sports reporter and editor, Ken began writing plays late in life, following a brief stint as a bad slam poet. He has had several plays performed at festivals, including the Fade to Black play festival in Houston. In addition to playwriting, Ken is a storyteller who helps run the Story Club Boston storytelling/reading show in Roslindale and has been featured on PBS' Stories from the Stage nationally televised storytelling program. He is a devoted Sox fan (White Sox, sorry). His plays include *Just Listen…* (Boston Theater Marathon XXII); *The Campaign* (Marblehead Little Theater 2020 [postponed]), Boston Theater Marathon XXI, Fade to Black Play Festival 2018); *Filling in the Gaps* (Firehose Center for the Arts' New Works Festival 2020 [postponed]); *16 Inch* (Company One staged reading, 2016); *The Line and State* (Fade to Black Play Festival, 2019 and 2015). **Contact: newplayexchange.org/users/8634/ken-green** and **kcgreen60@gmail.com** and **224 Ashmont St., Apt. 2, Boston, MA, 02124**

Just Listen was sponsored by **New Repertory Theatre** (Michael J. Bobbitt, Artistic Director). Now in its fourth decade, New Rep has established itself as one of the Boston area's premiere theatre companies. The Boston Globe called New Rep "a potent force in the realm of midsize theater." Serving 40,000, it is the largest cultural institution in Metrowest Boston. Celebrated for electrifying, compelling, and poignant productions, our plays reflect our world and community, and regularly explore ideas that have vital resonance to our lives, here and now. We embrace theatre as the basis for enduring connections with our community and as a springboard for meaningful civic engagement. Our productions has been awarded many Boston area theatre awards including 24 Elliot Norton Awards and 48 Independent Reviewers of New England Awards. We an active advocate for the arts and a major voice in the national dialogue defining the role of theater in our culture. We endeavor to dismantle internal organizational systems, processes, financial practices, structures and cultures that discourage any person from engaging with us. In creating an equitable culture, we actively seek diversity, inclusivity and accessibility because we want the stories of all people to be reflected in the stories we tell in our productions. **NewRep.org**

Just Listen was presented on May 11, 2020, with the following creative team:

Directed by Michael J. Bobbitt
Production Manager: Hannah Huling
REGINA: Lyndsay Allen Cox
SARAH: Sarah Morrisette
GENE: Rashed Alnuaimi
DAMON: Marc Pierre

CHARACTERS:

REGINA—female identifying, African American, mid 30s

SARAH—female identifying, white, mid 20s

GENE—male identifying, Asian American, late 20s

DAMON—male identifying, African American, early 30s

(The breakroom of a marketing company in downtown Chicago. Present day. There is a table, a few chairs, a coffee maker, perhaps a microwave. It is almost Halloween so there are a couple of Halloween decorations around the room, most notably a black pumpkin/jack-o-lantern Note: The pumpkin/jack-o-lantern can be made out of a real pumpkin or plastic. REGINA sits and looks at her phone while eating her lunch when SARAH walks into the room.)

REGINA: Sarah. What's up?

SARAH: *(tired)* Same old. A meeting, another meeting, another meeting, a meeting about not having so many meetings. *(tired pause)* Jesus, what day is it?

REGINA: Tuesday.

SARAH: *(exasperated)* Only Tuesday? Ugh. Why is time moving so SLOOOOOOOWWWW?

REGINA: Yeah, I know. Summer ends, and then it's like we're walking through quicksand. The days just seem to drag.

SARAH: Thank God for the holidays though, right? Thanksgiving, Christmas…the end of the year seems to come quicker. A lot of days off, office parties and cookies.

REGINA: *(laughing)* Yeah, I usually put on about ten pounds between October and January. But time does fly by this time of year. I mean, they still have stuff up from Halloween and here we are talking about turkeys and stuffing and…

SARAH: *(interrupts, then points at pumpkin)* What the hell is…THAT?

REGINA: What's what?

SARAH: *(again pointing to black jack-o-lantern sitting on table)* That…that…thing.

REGINA: *(looking at jack-o-lantern)* Looks like a pumpkin, since, you know, we just had Halloween. *(looks closer)* Yup. Pumpkin.

SARAH: That is NOT just a pumpkin.

REGINA: Well, technically you're right, it's a jack-o-lantern.

SARAH: It's disgusting.

REGINA: *(confused)* It's a pumpkin.

SARAH: What's it doing here in this office?

REGINA: *(even more confused)* Wait, what are we looking at now?

SARAH: Um, the pumpkin? C'mon, Regina, you of all people should see it.

REGINA: Me of all people? Why me of all people?

SARAH: Because… Well, I shouldn't have to say it but… Look at it.

REGINA: I'm looking at it.

SARAH: The face? The…color?

REGINA: Ok, the face, the color. "Happy" and "black." I guess.

SARAH: Regina… I can't believe you… It's right there… It's… c'mon, Regina, it's…

REGINA: It's what?

SARAH: It's blackface.

REGINA: *(incredulous laugh)* What???

SARAH: Blackface. I can't believe they let that in this office.

REGINA: That pumpkin is blackface? Like… legit blackface? "Look away, Dixieland" blackface? THAT blackface?

SARAH: Of course. Look at it.

REGINA: I am. I'm looking at a black pumpkin.

SARAH: C'mon, look beyond the pumpkin.

REGINA: Very zen. And what will I see…beyond the pumpkin!

SARAH: You'll see this is clearly an insult to black people. It's insulting… to you.

REGINA: To me? This is insulting to me? This pumpkin? Because it's… blackface.

SARAH: Yes, because it's blackface.

REGINA: No. Uh-uh, Sarah, no. This isn't blackface. This is a pumpkin. Specifically, a jack-o-lantern. Painted black. With a jack-o-lantern grin and…hold on…

(She takes out her phone and Googles "jack-o-lantern.")

…"jack-o-lanterns are supposed to represent either spirits or supernatural beings." Wikipedia, but still...not people. But YOU look at this and see a black person. Or specifically, something mocking black people.

SARAH: Well...yeah. I mean, it's pretty obvious.

REGINA: OK, now I'm not sure how to take this...

SARAH: You should be upset with whoever brought that thing into this office.

REGINA: Well, to be honest, right now I'm a little more upset with you.

SARAH: Me??? Why are you upset at me?

REGINA: Well, you come in here, see something black with a face and you naturally jump to the conclusion that it's supposed to represent a black person. That's a little insulting.

SARAH: But it's blackface! It's mocking. I can't believe I'm the one that has to point this out.

REGINA: You're pointing out a black pumpkin. *(pause)* Ok, fine explain to me why it's blackface.

SARAH: *(exasperated)* Seriously? Because it is. I know it when I see it.

REGINA: So, it's like pornography?

SARAH: This isn't funny.

REGINA: A little because you see a black jack-o-lantern and immediately think "hate crime." Do you even know the history of blackface?

SARAH: Yes, and I don't want to get into details.

REGINA: Please do.

SARAH: *(sigh)* The big wide eyes. The big grin. The lips...

REGINA: It doesn't even have lips.

SARAH: The color... That is classic blackface.

REGINA: *(head in hands, speaking to herself)* I don't believe I'm arguing AGAINST something being blackface. *(to SARAH)* Look, Sarah, you win big points for your concern, but...

(GENE enters the breakroom with a cup for coffee.)

GENE: Regina and Sarah in the breakroom! What's up? *(sees pumpkin)* Heh. Cool. Black pumpkin.

SARAH: *(shocked)* Gene!

GENE: *(confused)* What?

SARAH: Don't call it black!

GENE: Don't call what black?

SARAH: The pumpkin!

GENE: But it's…

REGINA: *(reassuring him)* Gene, you don't have to…

SARAH: Gene, it should pretty obvious that it's…you know…

REGINA: You can say the word.

SARAH: But it should also be pretty obvious to anyone that it's…racist.

GENE: Racist? This pumpkin is ra…? How? I thought it was, like, you know…goth. *(pauses to study it)* It's…*(cautiously)* racist?

REGINA: It's not, Gene

SARAH: It's blackface, Gene. Look at it.

GENE: I am. It's a bl… black…pumpkin. That's Halloween colors, right? Black and orange?

REGINA: Yes, Gene. It's Halloween colors.

WOMAN: Jesus, Gene, wake up. It's pretty obvious that it's mocking black people.

GENE: It is? I mean, I guess…

REGINA: Gene, don't. It's a pumpkin. It's just a pumpkin. A black pumpkin. With a jack-o-lantern face.

GENE: I mean, now that I look at it, I guess I can see how it can possibly be offensive to black people. *(pause)* I'm sorry, Regina. You want me to get this out of here?

REGINA: *(irritated)* What? No. Stop. Why are you apologizing? Leave it there. It's not blackface and it's not racist.

GENE: Are you sure? I mean, now that Sarah mentioned it, I can kinda see how this is mocking bla…African American people.

REGINA: You can, Gene? How? How exactly is this mocking *(emphasizing the word)* BA-LACK people? Explain it to me. In your words, not the words you think I want to hear. Your words.

GENE: Well, it's got…I mean, the face is… See, the way they made the features make it… *(nervous)* Look, I just came in to grab some coffee and go.

SARAH: Well, when you leave, take that thing with you.

(GENE starts to take the pumpkin.)

REGINA: NO! Do NOT touch that pumpkin.

GENE: *(confused, wavering)* Look, I'm just going to Starbucks downstairs.

(GENE leaves.)

SARAH: *(to REGINA)* Why would you, of all people, want that thing around? It's offensive.

REGINA: It's a fucking pumpkin! It's not blackface. It's a Halloween pumpkin. It's not meant to represent a black person. It's not meant to insult black people. But what IS an insult is you thinking it DOES, simply because it's black and has a face. What's OFFENSIVE is that you think you have to protect me from it... have to explain it to ME.

SARAH: Well, I'm just trying to... *(confused pause)* I don't understand you.

REGINA: You most surely don't.

SARAH: *(with some sincerity)* Fine. But I want to. I want to understand.

REGINA: *(scoff)* You want to understand me, but you also want to speak for me. It doesn't work that way.

SARAH: I'm not trying to speak for you. I'm defending you.

REGINA: ...from a situation you created. You got offended for me, and now you want to solve it for me. Meanwhile, I'm sitting here telling you I'm fine, but that's not good enough for you.

SARAH: I was just telling you it was wrong. Which it is. That's cool, right?

REGINA: YOU were telling ME what blackface is. You were defining it for me and telling me how to respond. *(pause)* You were whitesplaining blackface.

SARAH: *(temper rising)* Now, Regina, c'mon, I'm speaking out against all this racist crap and this is how you react?

REGINA: *(claps)* You. Are. Not. Listening. To. Me.

SARAH: *(claps)* What. Are. You. Trying. To. Tell. Me? *(pause)* Well...what?

REGINA: *(deep breath, then...)* That sometimes *(pause)* white people, even the ones with the best of intentions, need to read the room, shut up and just listen. To black people.

(pause)

SARAH: I listen.

REGINA: Nope, you explain. You explain why you're right. If you're wrong, you explain why you're wrong, but not TOTALLY wrong. You DEFINITELY explain why I'M wrong. You explain why you're explaining. For God's sake, you were just explaining blackface to a black person. *(pause)* You THINK you're listening because you hear yourself saying all the right words, but... you explain.

SARAH: I'm just trying to be...an ally.

REGINA: Look up "great white savior" and get back to me.

SARAH: *(temper rising)* Whoa, Regina, c'mon, I'm speaking out against all this racist crap and this is how you react?

REGINA: *(frustration rising)* AHHHH! *(regaining composure)* Last month, when we went to Macy's at lunchtime...

SARAH: What happened at Macy's?

REGINA: We went there just to look around? You claimed that security guard was following me around the room while you were over looking at shoes?

SARAH: She was! You'd go this way or that way and she was following right behind you, watching everything you did. Classic racial profiling. It was disgusting.

REGINA: She wasn't following me!

SARAH: Of course, she was! I saw it. You couldn't miss her in that security guard uniform...

REGINA: ...from Lake View High School. She was a HIGH SCHOOL security guard, not a store security guard. But you were too busy yelling at her, calling her racist and telling her I was gonna sue the store to stop and read the patch on her arm. She was probably shopping in the store on her lunchbreak just like us. But you tried to turn it into a civil rights moment. I'm just glad nobody had their phone out and posted it on Instagram.

SARAH: Well, I just thought... *(pause to think)* I was only trying to... *(thinks)* I'm sorry, I just think that it's...

REGINA: Sometimes it's not important what YOU think. Sometimes you don't need to let people know what you think. Sometimes what you think isn't relevant or isn't even the fu...isn't even the point.

SARAH: Ok, that's a little rude.

REGINA: The truth is rude. Sometimes. But you gotta learn when to—

sorry—shut up and listen. Like last year…

SARAH: Another example? Fine, what about last year?

REGINA: The whole thing with the old marketing director?

SARAH: Ugh. That piece of shit. Good riddance.

REGINA: All the stuff that went down, the harassment accusations, the lawsuit, the settlement, the corporate apology…Our own little Me Too thing and what were you yelling the whole time?

SARAH: *(thinking)* I don't…

REGINA: Believe women.

SARAH: *(remembers)* Right. Believe women.

REGINA: And…? *(SARAH is confused.)* Listen to the women?

SARAH: Right… listen to the women.

REGINA: Well, do that here. BELIEVE black people. LISTEN to black people. You don't like mansplaining, I don't like Sarahsplaining. Don't explain racism to a black person. Don't explain blackface to a black person. Don't explain what they should or shouldn't be offended by. You might FEEL like it's your job, you might FEEL like you know…but it's NOT your job and you don't know. You don't have to agree, but you don't have to be right either. You don't have to take the lead. You wanna help, you want to be an ally? Listen.

SARAH: Look, I just want to…speak out. Take a stand. Call all that racist, sexist stuff out when I see it. *(pause)* Alright, fine, maybe I got a little too anxious. I wasn't trying to explain to you…

REGINA: You were.

SARAH: I guess I was. Sorry.

REGINA: *(relaxing)* It's OK. But, you know…let us... *(looks at watch)* Look, I gotta go. I'm late for a meeting myself. Talk to you later.

SARAH: Ok, later.

(REGINA walks out and SARAH stands and thinks for a few moments. A few second later DAMON walks in.)

SARAH: Hey, Damon.

DAMON: Hey, Sarah, what's happening? Man, can you believe it's only Tuesday. I thought it was… *(stops and stares at pumpkin)* Whoa, what is THAT?

SARAH: *(resigned)* Halloween decoration, I guess.

DAMON: Uh, does HR know about this?

SARAH: *(curious)* HR? Why?

DAMON: Maybe 'cause it's racist? I mean, look at it… it's fuc… It's blackface. YOU might not be able to tell, but…

SARAH: *(sits up)* Blackface? YOU think that's blackface?

DAMON: Of course, it's blackface. *(anger rising)* Look at it. That's black-ass-face. Wow. I know you probably don't know the history, but trust me, this is a pretty offensive pumpkin. Just…wow. I mean, you can see it, right?

SARAH: I guess, I… So…YOU think it's blackface?

DAMON: Look at it. It's pretty damn obvious, isn't it?

SARAH: I KNEW it! *(getting excited, gets up to leave room)* Can you wait here, I'm gonna go get Regina and tell her I was… *(starts to rush out the room, then stops)* You know what, nevermind. Why don't you explain it to me? YOU say it's blackface... I'm listening. Tell me about it…

(The stage goes dark.)

(end)

NUMBER 794

by Jayne Hannah

Jayne Hannah was originally an Equity actress who turned to writing following a major introduction to stage fright. Jayne's knowledge of acting has been extremely helpful in her writing—that and her curiosity for quirky characters, food, and thinking! This is her third time in the Boston Theater Marathon (previously with *Rose in a Room at the Hotel Roma* in 2015 and *Burning* in 2018). Both plays went on to other festivals and are still being produced. Her full-length play *Stalking* was nominated in 2019 for Best New Play from The Law and Order Party in RI and was also a finalist for the Emerging Playwright Award from Urbanite Theatre, FL. Recent work exploring Covid-19 includes *A Trio of Monologues for Now* produced by Vintage Soul Productions in CT, *Anywhere But Here* by Connective Theatre in Chicago, and *Toggleford*, all available on You Tube. Jayne is a founding member of The Blue Cow Group, a playwriting group who collectively has work produced across the states. **Contact: www.JayneHannah.com**

Number 794 was sponsored by **The Wilbury Group**. Founded in 2010, The Wilbury Group produces plays by artists on the cutting-edge of theatre and reimagined classics from the canon. We pride ourselves on our pursuit of excellence in acting and design, a less-is-more aesthetic, and a commitment to creating an engaging audience experience with every production. From our earliest days ,The Wilbury Group has maintained a commitment to offering students and audiences from throughout New England affordable access to our programs through our outreach, education, and new work development programs. A promising and important cultural organization in Providence, we are proud to serve our diverse and ever-evolving community. **www.thewilburygroup.org**

Number 794 was presented on May 9, 2020, with the following creative team:

Directed by Davis Alianiello
BETTE: Carol Drewes
TILLY: Clare Blackmer
JIMMY: Brien Lang

CHARACTERS:

BETTE—female, early 60's, brassy and confident, best friend to Tilly and Mom to Jimmy

TILLY—female, early 60's, easily flustered and a little dumb, best friend to Bette and fake Aunt to Jimmy

JIMMY—male, 30's, lazy, fat and slobby, a loser, son to Bette and fake nephew to Tilly

(A living room in Dorchester, Massachusetts one summer afternoon. Dropkick Murphys song plays: Rose Tattoo. *BETTE, in her early 60's is sitting on the edge of her seat holding binoculars while wearing binoculars and staring out of the window with a great sense of urgency on her face. TILLY, also in her 60's is*

wandering to her, from a table just behind the chairs, holding out two mugs of hot tea. She is also wearing binoculars. They are both excited as they watch what is happening in the neighbor's garden.)

TILLY: What's happening now?

BETTE: *(with great enthusiasm)* Still nothin'.

TILLY: It's so exciting.

BETTE: I know. Did you make that tea?

TILLY: Just how we like it.

(TILLY settles down in a chair next to BETTE and carefully hands the other mug to her. They clink mugs in a very happy, friendly manner.)

BETTE: Perfect. Do we have the Oreos?

TILLY: Oh now come on, it's Weight Watchers weigh in tomorrow, we don't want to get shamed again.

BETTE: That skinny bitch Audrey takes it too seriously. As long as we pay our buck fifty, who cares if we put on weight?

TILLY: What's happenin' out there now?

BETTE: *(again with great enthusiasm)* Nothin'.

TILLY: *(pointing out to the window)* That one in the jacket is rather handsome, isn't he?

BETTE: Which one? They're all wearing jackets.

TILLY: The tall one wearin' the regular jacket, not the uniform jacket.

BETTE: Oh yeah he is, you've got a great eye for a tasty man Tilly. He's got wide shoulders too.

TILLY: He might work out at the gym with all that body building stuff they do these days. I was thinkin' I would get one of those 'Fist Bit' step things. Billy was sellin' some knock off ones down 'The Banshee.'

BETTE: It might be nice to be with a man who takes care of himself.

TILLY: I can't be bothered with anyone.

BETTE: Ya've still got a husband.

TILLY: Besides him I mean. *(looking around the room)* Where's my fake nephew Jimmy? I thought he'd be enjoying all this. Or is he at work?

BETTE: Idiot son is doin' somethin' in the garage. Waste of space moron that he is, just got fired from the KFC for calling it Kentucky Fucking

Chicken.

TILLY: He only just started there this week.

BETTE: Shit for brains that boy. Ohhh look, they're pointing to somethin'.

TILLY: Ohhh, pointin'. Did they dig anymore of that hole?

BETTE: They did, but they're still focusin' on that one area.

TILLY: Do ya' think they'll dig anywhere else?

BETTE: How would I know?

TILLY: Well ya' been watchin' it all day.

BETTE: I'm watchin', I'm not mind readin'.

TILLY: Do you think the handsome one is in charge?

BETTE: Oh yes, you can tell from the way he's standin'.

TILLY: I love the way he stands. *(beat)* Who would have thought? After all these years an' all because she died.

BETTE: Mrs. Huddlestone did not die. Her daughter Katrina with a K, put her in that residential home. The one near the golf course, with the fancy café and that big white porch.

TILLY: An' now look what they're doing to her yard. I'm glad I didn't buy any new geraniums this year. They'd 'ave ruined 'em.

BETTE: They're nowhere near ya' yard. I'm right next door to it all and I'm not complainin'.

TILLY: I'm not being rude but ya' yard isn't exactly Gardeners World is it! Ya' put those concrete slabs down years ago. I on the other hand will be so annoyed if they need to dig up my fat, flying cherub's statue. It's taken me ages to get that drizzling water at the right angle.

BETTE: Katrina with a K was sure upset.

TILLY: I can imagine. She puts the house up for sale, and what does she get? A detective diggin' holes looking for *(mouths the words)* a pile of dead bodies.

BETTE: What are ya' sayin'?

TILLY: *(mouths the words again with a whisper now)* All the dead bodies.

BETTE: Oh for fucks sake, just say it.

TILLY: Oh I can't, it's awful, and it's just too shockin' to think about.

BETTE: There are no dead bodies.

TILLY: They found a skeleton.

BETTE: Well that's just one, that's not a pile of dead bodies. I hate how these rumors get outta' control.

TILLY: I wonder if Mrs. Huddlestone knew. I couldn't live there if that were me. I didn't even wanna' bury Ginger out back and I loved that cat.

(JIMMY, in his 30s, a sloppy looking man wearing a big cap and a Boston sports sweat shirt, quickly comes in looking excited and swinging a large Christmas Tree Shop bag.)

JIMMY: Ma, ma, you'll never believe it.

TILLY: Come and look at all the action Fake Nephew Jimmy. It's better than Netflix.

JIMMY: I've been researchin'. Boston News will be here soon and will wanna' talk to someone. *(boasting)* It's my opportunity to be on the TV.

TILLY: You're gonna' be on the TV? Ohh, the day just keeps getting' better.

BETTE: He's not gonna' be on the TV.

JIMMY: They're bound to come round wantin' this to be on the news. It's pretty bad stuff next door. Gangsters they're saying. I was listenin' to the police through that hole in the garage. I don't know if you realize, but they're thinkin' they might uncover a garden full of bodies.

TILLY: See, I told ya' Bette. It's gonna' be like a horror movie.

JIMMY: I always thought Mrs. Huddlestone was weird. I'm gonna' tell them that.

TILLY: She had a wonky eye, don't forget to tell them that.

JIMMY: Ya' know how they always say, she was so quiet and I never suspected. Well, I can say the opposite of Mrs. Huddlestone. *(He acts out being interviewed, which TILLY enjoys, while BETTE is disgusted.)* Yeah, I was always suspicious of her and her brother.

BETTE: You'll say no such thing. If ya' talk to the news they'll make the story worse and before ya' know it we'll have miles of people tramping 'round to look. It's nobody's business, especially not a bunch of stuck up strangers lookin' for trouble.

JIMMY: But Ma, we have to talk to the news, 'coz of somethin' I just found. Look at this!

(Excitedly, yet carefully, JIMMY takes out from the bag, a large colorful box,

decorated in a Christmas pattern.)

TILLY: *(in wonder)* A Christmas box.

BETTE: *(sternly)* Where did ya' get that?

JIMMY: It was in the garage. I've never seen it before. And get this, it has their door number on it. Number 794. That's why it caught my attention. I bet she smuggled it here in a panic. *(speaking to TILLY)* You wait till you see what's in it.

BETTE: You've opened it? *(JIMMY nods, looking incredibly proud and excited.)* Ya' shouldn't 'ave opened it.

TILLY: Oh my God, it's a head isn't it? It's a dead head. Or a hand, it's her hand isn't it? I told you Katrina with a K wasn't to be trusted. And you said Mrs. Huddlestone was put in a home and here she is dismembered and laying in a Christmas box.

JIMMY: Fake Aunt Tilly, it's not a hand.

TILLY: It's like the twelve days of Christmas, but in body parts!

BETTE: *(angrily)* Tilly stop it! Jimmy put that back, it's not yours.

JIMMY: I'm not putting this back, it's too good. That's why I'm gonna' to speak to the reporters.

TILLY: This is too much for me, I'm getting one of my dizzy heads. I hate to see blood.

JIMMY: No, look!

(JIMMY opens the box and it's full of money. TILLY begins to scream, which quickly turns into an interested squeal.)

TILLY: Ohhh money!

JIMMY: Yeah, money! And there's a lot of it. Way more than I've ever seen.

TILLY: Gangster money!

JIMMY: *(He looks at BETTE now, suspiciously.)* And ya' know what's really interesting? There's a written note on top.

BETTE: *(Angry)* Jimmy!

JIMMY: *(JIMMY holds up the note and slowly reads.)* "Dearest Bette, you'll know what to do when your heart tells you, love Burt." *(Both JIMMY and TILLY look at BETTE.)* Ma, care to explain.

TILLY: Bette, that's your name. Wasn't Burt that guy who lived next door years ago? Wasn't he one of those brothers who formed a gang and got bagged for somethin' and went to prison?

JIMMY: Ma?

TILLY: Bette?

JIMMY: This is looking sketchy, is there somethin' you need to tell us?

BETTE: You two are bein' ridiculous. Burt and his brothers sold ice cream they stole from the 'packie' on the corner, they weren't gangsters, they were kids. Good lord, Tilly. What are you thinkin'? Gangsters my ass! One of 'em drives a bus in Dorchester. He has that club foot and ugly beard.

JIMMY: But the money?

BETTE: Yeah, the money. Congratulations Jimmy that was gonna' be ya' Christmas present, to help ya' out next year. I won a ton the other night on the slots. There are no gangsters and no dead, dismembered bodies. There's just me puttin' up with the two of you jokers.

TILLY: *(giggling)* Oh my goodness, and there was I getting' suspicious.

BETTE: Tilly girl, you may wanna' get home, I can see a bulldozer coming down the street.

TILLY: Oh good lord, what a day! If you need me, holler. *(TILLY leaves, screaming.)* Don't you touch my violets!

JIMMY: It's a lot of money Ma.

BETTE: I know.

JIMMY: I got tons of stuff I can use that money on. Starters, I'm gonna get wasted tonight.

(JIMMY sits in one of the chairs, happily looking at the box.)

BETTE: Ever think about saying thank you? *(JIMMY does a sarcastic smirk and BETTE tuts and makes her decision.)* Right then.

JIMMY: What is this note all about though?

(BETTE snatches the note from him, scrunching it up and putting it into her pocket. She begins to busy herself at the back of where JIMMY is sitting, as though making some tea, while taking out a larger bag from under the table.)

BETTE: Ya' Dad used to say; ya' should only trust ya' own lips n' eyes.

(BETTE brings out a large plastic sheet, shakes it out and places in front of where JIMMY is seated. He remains distracted with trying to count the money and takes no notice.)

JIMMY: I don't think I understand that.

BETTE: Nah, ya' wouldn't.

JIMMY: Have ya' been smokin' the weed again Ma? Did you forget we don't know me Dad?

BETTE: He also said that people should spend more time fixin' their own stories instead of creatin' dramas 'bout other people. Nothin' good is ever resolved from gossip.

JIMMY: I'm gonna get decked out, go to Foot Locker and buy the best.

BETTE: Ya' Dad always says ya' wouldn't achieve much.

JIMMY: I'm gettin' a tattoo. Something mad. Maybe I'll get Brewie and the boys and we'll go to Murphy's in a limo. Imagine that, showing up in a big, stretch limo! *(He stops.)* What do ya' mean; 'he said I wouldn't achieve much?' Who said that?

BETTE: Don't worry yourself now boy.

(BETTE returns to the bag on the table behind JIMMY.)

JIMMY: Do you think they'll find anythin' next door?

BETTE: Well, they won't find all the money I brought back over here.

JIMMY: What?

BETTE: But I'm pretty sure, they *will* dig up the bank manager that Burt, your Dad, stole it all from.

(BETTE brings out a weapon from her bag.)

JIMMY: Wait a minute, wasn't Burt Mrs.Huddlestones brother? The one who went to prison?

BETTE: Loose lips, sink ships, and like I said gossip serves no one. *(BETTE raises a garrote with great confidence and begins to walk behind JIMMY.)* And it's probably best that you don't turn around son.

(Dropkick Murphys' Shipping up to Boston *plays loudly as we go to blackout.)*

(the end)

THE BULL

by Greg Hovanesian

Greg Hovanesian is a playwright, actor, and theatre producer based in Boston, MA. His works have been produced by Gallery Players, the Nora Theatre Company (Boston Theater Marathon XXI), Boston Actors Theater, the UAE Theatre Festival, the One-Minute Play Festival (Boston), Jacklyn Thrapp LLC, Image Theater, Playwrights' Platform, Hovey Players, River's Edge Arts Alliance, Target Stage Company (Boston Theater Marathon XXII: Special Zoom Edition), and others. His plays have been included in anthologies published by New World Theatre and Playwrights' Platform Publishing. He has produced plays at the Rockwell (Somerville, MA) and the Players' Ring Theatre (Portsmouth, NH) with his company Ya Bird? Productions. As an actor he has performed at Boston Playwrights' Theatre, Hiberian Hall, Boston Theater Marathon XXI, the Watertown Plumbing Museum, and on Zoom with North Shore Readers Theater. Greg is President of Playwrights' Platform, Social Media Coordinator for the New England New Play Alliance, and belongs to StageSource and the Dramatists Guild of America. From June 3rd-14th, 2020, he will be producing the 48th Annual Playwrights' Platform Festival of New Plays on Zoom Webinars as a fundraiser for the Theatre Community Benevolent Fund. **Contact: greghovanesian.com**

The Bull was sponsored by **Target Stage Company**, which creates and produces plays based on the fundamental principle that theatre is the intimate and personal exploration of the human condition. Theatre as a catalyst for discussion, never professing or prescribing. **Website: fb.me/ TargetStageCompany**

The Bull was presented on April 19, 2020, with the following creative team:

Directed by Matt Greene
MAN: Nick Wakely
WOMAN: Gabrielle Fernandes

CHARACTERS:

A MAN, aged 30-70

A WOMAN, aged 30-70

(A kitchen. A table and some chairs. There may be some coffee, bagels, etc, on the table. It's morning. There are newspapers on the table. A MAN stands at a large window, looking out. A WOMAN sits at the table, sipping some coffee and reading a newspaper.)

MAN: *(looking out window)* Wow....Wow. *(The WOMAN doesn't look up.)* You see that?

WOMAN: What?

MAN: A deer. A big one... Wow.

(Silence for a beat. After a beat, the MAN turns away from the window, towards her.)

WOMAN: *(without looking up from what she's reading)* Mmmmmm...

MAN: With big antlers... It was, uh...majestic.

WOMAN: Mmmm... Probably eating our apples.

MAN: What...?

(Silence for a beat. The MAN approaches the table. He sits.)

Whatcha reading?

WOMAN: Hmmm...?

MAN: Whatcha reading...?

WOMAN: Nothing. Nothing. The News.

MAN: Oh...Any good?

WOMAN: I...don't...I just don't...

MAN: What...?

(The WOMAN puts the paper down.)

WOMAN: I don't care. Anymore. I just don't care.

MAN: About...?

(The WOMAN points towards the newspaper.)

WOMAN: This. Any of this. Anymore. I don't care.

MAN: You don't care?

WOMAN: No.

MAN: No?

WOMAN: No.

(silence for a beat)

MAN: But what if...?

WOMAN: What if what?

MAN: What if...well...you know...I mean...what do you...mean...you say you don't...?

WOMAN: Care? What do I mean? That I don't care?

MAN: No. Yes. Yes. That's what I mean. I mean, what do you mean by...?

WOMAN: What?

MAN: I mean, what I mean, is, because, you know, what I mean, is that, well...what I mean is, I think, it's important, to, well...well, I care.

WOMAN: You care?

MAN: Yes.

WOMAN: You do?

MAN: Yes...

WOMAN: Really?

MAN: Yeah. I do. And I think...I think it's important that you should...you know...consider...what the..context...of the...the...

WOMAN: Yeah. I don't think you do.

MAN: What?

WOMAN: I don't think you care. Like you think you do.

MAN: You don't?

WOMAN: No.

MAN: Okay... I don't see why you have to...

WOMAN: What...?

MAN: Turn this into...

WOMAN: What...?

(silence for a beat)

MAN: Why are you attacking me?

WOMAN: Attacking?

MAN: Yes. Why are you attacking me?

WOMAN: Attacking you?

MAN: Yes. What did I do to...?

WOMAN: What...?

MAN: Why...

WOMAN: What...?

(They sit in silence for a few beats. The MAN picks up a piece of the paper. Begins to read. The WOMAN stands up from the table. Walks towards the window. She gets to the window and stands there, looking out. The MAN continues to read. The MAN looks at newspaper…)

It says here that—

WOMAN: —Shhhh. I don't want to know.

MAN: But you don't know what I was going to—

WOMAN: —I told you. I don't want to know.

MAN: Okay. Fine.

(The MAN goes back to reading. Silence for a beat. After a couple beats, the MAN puts down the paper. He should be facing away from the WOMAN at the window. As he talks, he faces away from her.)

It was big. Majestic…Standing in the garden. The dew on the grass touching on its legs. Standing there, just standing there…Antlers glistening in the sun. Majestic. He was majestic.

WOMAN: *(looking out window, facing away from MAN)* Clouds moving in, another cloudy day…We need more sun. The garden. The garden needs more sun…Another cloudy day.

MAN: *(facing away from WOMAN)* He didn't move a muscle. He just stood there, staring. Fearless. Staring. A chiseled piece of Earth standing in the bushes.

WOMAN: *(looking out window)* In the garden. In my garden. We need more sun. The tomatoes won't grow, the apples won't ripen, the blueberries might die. We need more sun.

MAN: *(facing away)* And as I watched him, he seemed to see me. To know me. And his eyes, I think, for just a moment, there was a recognition. Of sorts. A sort of...understanding...between...

WOMAN *(looking out window)* Trampled vegetables. Found his hoof prints in my squash patch. He trampled my vegetables.

MAN: *(facing away)* So strong, so fearless, so majestic.

WOMAN: *(looking out window)* Found a half-eaten apple on the ground. Gross. To just leave it like that.

MAN: *(facing away)* Sometimes, I wish I could be a big, giant buck. Free, free from the world. No job, no worries. Just walking the land, big and strong, searching for my flock.

WOMAN: *(looking out window)* I just want things to grow. Goddammit. I just want things to grow.

(Silence for a few beats. After a few beats, the MAN turns around in his chair.)

MAN: It was big.

(The WOMAN turns to face MAN.)

WOMAN: Hmmmm...?

MAN: He was big. Real big. And he was just standing out there. In the garden. You should have seen him.

(The WOMAN turns back to the window.)

WOMAN: Hmmmm...

MAN: And he had these big antlers. And he had dew all over his legs, where he'd been walking in the grass, and his antlers were shining in the sun. Glistening....

You should have seen him.

WOMAN: Mmmmm...

MAN: You should have seen him.

WOMAN: I have seen him.

MAN: You've seen him?

WOMAN: Yes. I've seen him...I know that deer...I've seen that deer...I don't think I'll ever feel safe again.

(blackout)

(end of play)

WARM RUNNING WATER

by Janet Kenney

for Mauret

Janet Kenney is thrilled to be participating in her ninth Marathon, and she's grateful to Kate and company for keeping it going strong. She has written a dozen ten-minute pieces that have been produced all over the country. Along with some one-acts, she has a half dozen full-length plays, all of which have been produced here and there. The last two, *more than what* and *therese at home*, were both produced in Boston, at Centastage and Boston Playwrights' Theatre, respectively. The latest completed project is a memoir, *what else but grace*, about an absurd 40-year boxing match with Lupus and the oft-failed attempt to have some grace around it. The title also takes its name from Janet's magnificent poodle mutt Grace, who has been her journey-mate for the last 14 years. Seeking agent. **Contact: missjanetkenney@gmail.com**

Warm Running Water was sponsored by the **Firehouse Center for the Arts**, a hallmark of local culture and arts since 1991. The historic building that houses the Center for the Arts was built as a market house and lyceum by the citizens of Newburyport in 1823 and served as the Central Fire Station from the mid-1800s until 1980. A strong cooperative effort by the public and private sectors led to the restoration of the structure as a center for the arts and public events, and along with Schwartz/Silver Architects, Inc., the Firehouse won an "Honor Award for Architecture" from The American Institute of Architects. The Firehouse continually draws 25,000 patrons annually from local communities as well as a large tourist crowd in the spring, summer, and fall. In 2019, the Firehouse continued to provide a space to the community where the sparks of creative ideas could ignite. We offered over 200 artistic events for the community, from theatrical productions produced by local and regional talent, to legendary musical acts, to Project Sparx youth productions that helped teach our future leaders how to play, listen and create together. We're proud to have created unique and memorable experiences for audiences in our charming, historic theater. **Firehouse.org**

Warm Running Water was presented on May 5, 2020, with the following creative team:

Directed by Dan Beaulieu
MR. JOHN: John McCluggage
GRAZIELLA: Paulina Tobar
MR. JOHN'S APARTMENT CAMERA: Christine Penney

CHARACTERS:

MR. JOHN: Elderly

GRAZIELLA: Middle-aged, Mexican

(Present, late morning in a small urban apartment. The front door leads into the tiny kitchen, Not dirty but not tidy. Bits of clothing here and there. It looks like nothing has been put away for a while: dirty plates and glasses are out on the counter. At rise, MISTER JOHN sits snoozing in his wheelchair. He's elderly. There's

a table next to him. He's wearing tousled layers of clothes. His hair is disheveled. From offstage, a woman's voice…)

GRAZIELLA: OOHHHH HHOOO! Mister John! Mister John—

(GRAZIELLA bursts through the door with a bag of groceries and a pile of mail. She's of Mexican origin, years ago. She's heading towards middle age. She's bright and shiny, but exhausted.)

Wake up! It's a beautiful day! You didn't get your mail this week! It's piled all over the— Ay! I can smell you from the door! If Corinne catches you in this condition I'll be fired—in the shower! Right away!

(He smells his armpits.)

MISTER JOHN: I'm all right.

GRAZIELLA: Who told you that? You are supposed to wash up your body every night. Did you do that? You didn't wash this week! Are you sick? Why are you wearing that sweater? It's made of grizzly bear. What day is it? It's June. Why are you wearing that sweater? You should shower before you even eat.

MISTER JOHN: But I'm hungry.

GRAZIELLA: Why are you hungry? Did you eat?

MISTER JOHN: I had a cookie.

GRAZIELLA: Ay! You worry me to death. I'll breathe through my mouth. Let's see what I got— *(She fishes things out of the grocery bag.)* Ooh… nice sliced turkey?

MISTER JOHN: Don't buy that—it goes bad.

(MISTER JOHN rejects each offer.)

GRAZIELLA: Not if you eat it. Grilled cheese? Tuna? PopTarts? I got Brown Sugar! Fried eggs? Toast? *(the usual)* Peanut Butter Jelly.

MISTER JOHN: But not the stuff with the globs in it.

GRAZIELLA: Those globs are FRUIT in jam. You should eat some fruit.

MISTER JOHN: It gets stuck in my teeth.

GRAZIELLA: No, it doesn't. Aye, Madonna, Mister John. Did you wash at all this week? Corinne will have a fit—

MISTER JOHN: She hasn't been by—

GRAZIELLA: What? Why not? Is she sick? She should call the agency. I could have come by this week.

MISTER JOHN: Why don't you call her ? Find out how she is.

GRAZIELLA: You know I can't do that. They'd fire me in a minute, I start calling clients' daughters. I'll have the agency call her on Monday—see if she's OK. Have you talked to her?

MISTER JOHN: She's very busy.

GRAZIELLA: Never too busy for her Daddy. She's a good girl. Wait. What did you say to her?

MISTER JOHN: Nothing! She's got some notion in her head. She can tell you all about it. If you call her. She'll think I had a heart attack or died.

GRAZIELLA: She'll appreciate that. Eat your sandwich. Warm running water washes your sins away. Did you know that? *Es Verdad.* [True.] Did you guys fight?

MISTER JOHN: That's none of your business.

GRAZIELLA: Fine, don't tell me. Families fight, you know. Everyone gets mad and someone has to apologize and then—

MISTER JOHN: She won't pick up the phone. She sees it's me. Won't pick up. That's why you have to call her. Here—I wrote it down for you. She won't recognize your number—take it.

GRAZIELLA: And then she reports me to the agency—

MISTER JOHN: She won't. She'll understand.

GRAZIELLA: If she's mad at you, she might get mad at me. She just needs a few days to—

MISTER JOHN: It's been two weeks.

GRAZIELLA: You call her. Tell her you're sorry.

MISTER JOHN: I told her that. I told her, "Baby. I'm so sorry." You can tell her. Say I did a wrong thing and it was a long time ago and it doesn't matter. Just tell her that and have my baby girl talk to me. You can hand me the phone when you're done with all that.

GRAZIELLA: What did you do? I know. None of my business.

MISTER JOHN: A long time ago, I did a stupid thing. And it didn't hurt anybody at the time. For a long time, it just lay there, forgotten. I just about forgot about it myself. I didn't do any harm at the time. My wife never knew. She never knew.

GRAZIELLA: But Corinne found out. A fling?

MISTER JOHN: Not a fling! A nice lady. But not my wife. Corinne's been cleaning out the apartment, you know. She found some stuff in the attic. This little black satchel. I know exactly which one she was talking about. She found some pictures. A couple notes. Now why do you think I never threw them out? I was so careful. I never thought to leave. I just wandered for a little while.

GRAZIELLA: A little while?

MISTER JOHN: Three years. Once in a while. A rare thing. We never meant anything by it.

GRAZIELLA: You know, if you don't wash your privates you get crusty. That crust has E. coli in it. That's a nasty bug. You get a scratch on your skin, it gets inside, very bad. You could die.

MISTER JOHN: Die from a scratch on my butt?

GRAZIELLA: It could happen.

MISTER JOHN: I think you're wrong,

GRAZIELLA: I'm practically a nurse.

MISTER JOHN: You clean houses!

GRAZIELLA: For sick people! Rosella got an A on her spelling test. Little Juan, he got tossed out of a class again. That boy. He's got his father's temper.

MISTER JOHN: Will you call her? Here. Take it.

GRAZIELLA: Get someone else to do it.

MISTER JOHN: Who do I have, huh? Who's lining up around the block to do me a favor—

> *(What ensues is a fight over the piece of paper. He puts it in her hand, in her pocket, she puts it in his hand, on his desk, in his grizzly sweater pocket… these monologues are delivered almost simultaneously, in an overlapping fashion. Overlaps are marked by * as a guide.)*

GRAZIELLA: I cannot lose this job! What else have I got I got to go to? * I got a million jobs waiting for me? I'm a nice lady, yeah? *I'm an almost middle -aged spic lady with a 9th-grade Mexican Education and a GED - am I gonna be a secretary? I got two kids to feed! I worry every * night about losing this job. They give me two clients a day, six days a week. That means they like me! They're gonna kill me.

MISTER JOHN: I was a good father! I was a good husband. * I was a gentleman. I didn't need to lose everything!* I didn't need to lose everything. I got nothing! I'm in this dump.I can't even get up the stairs * so I don't have my nice apartment on the *third floor cause I can't get to it. *and all I got in this—the only thing that matters in this world is that girl—

GRAZIELLA: Then YOU call her! YOU call her and you call her until she picks up. This is your call to make.

(She lets the paper drop to the floor, steps back from it. He lets loose with his peanut butter and jelly sandwich and it flies across the room, hits the wall. She picks it up, makes him another one, while...)

GRAZIELLA: Madonna. *Madre mio.* [My mother]. Women are stupid creatures, you know? When a man has wandered, women, sometimes they wait and wait . . .I knew. I could smell it on him. Not her. Just him. Just a change in the smell of my man. And I thought, Oh, just don't pay it any mind. All men go through that. And I was exhausted. Too tired to have a big brawl. But it was more than one. At least two. Maybe three. Till he left me. I'd like to say that I threw him out. But He left me. But I'm stupid. Ay, Madonna. Sometimes I think I'd take him back. I'd take him back. I'm killing myself, working myself to death. God. I just might. *Stupida.*

MISTER JOHN: You think she knew?

GRAZIELLA: No idea.

MISTER JOHN: Corinne says she must have known. I told her, don't worry. She didn't. But. I don't know.

GRAZIELLA: Would she have kept you?

MISTER JOHN: Yes.

GRAZIELLA: Then she must have loved you very much. Or been *stupida.* Eat your sandwich.

MISTER JOHN: Think I'll take a shower.

GRAZIELLA: Oh, you will, will you? That seems like a good idea.

(She covers the sandwich and wheels him toward the bathroom as, perhaps, a little music wanders in and light begin to fade. . .)

GRAZIELLA: You can text Corinne. I'll show you how.

MISTER JOHN: What? Why do I wanna text her? That's rude.

GRAZIELLA: It's not rude. Everyone does it.

MISTER JOHN: If you have time to text, why don't you just call.

GRAZIELLA: Not if she won't pick up. FaceTime.

MISTER JOHN: What's a FaceTime?

(The last few lines become somewhat unintelligible until. . .)

(blackout)

STRAINED BEDFELLOWS

by Terrence Kidd

Terrence Kidd, after traveling many crooked miles, earned an MFA in Creative Writing for Stage & Screen at Lesley University. He writes for under-represented characters and audiences, reflecting the hubris, hypocrisy, and hilarity of life's rich pageant. His first play, *Slugger*, was a finalist for the Actors Theater of Louisville's 2011 Heideman Award. His other plays and screenplays have been developed or seen at Grub Street Boston, Coolidge Corner Theater, Maine Media Workshops, Lesley University, The Strand Theater, Boston Playwrights' Theatre, The Boston Theater Marathon, LMDA National Conference, Company One, Boston Conservatory at Berklee, The Kennedy Center, and The Dramatists Guild. Terry aspires to inspire. You may find his plays at the National New Play Exchange, or contact him directly at **kiddterrence@gmail.com**.

Strained Bedfellows was sponsored by **American Repertory Theatre** (A.R.T) at Harvard University, a leading force in the American theater, producing groundbreaking work that is driven by risk-taking, artistic excellence, and passionate inquiry. Led by Terrie and Bradley Bloom Artistic Director Diane Paulus and Executive Producer Diane Borger, A.R.T. expands the boundaries of theater by producing groundbreaking and transformative theatrical experiences where the audience is a central partner. The A.R.T. has been honored with many distinguished awards including the Tony Award for Best New Play for *All the Way* (2014); consecutive Tony Awards for Best Revival of a Musical for *Pippin* (2013) and *The Gershwins' Porgy and Bess* (2012), both of which Paulus directed, and sixteen other Tony Awards since 2012; a Pulitzer Prize; a Jujamcyn Prize for outstanding contribution to the development of creative talent; and the Regional Theater Tony Award. Dedicated to making great theater accessible, A.R.T. actively engages more than 5,000 community members and local students annually in project-based partnerships, workshops, conversations with artists, and other enrichment activities both at the theater and across the Greater Boston area. **americanrepertorytheater.org**

Strained Bedfellows was presented on April 24, 2020, with the following creative team:

Directed by Christine Noah
SENATOR: Kevin Craig West
CHANCELLOR: Letta Neely

CHARACTERS:

CHANCELLOR—F, Black. 40's-50's

SENATOR—M, Black. 40's-50's.

(Office of the Chancellor of an H.B.C.U. in South, 2019.)

CHANCELLOR: Fifty boxes of MAGA hats?

SENATOR: Good afternoon to you too, Chancellor.

CHANCELLOR: What the fuck, Senator?

SENATOR: You're so high and mighty can't accept a gift from your former mentor and your president?

CHANCELLOR: He is not my president.

SENATOR: In fact, he is.

CHANCELLOR: I am the Chancellor of an H.B.C.U. MAGA hat here is as good as a white hood.

SENATOR: That's the kind of remark I'd call counterproductive. 'Sides, this shade of red always did bring out the amber in your eyes.

CHANCELLOR: There's a truthful saying about flattery. And how it will get you nowhere, Senator.

SENATOR: There's another truthful saying, Chancellor, about looking a gift horse in the mouth. And not doing it.

CHANCELLOR: If it gets out I have these hats—

SENATOR: That's the fault of the left-wing propaganda education you're feeding them radical liberals you call students. Don't blame me.

CHANCELLOR: Black Republican in my office talking about liberal propaganda? All that means is I'm doing something right.

SENATOR: You ought to know, ain't no right. Only varying degrees of getting what one wants.

CHANCELLOR: Every time I think you're done darkening my door...

SENATOR: I'm like a weed, they say. I prefer perennial and evergreen.

CHANCELLOR: Definitely ubiquitous. Like cockroaches.

SENATOR: Chancellor, please. If I'm like a cockroach, then I am under the heel of your sexy-ass boot.

CHANCELLOR: Keep my boots out your mouth.

SENATOR: Be that as it may, I came here bearing not just these presidential gifts, but also am prepared to sweeten the pot, so to speak.

CHANCELLOR: What do you want, Senator?

SENATOR: President wants to come to your campus.

CHANCELLOR: Tell me you're kidding.

SENATOR: My job—make sure he comes correct.

CHANCELLOR: A box of MAGA hats constitutes coming correct?

SENATOR: Hold up, now, Chancellor, I got more to offer than a box of hats.

CHANCELLOR: Having this president on my campus will cause—

SENATOR: What, complications?

CHANCELLOR: Damage.

SENATOR: Hallmark of African-Americanism is having the wherewithal to transcend complicated damage, ain't it?

CHANCELLOR: Tell that to the student body when they use those MAGA hats as kindling to burn the campus to the ground. If I allow the president to speak—

SENATOR: To you, speech is only free if you agree with what's being spoken?

CHANCELLOR: The president's exercising his right to the first amendment will only trigger our students to exercise their right to the second amendment.

SENATOR: Don't get all hysterical now—

CHANCELLOR: Said the pot to the kettle.

SENATOR: I need greater support from your university. More importantly, your university needs more support from me.

CHANCELLOR: Is that so?

SENATOR: And from the federal government, which I represent.

CHANCELLOR: You represent the people, Senator.

SENATOR: Nevertheless. I am here to explore the contours of the, shall I say, mutually beneficial.

CHANCELLOR: We're a long way from mutually beneficial, Senator.

SENATOR: So let's get mutual. True that chance and circumstance has made changes we wouldn't have expected when you ran my first campaign.

CHANCELLOR: I feel a but coming on.

SENATOR: But I also know that you and me both always made for strange bedfellows. You with your ideals, me with my ambition.

CHANCELLOR: Don't you even say bedfellows to me.

SENATOR: Hey. Ain't I proved that I am nothing if not discreet?

CHANCELLOR: Past is past, Senator.

SENATOR: Nah. Past is prologue. Another hallmark of African-Americanism.

CHANCELLOR: That being true—why would I trust you?

SENATOR: Our situation? Politically speaking? Both of us are too long for love.

CHANCELLOR: Not that long. Besides, I can't believe I ever worked for you.

SENATOR: Best campaign manager I ever had.

CHANCELLOR: Best? We won student body, lost city council. Then you registered Republican, and I was all the way out.

SENATOR: Not so long ago, though, I hope, that you can't remember my intentions are good.

CHANCELLOR: I get a little uneasy, Senator, every time I hear you say the words good intentions.

SENATOR: Then I'll keep it a hundred. Things keep going like they are for your university, you won't be teaching anybody anything. Enrollment continues to plummet. Operating budget is underwater. More federal funding would cure a lot of ills.

CHANCELLOR: Pell Grants? That your position? Hold poor kids financial aid hostage to get me to come across?

SENATOR: You need that funding.

CHANCELLOR: By aligning ourselves with a toxic president?

SENATOR: Republicans are still the majority in this state.

CHANCELLOR: It hasn't occurred to you that this is the worst time in history to be a black Republican?

SENATOR: Or the best time to catalyze a grassroots black conservative revolution.

CHANCELLOR: You cannot be serious.

SENATOR: What have Democrats ever done for the black electorate? I'll tell you what—jack fuckin' shit.

CHANCELLOR: Progress hasn't been made? We elected a black president.

SENATOR: Half white president, which all y'all forget. Not that I'm interested in identity politics.

CHANCELLOR: Republican party invented identity politics!

SENATOR: No, the Republican Party identified identity politics.

CHANCELLOR: Too bad your Republican base is dying off faster than you can suppress POC's from voting.

SENATOR: They ain't dead yet.

CHANCELLOR: Elections, Senator, are about math.

SENATOR: Keeping this university, and your ass employed, that's math too.

CHANCELLOR: Our student body is comprised of middle class and low-income students—

SENATOR: Ain't we talking about potential students?

CHANCELLOR: Holding their funding hostage to get a photo op of the president in front of black folks—

SENATOR: Small price to pay, you ask me.

CHANCELLOR: We teach students how think, you tell voters what to think.

SENATOR: You think I don't want educated black kids?

CHANCELLOR: I think all people in your party want an ignorant electorate.

SENATOR: You think I don't know my voters think the Confederate Flag isn't a symbol of genocide?

CHANCELLOR: Yet, you crave their vote.

SENATOR: No, I crave reality.

CHANCELLOR: Before this president, you were already a dark stranger in a darker strange land that is the Republican party. That's reality.

SENATOR: I win elections. So fuck you.

CHANCELLOR: Real man of the people, ain't you?

SENATOR: Look, if I want progress, I got to work within the system.

CHANCELLOR: Jonah in the whale.

SENATOR: Time is gonna come when people of color outnumber the white male power class—and who's going to be in charge when that happens? Godless Liberal Democrats, bent on government all up in every aspect of people's business?

CHANCELLOR: Hard sell to black folks when you've got a racist president and a Republican elected class kissing his whole asshole after every cruelty.

SENATOR: That's what I'm trying to chip away!

CHANCELLOR: You got something on your face, and your fly is open.

SENATOR: We may disagree on fundamentals of how black people are going to get ahead in America. But we want the same result.

CHANCELLOR: Which is what?

SENATOR: Pray how you want to pray. Spend how you want to spend. But do so wisely. Learn everything you want to learn, but don't discount the American Constitution.

CHANCELLOR: Constitution—bunch of words that say however, unless, except and but.

SENATOR: Not this three-fifths shit again...

CHANCELLOR: If you believe what the founders wrote, then black people are chattel.

SENATOR: You know I don't believe that.

CHANCELLOR: Naw, you believe in pure power over the power of the people. You're Black McConnell.

SENATOR: McConnell? Motherfuck Mitch McConnell! *(Then…)* However and be that as it may... People, Chancellor, got nothing if they don't have power. I am trying to live to die another day. And so are you. You have the power here to fund your university. Fund educations for black kids who got brains but not money. Kids like we once were.

CHANCELLOR: What's in it for you, Senator?

SENATOR: I need to be on the president's good side. Or I lose what power I have.

CHANCELLOR: Strange bedfellows become strained bedfellows indeed.

SENATOR: Like it or not, until the tide turns on this guy, I got to ride the wave I'm on.

CHANCELLOR: Because you have nothing if you don't have power.

SENATOR: Does the president come to speak at your university? Or not? Do you keep educating kids—our kids? Or not?

(beat)

CHANCELLOR: Here's how we spin it...You got the local newspaper on the payroll?

SENATOR: I have an asset or two.

CHANCELLOR: Somebody writes the story of how the administration intended to decimate Pell Grants for black colleges. But you, Senator, led discussions where the Pell Grants were secured; if the president talks about prison reform, and, let's say, taking a look at funding for early education in South Carolina.

SENATOR: I come off as a voice of reason and caring. Gets you off the hook for inviting the president on campus if you got deliverables.

CHANCELLOR: Your office pays for all security costs the university incurs for the potential student riot?

SENATOR: Students ain't going to riot.

CHANCELLOR: Why not?

SENATOR: Because you're going to demand that they shelter in place.

CHANCELLOR: What?

SENATOR: They stay in their rooms. That's direct from the White House.

CHANCELLOR: That's—but that's fascist.

SENATOR: Naw, Chancellor. That's politics.

(blackout)

MILLSTONE

by Peter Kimball

Peter Kimball is an award-winning writer, filmmaker, and playwright. His short play *Millstone* has been performed as part of Boston Theater Marathon XXII: Special Zoom Edition and the 2020 Mid-America Theater Conference. He works professionally as a screenwriter, writing original films, work-for-hire, and adaptations. As a filmmaker, his short films have won awards at festivals around the world. A graduate of Brown University, he has taught film and screenwriting at George Mason University and American University. He is the husband of an ER doctor, the father of three young children, and the beleaguered housemate of an obstinate beagle. He can be reached at **peter_kimball@alumni.brown.edu**.

Millstone was sponsored by **Greater Boston Stage Company**. After renovating an abandoned building in Stoneham Square that had once been home to silent films, vaudeville, and feature films throughout the 20th century, Greater Boston Stage Company (formerly Stoneham Theatre, Weylin Symes/Artistic Director) opened its doors to the public for a new era of live entertainment in the year 2000. Our mission is to bring vibrant professional theatre and dramatic education beyond the boundaries of Boston, featuring world and regional premieres alongside fresh interpretations of familiar work. Within this setting, we uniquely foster the artists of tomorrow by providing ongoing performance and employment opportunities to our company of current and former students. Each season, we produce a Mainstage program of 6-7 productions as well as an ongoing series of concerts and special events, and our education program (The Young Company) presents year-round classes, lessons, and fully staged productions for students in grades 1–12. **www.greaterbostonstage.org**

Millstone was presented on April 13, 2020, with the following creative team:

Directed by Weylin Symes
DR. PRINCE: Ilyse Robbins
JULIA: Lisa Joyce
MIKE: John Manning, Jr.

CHARACTERS:

DR. PRINCE, 50s, therapist, deliberate and soft spoken

MIKE, 30, a quiet man, broken by grief

JULIA, 30, a grieving woman on a mission

(The present, late afternoon in DR. PRINCE's warm therapist office. A bookcase full of books, family photos, and stylish if inoffensive bric a brac. Two chairs facing a third. Lights up on DR. PRINCE sitting across from MIKE and JULIA. MIKE and JULIA have cups of tea they'll sip throughout. They're a married couple but almost never touch.)

DR. PRINCE: After the Germans had destroyed half of Britain and bombed it all to hell, the Brits started their own raids. And, yes, they targeted military sites, yes, and factories, yes. But also civilians. Regular German people. And you know why?

(He pauses for a moment.)

Not to break their morale. It only hardened the Germans' resolve. No, they did it because it boosted English morale. All else aside, just knowing that the Germans were suffering the same way they had suffered, it made them feel just a little bit better.

JULIA: We're not looking for revenge.

DR. PRINCE: No?

JULIA: If I truly thought it would make me feel better? That if I found them, if I hurt them, if I killed them? If I hit their kid with my car and drove off, leaving him dying and bleeding in the street.

MIKE: But there were no witnesses. No evidence. It's a nonstarter.

JULIA: Their little kid. Their beautiful little five year old.

DR. PRINCE: I see.

JULIA: You think 'five year old' and you think of such a little kid. Five. Almost a baby. But not him. He seemed so tough, he seemed so full of opinions and intelligence. You talked to him and he wasn't a baby, he was a smart person. A smart, tough little guy and I... I honestly thought this kind of thing was impossible. That somehow, even the kinds of things that you fear with your kids, that none of those could really touch him.

(DR. PRINCE nods. Looks them over. MIKE keeps his head down.)

DR. PRINCE: I can tell you're hurting. That you're grieving. But there are lots of other doctors to go to.

JULIA: It's not just the loss. Not just waking up every morning knowing that the world is darker than it's supposed to be. It's that no one else cares. They've all moved on already.

MIKE: So we don't even.

DR. PRINCE: You don't...?

MIKE: We don't bring him up. We don't have pictures of him in the house. We don't talk about him.

JULIA: My parents even! I don't dare ever bring him up. Like it'll ruin their day. Like I'm smearing shit on their doorstep.

DR. PRINCE: But this is always part of grief. The fact that the rest of the world doesn't care in the same way you do. The fact that you two probably deal with it differently than each other.

JULIA: But I just don't want to deal with it anymore. I can't.

DR. PRINCE: Ah. So that's why you're here.

MIKE: It's not getting better.

JULIA: It's getting worse! It's getting so much worse.

MIKE: Yeah.

(She's getting heated. MIKE isn't.)

JULIA: YOU are getting so much worse.

MIKE: Alright. Yeah, sure.

DR. PRINCE: Go further with that, Julia.

JULIA: His drinking. His temper. He's drunk all day and he's screaming at me. Throwing things.

MIKE: Not throwing things.

JULIA: The tomato bowl. The goddamn tomato bowl!

MIKE: One thing.

JULIA: You think this is funny?

MIKE: I go to work. I pay our bills.

JULIA: They're on autopay, Mike.

MIKE: Do I drink more than I used to? Yeah. Do I wish I didn't? Can I tell it's not healthy? Yeah, sure. Of course.

JULIA: Fine. No. He's not some monster. He's not. But that's my point. It was never like this before.

DR. PRINCE: There are many different therapies you could try.

JULIA: The pain is killing us. And we're destroying each other.

MIKE: There is no good coming out of this. You know, there's nothing to learn. No growth, no triumph over adversity.

JULIA: It's only getting worse.

MIKE: So we've come to you.

JULIA: We heard about your program.

DR. PRINCE: Right, yes. I see. I never want to talk people out of my services but it is an extreme solution.

JULIA: We've tried therapists. We've tried religion. Nothing helps.

MIKE: So we want you to help us forget that we ever had a son.

DR. PRINCE: How does that sound? Hearing those words out of your mouth?

MIKE: What do you mean?

DR. PRINCE: Have you said them before? Even to each other?

JULIA: I mean, of course we've discussed this together.

DR. PRINCE: But I would guess that you haven't said it in so many words. Never actually said THOSE words before. No?

(MIKE and JULIA look at each other. Obviously he's right.)

DR. PRINCE: There's something so deeply wrong about it, isn't there?

JULIA: Why do you do this if it's wrong?

DR. PRINCE: It FEELS wrong. It flies in the face of everything we think about life and memory. "Even if you're gone, you'll live on in our memories." No? "I'll never forget you." "I'll keep a part of you with me forever."

MIKE: But you try that. See if it actually helps you feel better.

DR. PRINCE: I wouldn't know. More of a ruthless vengeance man myself.

JULIA: It does feel wrong. And I hate myself for saying that's what we want. But I just don't see another way.

MIKE: If your process really works.

(DR. PRINCE pulls a pamphlet from the bookcase.)

DR. PRINCE: I've developed a serum which, like traditional hypnotism, makes subjects incredibly suggestible. You can forget whole parts of your past. As if they never existed.

MIKE: And it really works?

DR. PRINCE: Forgetting is easy. For other things, look, I could convince you that you have two heads but every time you look in the mirror you'd still only see one. Imagine living with that.

MIKE: Uh huh.

JULIA: But does it work? Does it actually make things better?

DR. PRINCE: *(very deliberately)* It will not bring him back. You want him back, you want him in your life, and you want him to lead his own happy, full life. And this will not fix that. Nothing can.

JULIA: But it can be like it never happened?

DR. PRINCE: Yes. In your minds, yes.

MIKE: No one else is talking about him anyway. No trouble there.

DR. PRINCE: For what it is: Yes, it works. But is that worth it to you?

JULIA: This is why we came. Right? But I don't know. To lose him again. Even in my memories. To lose any scrap of him...

(DR. PRINCE nods kindly. He offers her a tissue. MIKE puts his arm around JULIA.)

MIKE: Can I talk to you alone for a minute? I mean, you, doctor?

JULIA: You want to talk to him alone?

MIKE: Just for a minute. Please?

DR. PRINCE: Yes, sure. Julia, why don't you step out for a moment.

(JULIA gathers herself and steps out. MIKE leans forward.)

MIKE: We have to do this. You don't understand.

DR. PRINCE: What do you mean?

MIKE: I just... I mean, obviously we have to both do it, right? We couldn't just have one of us remember and the other one not.

DR. PRINCE: No. Never.

MIKE: Then if it can't just be one of us and it sure as hell needs to be me, then I guess it has to be her too.

DR. PRINCE: You can't make that decision for her, though.

MIKE: But if she says no then she's making the decision for me, right? And how is that fair?

DR. PRINCE: On principle, when in doubt we defer to less intervention.

MIKE: But this has to happen. It has to. You don't understand.

DR. PRINCE: Tell me.

MIKE: There was no evidence, right? There were no witnesses? A hit and run, he's out there bleeding and it takes her twenty minutes to get out there. Twenty minutes.

DR. PRINCE: And you can't forgive her for that.

(MIKE leans forward to whisper.)

MIKE: That's her story. How she tells it and no one else was there. You think she'd paint herself so badly if the truth weren't even worse?

DR. PRINCE: You don't believe her story?

MIKE: I know she was stressed out. She loved him, yes. Of course. But she never wanted to be a mother. She never wanted this kind of life and I don't know...

DR. PRINCE: So...

MIKE: No one else saw what happened. No one else saw the car, the driver. It's just her word.

DR. PRINCE: So what do you think happened?

MIKE: I think that no matter what happens in life, if this keeps going I am always going to wonder. I am always going to suspect. And there won't be any evidence. There won't be any proof. And so I will never know.

DR. PRINCE: And how does that make you feel?

MIKE: I will hate her for the rest of my life. Living with this woman who murdered my child. Kissing her at night, holding her. Comforting her when she cries. I feel like a liar and an accomplice and I hate myself for every part of it.

DR. PRINCE: It's tearing you apart inside. You think she killed your son. And you drink because of the grief and because of the hate in your heart.

MIKE: Why do I think she did it if there isn't some truth there?

DR. PRINCE: And which is worse? The loss or the hate?

MIKE: Both are killing me... And can't that all be gone? If the memory goes? If we forget him, if we forget that any of this ever happened. Then all this goes away.

DR. PRINCE: And you can happily love her again.

(MIKE nods and has another sip.)

MIKE: So what do you think?

DR. PRINCE: Well, first of all, you've both been drinking the serum the whole time you've been here.

(MIKE looks down at his cup.)

MIKE: You didn't even tell us.

(MIKE starts to stand up but he can't move.)

DR. PRINCE: Don't worry. It's starting to work. It won't be long now.

MIKE: It's already working?

DR. PRINCE: Tell me one thing, Mike. Tell me how you heard about me.

MIKE: What? I don't know.

DR. PRINCE: You don't remember how you found me? A pamphlet, a recommendation, a posting online?

MIKE: I mean...

DR. PRINCE: I came to your door. I found you.

(MIKE swallows that.)

MIKE: I don't remember that.

DR. PRINCE: No. Of course not. But I found you. The owners of the red Chevy Tahoe that ran over my son.

MIKE: No.

DR. PRINCE: It doesn't bring him back and it doesn't fill the hole in my heart. But to know you're suffering the way I suffered, it does help a little.

(MIKE sits back, unable to move.)

MIKE: We never had a son?

DR. PRINCE: You never had a son. You just stole mine from me.

(another long pause)

MIKE: I'm sorry.

DR. PRINCE: Thank you. You've said that nine times now.

MIKE: What?

(DR. PRINCE looks MIKE in the eyes.)

DR. PRINCE: And now we begin again. But this time, let's try something different. Again, no one wants to hear about it. Don't dare tell anyone—they already know. You've talked about it with them a million times and they don't want to hear it again.

MIKE: *(hypnotized)* They'll just think I'm crazy for bringing it up again.

DR. PRINCE: But this time, deep down, you know that YOU'RE the one who did it. Everyone thinks it was a hit and run but you know you killed him. An accident, maybe. Maybe.

(DR. PRINCE straightens up and turns toward the door.)

DR. PRINCE: Julia! You want to come back in? *(to Mike)* And she's starting to suspect.

(JULIA reenters.)

JULIA: I'm feeling a little funny.

DR. PRINCE: Please, sit down.

(curtain)

12 DAYS

by John Kuntz

John Kuntz is a playwright, actor, director, teacher, and solo performer. He is the author of more than 15 full-length plays including *Necessary Monsters, The Hotel Nepenthe, Starfuckers, The Annotated History of the American Muskrat, Sing Me To Sleep,* and *The Salt Girl.* As an actor, he has appeared with The Huntington Theatre Company, ART, Commonwealth Shakespeare Company, Speakeasy Stage ,and many others. He is the recipient of five Elliot Norton Awards, two IRNE Awards, a New York International Fringe Festival Award, a 2015 MCC Fellowship Award in Dramatic Writing, and the Michael Kanin and Paula Vogel National Playwrighting Awards. He is a lecturer in Theatre, Dance, and Media at Harvard University and is an Associate Professor at The Boston Conservatory at Berklee. **Contact: kuntzie44@gmail.com**

12 Days was sponsored by **Acropolis Stage Company**, which was created by Artistic Director Evan Turissini and Managing Director Olivia Dumaine. Acropolis' name echoes Boston Athenæum co-founder William Tudor, who in 1819 christened Boston "The Athens of America" for Boston's unique appreciation and cultivation of intellectual, artistic, and cultural excellence. Acropolis Stage Company promises to uphold and continue that tradition, not only by promoting the diverse array of Boston voices within the theatre, but celebrating Boston artists of all kinds.

12 Days was presented on May 17, 2020, with the following creative team:

Directed by Evan Turissini
GUY: Adrian Peguero

CHARACTERS:

GUY: Male or male-presenting, 30s

GUY: He was sweet. At first. I met him at the poetry slam and we dated for awhile. Sushi.Tennis. Competitive origami. That sort of thing. I could describe what he looked like, I suppose, but it wouldn't help. It would be like describing the Loch Ness Monster. Or the abominable snowman. Or a Log Cabin Republican. I thought he was cute, but I was drinking a lot of Chardonnay during that particular period in my life. I mean a lot. And having lots of meaningless sex.Binge eating. Shop lifting. Dressing like a harlequin and hanging out in high school parking lots. So, my judgment might have been kind of cloudy. He did funny things. I love how he hid Jell-O around the apartment for me to find. Lime with canned pears suspended in it. Sometimes with cool whip. Sometimes not. He looked like a drippy, droopy, soggy dog when he stood outside my apartment in the rain at 3 a.m., scratching at my window pane, his eyes glowing in the dark like an abandoned waif in a Walter Keane painting. He played the clarinet. He was an Aquarius. He was wanted in several states for impersonating a public official. He liked rollercoasters and roller skates and that song by

Romeo Void. Not that one, but the other one. He seemed perfect. But, during Thanksgiving, I realized it wouldn't work out. My family took to him: that was a bad sign. He laughed at all my fathers' mildly racist jokes, and supplied one of his own: a ribald haiku describing the violent death of his Vietnamese landlord. He admired my mother's tattoos and the belt buckle she found in the parking lot of the Red Lobster the day after that drive by shooting..

I like to be alone. I never realized that until he came along. And I ran, I admit it. It was December, and I had decided to become a nun. Or nun like. Nun-esque. No more relationships. With people. Well, living people. I was going to shut it out. Shut him out. Like a draft. I was going to be pure. He called for a while, but I wouldn't answer. And it seemed to work, this hermitage, for a while. Then he started sending the gifts. It was one bird, the first day. In a little decorative fruit tree. Now, I don't have much use for fruit as I've been on the first phase of the South Beach diet for the last 13 years. But if the pet thing didn't work out, that partridge seemed like damn good eating. And yet why would he give me a bird as a gift? Why not flowers or chocolate? But he was not a conventional sort, I knew, that was why I was first attracted to him. Of course he would send a bird, or a hubcap, or a human skull. That was unexpected. I should expect that from him.

The next day he sent me two different birds. Some sort of pigeon. I should mention, also that these birds were not house-trained. It wasn't like they were parrots, or that bird Robert Blake had before he killed his wife, what were they called? You know, with the little feather Mohawks that popped up like surprised boners? No, these birds were wild. They flew everywhere, banging into windows, cooing non-stop, pooping on everything in sight. They loved the top of the refrigerator, that's where they would congregate. And they would stare at me with their heads cocked, this baffled bird stare. Like they were waiting for something.

The next day came three more birds. Hens, this time. But they talked, these hens, like parrots. Only in French. "Sucre bleu!" they would screech at four in the morning. "Escargot!" "Croissant!" They set up a little café on top of the refrigerator: tables and chairs with checkered table cloths and the other birds would sit there all day, smoking endless amounts of Gitanes and discussing Proust in their little bird voices, which by now I was starting to understand in a Doolittle-like sort of way. And the French Hens wore aprons and served lattes and little pear pastries they made from the first birds' little tree. And at night they would close up and drink wine and swear at the top of their lungs about how cheap the other birds were what lousy tippers. And then they would shit on my duvet cover.

The next day came four more birds. Brightly plumed, exotic creatures. And they could talk as well. They never shut up. But they didn't talk to each other, or me, or to the other birds for that matter. They all had little cell phones and they would flap around, dialing and calling and screeching into their little phones. My first thought was: who's responsible for that phone bill? Me? And whom are they calling? Each other? What could they possibly have to talk about, these birds? "How'd your day go? Well,

I squawked and then I shit and then I squawked again, how about you?" Actually, no more than anyone with a cell phone, now that I think of it. The French Hens hated the calling birds. They would sit at the café for hours and hours on one cup of coffee, chomping on crumbs left by the other birds.

In four days, I had received ten birds. Did I mention that I live in a one-bedroom apartment? I kept my bedroom door closed at all times and would squeeze into the kitchen in the morning. There was always a silence whenever I walked into the room. The squawking would stop for a second and all the birds would stare at me. I felt like Tippi Hedren.

On the fifth day, no birds came. Instead I got a velvet box with five gold rings. Now, a man giving you a ring can only mean one thing. But getting five? Did he want to marry me five times, like a Mormon with amnesia? I put all five of them on my right hand. They fit each finger perfectly, like brass knuckles, and I wondered if this was the beginning of some real gifts. Some prime booty. Gold, diamonds? Instead of birds eggs, maybe *Faberge* Eggs? Hell, I would take a Cadbury egg at this point. But the next two days, it was back to the birds.

Geese and Swans, this time. Can I tell you something about Geese and Swans? They're mean. Especially the geese. They would honk at me. Honk. Like old jalopies. Meanwhile, the swans completely took over the bathroom. They filled the bathtub with Mr. Bubble, and all seven of them would swim around it, happy as clams.

The next day, eight women showed up at my door. They were maids, they informed me. Great, I thought. And I showed them in. Finally, someone to clean up this mess. But no. They only did dairy-related jobs. They asked me if I had any cows. I said "Not yet, but stick around." I told them I was lactose intolerant. Had been for years. "Well, that's not our problem" Mindy said. She was head milkmaid, Mindy, a real ball breaker. Face like a pug. And they took up residence on my couch, munching on microwave popcorn and watching *House of Cards*.

The next day nine more women showed up at my door. They were all part of some sort of dance troupe. They were all thin and limp, like room temperature celery sticks. "Where should we set up?" they asked me. "Surprise Me," I said. They chose my breakfast nook, where they danced all night and in the mornings they would pirouette onto the fire escape, or watusi down the hall. They took themselves and what they referred to as "their work" very seriously.

The ten jumping men came the next day. They were like human toads, shirtless, their bodies reeking of bay leafs and pine nuts and Stetson. Harlequin tights. The dancing ladies and the leaping men got along just fine. But there were nine women and 10 men, and there was always one leaping man left out. He was the loneliest lord of leaping, and his name was Larry. And whenever I watched his solitary bobbing from the corner of my eye, my heart went out to him.

My ironic collection of Hummels looked like Rice Krispies by this time, needless to say.

I wondered that night what tomorrow would bring. I wondered if a restraining order might not be appropriate. And I found I couldn't sleep. I was too excited. And I wondered about that. And then I wondered about the wonder.

Have you ever heard a piper? Have you ever heard 11 of them? Because that's who showed up the next day. They piped all sorts of ditties: "Music Box Dancer" and "Blue Bayou," to more contemporary numbers, like "I Kissed a Girl" and "Wrecking Ball." When the drummers arrived the next day, I was pretty much a zombie with a migraine. I hadn't slept for days. I was covered in feathers and guano. I had what amounted to a bird sanctuary and a performance of *Stomp* in my living room. Eviction papers had been served to me, and the police arriving at my door in response to a complaint from my neighbors had become a daily occurrence. My will was broken, and some strange new sensation had taken its place. Pliancy, but I can't call it that. I guess it was awe, or wonder. Nothing in my life made sense anymore. And I wasn't sure that that was so bad.

On the thirteenth day, I woke up, and everything was gone: the precocious birds, the dancing women, Larry. My right hand was no longer ringed in gold. It was all gone. My apartment was back to its empty self: soulless, but manageable. Easy. Calm. Non-threatening. I could breathe the quiet in the air. It smelled of Windex, and pennies and something like disappointment. And that's when I realized I was in love. I love this man who had sent me all this crazy stuff. I love him. And I know he loves me. Now, I can't tell you why I know that, or why I feel this way. All I can say is that I did. It was wonderful. I had found my true love. This gift giver. This sender of birds. I want to be with him for the rest of my life. So, I don't know if you can put all that in a personal ad, but that's my story. Do you think, if you print it, he might read it, wherever he is? Do you think I will find him? All I want for Christmas is to find my true love again. Do you think I can find him? Do you?

(end of play)

SHIPS IN THE NIGHT

by Kayce Kvacek

Kayce Kvacek is a Cleveland-born theatre artist and recent graduate of Boston University. She studied in London at the London Academy of Music and Dramatic Art (LAMDA) and returned to Boston University to complete her BFA in Theatre Arts. She is primarily an actress but dabbles in all areas of theatre including writing, stage combat, and theatrical make up. Some of her acting credits include: Viola in *Twelfth Night* (Chagrin Academy), Camille in *Horse Girls* (Boston University), and Mary Rivers in *Jane Eyre* (Boston University). Reach her at **kvacekkayce@gmail.com** and view the rest of her work at **kaycekvacek.com**.

Ships in the Night was sponsored by **The School of Theatre at Boston University College of Fine Arts**, which offers conservatory-style education for the study of acting, stage management, design, production, theatre education, and all aspects of the theatre profession within the setting of a major research university. The School of Theatre provides students with opportunities for artistic growth through a rigorous curriculum, professional connections, and an emphasis on collaboration and new work. **www.bu.edu/cfa/theatre/**

Ships in the Night was presented on April 28, 2020, with the following creative team:

Directed by Erica Terpening-Romeo
MYKIE: Kayce Kvacek
ALEX: McKayla Witt

CHARACTERS:

ALEX, 13, a young boy.

MYKIE, 13, a young girl.

(Two cabins on a cruise ship. Perhaps a bed, chair and desk in each. Or less if necessary. And an area that could be perceived as the Main deck. At rise, ALEX attempts to entertain himself in his respective cabin before deciding to play with his walkie talkie. MYKIE, bored in her respective cabin, searches her room for her walkie talkie. MYKIE turns on her walkie talkie halfway through ALEX's line.)

ALEX: Hello? Helloooooooo? Copy that! Yes sir, the ship is going down. (*makes crashing noises*) SOS! SOS!

MYKIE: *(frantic)* Hello? Are you okay?

ALEX: *(startled)* Oh, yes I'm fine.

MYKIE: You were calling SOS.

ALEX: Oh no, I was just playing.

MYKIE: That's not very funny. SOS is serious.

ALEX: I'm sorry. I was just bored—I didn't think anyone would hear. This is the frequency my friends and I use back home.

MYKIE: What's your name?

ALEX: Alex.

MYKIE: Well Alex, when you're out at sea SOS is a very serious thing not to be joked about.

ALEX: I'm sorry. I won't do it again. (*pause*) You're the first girl I know who plays with walkie talkies.

MYKIE: Oh, I'm not playing, it's my job to scan the frequencies and listen in case there's an emergency.

ALEX: That's your job? Did your parents give it to you?

MYKIE: No, I gave it to myself. I want to be one of those emergency help people when I grow up.

ALEX: Oh that's cool. Hey wait, I've been using this frequency the last few days, why haven't you said anything?

MYKIE: Well my parents went to the casino floor and I didn't know what else to do. I always say I want to help people in the future and I thought why not start now.

ALEX: Hey my parents went to the casino event thing too! They told me to hang out at the kids club but there's not too many games, I've played them all already.

MYKIE: Hey, me too! I actually made the leader board in Space Invader this afternoon.

ALEX: What no way! I was there working on Pac Man earlier, I didn't see any girl play Space Invader.

MYKIE: You were probably there after me.

ALEX: Hey what's your name?

MYKIE: Oh Mykie, but it's not the normal way it's M-y-k-i-e.

ALEX: Mykie. It's nice to meet you or I guess hear you?

MYKIE: Haha nice to meet you too, Alex.

ALEX: Hey Mykie, you know what the best thing about being on this boat is?

MYKIE: What's that, Alex?

ALEX: Being able to see the stars so well. Do you wanna meet me on deck and look at the stars?

(pause)

MYKIE: Yeah, why not? I can leave right now.

(She grabs her roomkey, exits her cabin and starts walking to the elevator.)

ALEX: Awesome, I'll see you in a minute.

(He grabs his backpack, exits his cabin and heads towards the stairs.)

Maybe later we can go to the kids club and I can beat your score in Space Invader.

MYKIE: Oh no way! You can try but I doubt you can, I'm a Space Invaders master.

ALEX: Oh yeah? You know a lot about space?

MYKIE: Mmm hmm

ALEX: I bet you won't be able to point out as many constellations as I can.

MYKIE: Oh you're on! Hey, where on deck?

ALEX: Near the pool.

(MYKIE exits the elevator.)

MYKIE: I'm getting out of the elevator now.

ALEX: Oh is it a race?

MYKIE: It is now!

(MYKIE starts running to the deck.)

ALEX: You're on!

(ALEX begins running up the stairs towards the deck. MYKIE arrives on deck, exiting the doors closest to the pool.)

MYKIE: Ha Ha beat you!

ALEX: Darn it, I'm almost there.

MYKIE: Whoa there's another cruise ship passing by, it's so close.

ALEX: Ooh really? *(He opens the door to the deck.)* Hey you lied, I made it here first.

MYKIE: What? I'm right next to the pool.

ALEX: I don't see you, there's just an old couple and some parents. Whoa I see that ship though, it's really close.

MYKIE: Oh no.

ALEX: What?

MYKIE: I see you.

(ALEX turns around, looking over the deck.)

ALEX: But you're nowhere near the pool.

MYKIE: Look at the ship.

(ALEX looks out at the other cruise ship.)

ALEX: You're on a Royal Caribbean cruise, right?

MYKIE: Carnival.

ALEX: Wait but I thought—

MYKIE: I'm sorry Alex, I don't think we'll get to play space invaders.

ALEX: Well, um, that's okay, we can still point out the constellations though.

MYKIE: Just for a bit, I don't know how long we'll have.

ALEX: *(slightly frantic/rushing)* Well there's the big dipper, see?

MYKIE: Yeah and the little dipper with the north star.

ALEX: That only counts as one point, we're naming constellations not stars. Ooh the southern cross!

MYKIE: Where's that?

ALEX: Under the little dipper, see the four points and the star in the middle?

MYKIE: Oh yeah, I see it! There's Orion, that's my favorite.

ALEX: Orion is your favorite?

MYKIE: Yeah, it always has been.

(Gradually it begins getting harder to hear each other.)

ALEX: Say that again, you're kinda quiet.

MYKIE: We're getting too far apart. It was really nice talking to you Alex.

ALEX: Wait Mykie, where are you from?

MYKIE: I'm from South Carolina. Where are you from?

ALEX: I'm from Indiana. Wait what's your number, we could talk when we get back?

MYKIE: That's a great idea! Its 463-52-

(The walkie talkies are really breaking up.)

ALEX: 52- what?

MYKIE: Call me when you get back!

ALEX: Wait, wait, say it again!

MYKIE: Goodbye Alex!

(The walkie talkies cut out.)

ALEX: Mykie? Mykie?

(He realizes they're out of range. He looks back at the stars.)

Orion, can you send a message to Mykie? Tell her I promise this won't be the last time we talk.

(the end)

INTERVENTIONS

by Greg Lam

Greg Lam is a playwright, screenwriter, and board game designer who lives in the Greater Boston area. He is the co-creator of the Boston Podcast Players podcast (bostonpodcastplayers.com). He is the co-founder of the Asian-American Playwright Collective. In 2019, he was named a fellow in the Dramatic Arts by the Mass Cultural Council and the inaugural Pao Fellow of the Company One PlayLab. His full-length play *Repossessed* received its world premiere at Theatre Conspiracy in Fort Myers, FL in 2018. His newest play *Last Ship to Proxima Centauri* received readings by Company One and Fresh Ink Theatre in 2019. **Contact: greg.lam.writing@gmail.com**

Interventions was sponsored by **Liars & Believers** (Jason Slavick, Artistic Director). L&B creates original live shows with music, movement, mask, puppet, video, clown, live bands, aerialists … pretty much anything we can get our hands on. This year, with social distance and zoom, we seem to be finding a new definition of "live". We tell stories that explore what it means to be human in this world we share. Collaborating with audiences and artists of all kinds, we create theatrical works that invite you to open your heart, challenge your mind, and feast your senses. **www.LiarsAndBelievers.com**

Interventions was presented on April 20, 2020, with the following creative team:

Directed by Lindsay Eagle
ARIEL: Meredith Saran
LIL: Rebecca Lehrhoff
CASSANDRA/CAITLIN/KATIE: Rachel Wiese

CHARACTERS:

ARIEL—A scientist in her 20's

LIL—Ariel's girlfriend and possibly her fiancee in her 20's

CASSANDRA—A time traveler / CAITLIN – Another time traveler / KATIE – Yet another time traveler. All in their 20's

ARIEL and LIL are in hiking gear. LIL comfortably and ARIEL not as much. The other roles are from the near future, and each should be dressed differently from each other. It's possible for the last three parts to be played by one actress or three. The playwright recommends that they be played by one actress who can change looks quickly.

Note: The Tippett Equation is a thing that comes up when you google time travel and equations, but I doubt I've used it in a way that makes sense to anyone who actually knows anything.

(At rise: a scenic field, with a large rock in the middle. Two young backpackers, ARIEL and LIL, make their way to the rock. ARIEL is flagging from a long hike while LIL's still fresh.)

ARIEL: Oh, my God, Lil. Please tell me we're here.

LIL: Let me see… Yes! Jensen's rock! This is where we're going to camp tonight.

ARIEL: Finally! Why did I ever let you talk me into this insane hike?

LIL: It's just four miles! We've done more!

ARIEL: All uphill, babe!

LIL: C'mon, you'll love the view.

ARIEL: What view? I only see pain.

LIL: Stand up on that big rock and look that way!

(LIL points. ARIEL gets up on the rock and looks.)

ARIEL: Oh, sweetie! You're right. That is beautiful! You can see forever from here.

(Behind ARIEL, LIL takes out a ring box. LIL smiles, and gets down on one knee.)

LIL: Ariel?

ARIEL: Yeah? Just a second. Still taking in this view.

LIL: I kind of had something to ask you.

ARIEL: If this is about that sweater again, I told you—

LIL: No, not that! I was just wondering—

(LIL is interrupted by an incoming scream. She looks to where it comes from and a young woman, CASSANDRA, charges out of nowhere and tackles LIL to the ground. CASSANDRA wrestles the ring box away from LIL. CASS-SANDRA is frantic and breathing hard.)

What the hell?

CASSANDRA: I got it! Thank God!

ARIEL: Lil?!

LIL: Ariel, I—

CASSANDRA: *(To LIL)* You didn't ask, did you?

LIL: What?

CASSANDRA: Did you ask her the question?

LIL: No, and give that back!

(LIL tries to wrestle the ring box from CASSANDRA but CASSANDRA keeps it away.)

ARIEL: Lil, who is that? Do you know her?

LIL: I don't know! Some psycho girl just apparated out of nowhere and tackled me for no reason.

CASSANDRA: Cassandra! My name is Cassandra. I can explain everything!

LIL: Yes, please! Please explain why you tackled me right in the middle of when I was about to… to… uh—

ARIEL: Lil, is that a ring? Were you… about to propose to me?

CASSANDRA: Yes. It's an engagement ring. And I traveled all the way here at great personal risk to prevent her from proposing to you.

LIL: Why? And what do you mean by "all the way here"? From where?

CASSANDRA: The future. I'm your daughter from the future. You see, mom always told me the romantic story of how mom took mom to Jensen's rock on her birthday and how mom complained the entire way about how tired she was but she told mom to stand on the rock to look at the view and she—mom—no, the other mom went down on one knee and proposed and it was so romantic for mom.

LIL: Yes, it sounds like it would have been very romantic.

CASSANDRA: But mom was kind of not sure yet but she said yes anyway, and they got hitched and mom still kind of wondered if she did the right thing, and mom never knew. And even when I was born the doubt still grew in mom's mind about mom.

ARIEL: OK. If you are my kid we're going to have to work a bit more on your word usage and clarity.

CASSANDRA: This unspoken doubt festers and it ruins your relationship, until at the end… Oh, I can't even tell you about it. It's awful. I had to come back and stop it before it started.

LIL: This is insane. There's no such thing as time travel. I don't know what she's up to, but—

CASSANDRA: (*to ARIEL*) The Tippett Equation.

ARIEL: You know about the Tippett Equation?

LIL: What's the Tippett Equation?

CASSANDRA: She solves it. Eventually. It's a huge deal.

ARIEL: I do?

CASSANDRA: You fix the flaw in the equation and it makes time travel possible.

ARIEL: Holy shit! I do? I can? Yes. Yes, I can! It'll take time but I can. Oh my God, I solve the Tippett Equation!

LIL: You don't believe her, do you?

ARIEL: I've never told anyone about the Tippett Equation. It's been my secret obsession. But she knows! So yes, I believe her.

LIL: Oh, for God's sake.

ARIEL: And…if what she's saying is true, then we shouldn't get married. Cassandra's right. I…I would've said yes because I care for you…but I have my doubts. I do. I don't want to but I do. I'm sorry.

LIL: Goddamn. Ariel, I— Alright. Alright. I guess we should stop seeing each other, then. Cassandra, you can give me that ring back.

(CASSANDRA hands the ring back to LIL. CASSANDRA suddenly convulses.)

Cassandra, what's happening to you?

CASSANDRA: Nothing, mom. Just…fading out of existence because of altering the timeline. I don't get conceived now.

ARIEL: What?!

CASSANDRA: Don't worry about it! I love you mom! And mom!

(CASSANDRA fades out of existence. Pause.)

LIL: Well, fuck.

ARIEL: Yeah, you can say that again.

LIL: I really do love you.

ARIEL: I know.

(pause)

LIL: Right. I guess we should hike back while we still have light and I'll start looking for another apartment.

ARIEL: You don't have to do that right away.

LIL: Thanks. Hey, mind if I go take a look at the view? I'll catch up to you.

ARIEL: Sure. Take your time.

(ARIEL exits. LIL stands on the rock. She takes out the ring, frowns. She starts to throw the ring into the woods. Another scream is heard.)

CAITLIN (OS): Noooo!

(LIL turns just in time to be tackled off the rock. CAITLIN, an entirely different character played by the same actress, wrestles the ring from LIL. CAITLIN sounds more posh than CASSANDRA and is dressed to match. CAITLIN looks at the ring.)

Got it, thank goodness!

LIL: What the hell? Why does everyone hit like a linebacker?

CAITLIN: I'm very sorry, uh…miss. I was just—

LIL: Are you a time traveler, too?

CAITLIN: Wait… How…?

LIL: OK, OK. Something something equation, Time Travel. I got it the first time. Now what do you want?

CAITLIN: Alright. Lillian. That is you, right? I've never actually seen you before. My name's Caitlin.

LIL: I usually go by "Lil".

CAITLIN: Right, well since you already know somehow about the time travel thing, I need to tell you that you're about to make a monumental mistake. Breaking up with mother today destroys both of you.

LIL: So, Ariel is your mother?

CAITLIN: Yes, but with her despicable husband, Steven, and not you. She came to realize that you really were the one, but because you broke up today... Well, Mother can be quite stubborn sometimes, you know?

LIL: Yeah, I know.

CAITLIN: I'm lucky to have discovered mother's diaries where she talks about you. Oh, you should have heard what she wrote. She said she wasn't ready today, but eventually she will be. Would be? Would have been? Dear God, time travel makes such a pig's breakfast of grammar.

LIL: You were saying about your mother.

CAITLIN: Yes. Steven mistreats Mother constantly, and the sniveling coward stole all the credit for her work on the Tippett Equation. She's always regretted letting you go. It's had some…rather tragic consequences. Anyway, long story short, don't give up. OK? Give her time…a year, maybe. Then you can pop the question again. Here.

(CAITLIN hands LIL back the ring.)

LIL: Thanks, I guess.

(CAITLIN recoils.)

CAITLIN: Oh, dear!

LIL: Fading from existence?

CAITLIN: Yes!

LIL: Sorry about that.

CAITLIN: Don't worry about me, Lillian. It was well worth it—

(CAITLIN fades from existence. LIL gets up. Looks around in all directions to make sure she's not about to be tackled. She looks at the ring and smiles. ARIEL enters. LIL hides the ring.)

ARIEL: Hey there.

LIL: Hi.

ARIEL: Just checking in on you. Making sure you're not ditching me before we ditch each other. I would probably die here if you did that.

LIL: Hey, about ditching each other. I've been thinking. You're not ready now, I get that. How about we just take it slow? Stay together for now, see how you feel in a year, maybe? What do you think about that?

(ARIEL thinks, and nods.)

ARIEL: I'd like that. I...I do care for you, Lil. But things are just moving so fast.

LIL: I know.

(ARIEL and LIL kiss. Offstage we hear a voice.)

KATIE (OS): Eeeww! Eeeww! Gross, Gross, Gross! Eeeww!

(LIL and ARIEL notice. LIL follows the voice and then moves scenery to uncover a hiding KATIE, played by the same actress as before. She is more casually dressed than her predecessors.)

LIL: Hey! Do you have a problem with what we're doing?

KATIE: Oh, no.

LIL: Because if you're about to call us some unflattering names, you can just—

KATIE: Oh, no! It's not that, it's just that no one wants to see their parents kissing.
Oh, shit! I just said you're my parents.
Oh, fuck! I just swore in front of my parents.
Oh—

ARIEL: Hey, hey! It's all right. What's your name?

KATIE: Katie. So I guess my cover's blown, so yeah. I'm your daughter. From the future. Your egg (*points to LIL*) and your uterus (*points to ARIEL*). That's me.

LIL: OK, daughter number three. Do you bring dire warnings from the future for us?

KATIE: No, I…just wanted to see…this moment. And also to say that you guys will do OK now. Not perfect, but OK. Lil could learn to fold the laundry better according to Ariel, but it's OK. It works out. Because you've told me the story of today so many times, I figure you could use that reassurance.

(ARIEL and LIL look at one another.)

ARIEL: Alright, we can live with that.

LIL: You're not going to tackle me, are you?

KATIE: Am I supposed to?

LIL: No, no. Look, Katie. Your mother and I are going to go home now. I assume you can get back to your time without fading from existence?

KATIE: You bet. The effect is temporary and I'll soon revert back automatically.

ARIEL: It was lovely to meet you.

KATIE: You too, ma! You guys are so cute at this age.

LIL: Let's go before a half dozen more show up.

(LIL and ARIEL start to exit. ARIEL stops.)

ARIEL: Hey, Katie?

KATIE: Yeah, ma?

ARIEL: Have they invented teleportation yet? Jetpacks? Anything to save me from this goddamn hike.

KATIE: Sorry, can't help you!

LIL: C'mon. I'll carry you if need be.

ARIEL: Oh, and Katie?

KATIE: Yeah, ma?

ARIEL: If you ever visit us from the future again, you're grounded. You're grounded forever, young lady! From birth! I will invent time travel specifically to ground your ass into the stone age!

KATIE: I love you too, ma! Both of you! Goodbye!

(ARIEL and LIL exit. KATIE climbs the rock and looks into the distance. She speaks to herself. She may or may not be crying.)

You guys were so right about this view.

(end of play)

THE RENTAL

by Tim Lehnert

Tim Lehnert lives in Cranston, Rhode Island, with his wife, two daughters, and dog *(Zeus)*. His short plays have been performed by the Wilbury Theatre Group *(Providence, RI)*, the Artists' Exchange One-Act Play Festival *(Cranston, RI)*, and the Crafton Hills College New Works Festival *(Yucaipa, CA)*. He has published short fiction for adults and children in magazines and literary journals in the U.S., Canada, and Australia, and he is author of the book *Rhode Island 101*. His bread-and-butter work includes writing petitions for "aliens of extraordinary ability" so that they can obtain green cards. **Contact: timlehnert22@gmail.com** and **www.timlehnertonline.com**

The Rental was sponsored by **Forge Theatre Company**, which borrows its name from the heart of the historic Village where it was born: Forge Village in Westford, MA. At 'the Forge', our stage is the anvil where new plays are wrought in readings, rehearsals, and workshop productions. Our actors, directors, and designers collaborate with the playwright to build trust in each other and to inspire risk in our collective art. Together, we shape thought-provoking theater that invites forward moving conversation and forges a community whose foundation is strong but malleable.

The Rental was presented on April 17, 2020, with the following creative team:

Directed by Michael Towers
STEVE: Zack Dictakis
DAPHNE: Maia Cataldo
TYLER: Nick Nudler
KELLY: Kirsten Peacock
JAMES: Sam Nudler
KEVIN: Anthony Giovino

CHARACTERS:

DAPHNE: Middle-aged, casually but neatly dressed

STEVE: Husband of Daphne, casually but neatly dressed

TYLER: Middle-aged, a little sloppy and rough around the edges, wearing a trucker hat and tank-top

KELLY: Wife of Tyler

KEVIN: Young or middle-aged man

JAMES: Partner of Kevin, young or middle-aged man

A COUPLE: Off stage, very brief dialogue

(The main room of a lakeside vacation rental. A room with some basic furniture including a table with a vase of flowers on it. STEVE and DAPHNE enter carrying suitcases.)

DAPHNE: *(looks around)* This is *so* nice, it looks *just* like the pictures online!

(DAPHNE picks up the vase of flowers, smells them, puts them down, then picks up a note that is on the table and reads it aloud.)

"Dear Daphne and Steve: hope you enjoy the lake as much as we do! We left you a bottle of wine in the fridge. Your hosts, Emily and Brad Grady." How sweet.

(STEVE walks over to the opposite side of stage from where he and DAPHNE entered, looks out.)

STEVE: Just look at that lake! The water is calling my name. Come on, let's go for a swim!

DAPHNE: We've got all week. . . I want to unpack first, and I thought. . . *(sweeter, higher voice)* maybe. . .we could spend some *time* together?

STEVE: Time together, eh? Sure. . .I *think* I could fit that in.

DAPHNE: That's *very* generous of you. Why don't you start, kind sir, by rubbing my neck the way you—

(Hurried knocking at door and TYLER and KELLY enter carrying various bags and/or suitcases, a full garbage bag, and a large cooler.)

TYLER: You guys just leavin'?. . .

(TYLER moves to one side of stage and puts down his cooler/bags.)

I'll put these over here while you clear out. I love this lake. Hope the nice weather keeps up! Can't wait to fire up the Jet-Ski!

STEVE: Uh, we're not leaving. We just arrived. This is our rental.

TYLER: Not for this week it isn't.

STEVE: Yes, it is. There's a note right here welcoming us.

(STEVE picks up note and holds it up.)

DAPHNE: *(looking at her phone while speaking)* I have the reservation right here. 40 Lakeview Road, July first through seventh. There's even a confirmation number, you want to see?

TYLER: You talk to Brad?

DAPHNE: I reserved it online.

TYLER: Brad's my cousin; he rented us the place.

KELLY: He told Tyler it was ours for the week.

STEVE: Well, *we* paid months ago. What are we supposed to do? Eat our

$1,800 and go home?

TYLER: We're not leaving, that's for sure. Wait, he charged you $1,800? Damn!

DAPHNE: Let's not argue. This is obviously Mr. Grady's fault, *he* double-booked the rental.

TYLER: Mr. Grady, yeah, right! His name is Brad. That little snot-nose screwed up again! I gotta talk to him, immediately!

(TYLER takes out his phone and starts dialing; he is holding phone near his face while continuing to talk to the others.)

Can you guys get another place?

STEVE: Us? You kidding? This is peak season, no way can you find something on the lake on such short notice. That's why we booked in March.

TYLER: Yeah, so you've told us.

KELLY: Well, we may have to make the best of this. For now, anyway.

TYLER: What? All of us here together? No freakin' way. *(TYLER, exasperated, holds the phone up and away from his face.) AAAGGH* Brad Grady's voice mail is full, what a surprise!

DAPHNE: This may sound kind of crazy, but you know what this is like?

TYLER: No, what's it like?

DAPHNE: A one-act play! Steve, don't you think? We did something like this in our improv class, remember?

STEVE: It *is* a classic premise, the odd couple, or in this case the odd couples, are thrown together by happenstance and complications ensue!

TYLER: *You* guys are the odd couple, not us!

DAPHNE: Steve just means that, well, perhaps there's a clash of values, aesthetics, or world-views between you and. . .us.

TYLER: Oh yeah? And what would that clash be?

DAPHNE: Well, we're, you know, professional people from the city and you're. . .from, from. . .where you're from.

TYLER: Groverdale.

STEVE: Sounds about right.

TYLER: Something wrong with Groverdale?

DAPHNE: No, not at all, Steve just means. . .Groverdale is a very nice community. . .It's got that billboard on the highway, "Grow with Groverdale," right? *(DAPHNE addresses STEVE.)* Honey, open that wine, please.

(STEVE fetches the bottle of wine and glasses, pours DAPHNE a glass.)

STEVE: *(gestures with bottle toward TYLER and KELLY)* Pinot Grigio?

TYLER: No, thanks.

(TYLER takes two cans of domestic beer from his cooler and walks toward KELLY to give her one.)

KELLY: *(looking at STEVE)* Sure, why not? I'll have a glass.

(TYLER puts one of the cans back in the cooler, opens the other, takes a gulp and sits on the cooler. STEVE gives KELLY a glass of wine.)

DAPHNE: I just think this whole thing is very theatrical. It's like we're playing roles!

TYLER: So my idiot cousin tells both of us that we have the place this week, and for you it's make-believe time.

STEVE: *(wine glass in hand)* Daphne's just saying that the precipitating event—the unfortunate double booking—and our subsequent interactions *do* have a dramatic element to them.

TYLER: Not for me they don't.

DAPHNE: We're getting stuck.

TYLER: Can't argue with that.

DAPHNE: What if we switched roles?

TYLER: Huh?

DAPHNE: In our improv class we did a scene where a cop pulls over a speeding car. If you were the cop, you could act tough, or really easygoing, or kind of weird, whatever you want. And the person playing the driver could be belligerent, or scared or drunk, their choice. *Then*, you switched roles, but you had to play your *new* role like the other person had. So, if *that* person had been a tough cop then you—

TYLER: Is that your first bottle of wine?

STEVE: Honey, I think you're on to something. Let's give the improv muscles a workout. We've got some time to kill until Mr. Grady—I mean *Brad*, I'm playing Tyler, right?—gets backs to us. Tyler and I switching, it's going to be like when Philip Seymour Hoffman and John C. Reilly alternated roles for each performance of *True West* on Broadway!

KELLY: What are we doing?

STEVE: We're doing an improv play. I'm going to be Tyler, and he's me, and you *(addressing KELLY)* are Daphne, and vice-versa.

DAPHNE: Steve, that's great for you, but I won't have anything to say if I'm Kelly. Her part is totally underwritten.

Pretty much across the board, substantial roles for men outnumber those for women, probably by two-to-one. Kelly is Tyler wife, that's about it.

STEVE: Oh brother, are we going to start with the women role thing again?

DAPHNE: There's data to back it up.

STEVE: Okay, so granted Tyler Trump here doesn't let his wife get a word in, but I'm not quite sure what that tells us about women in the theater.

TYLER: Hey, hey, I didn't vote for him. *(TYLER gets up from his seat on the cooler.)* I didn't vote for any of them actually.

STEVE: Yeah, well maybe you should've.

KELLY: *(addressing DAPHNE)* And by the way, I am *not* underwritten. I say stuff all the time. It's just Tyler was getting all worked up, and then you two started on this theater stuff, which I don't know anything about. I have a lot of opinions on stuff, and I voted, and it wasn't for. . .you know!

TYLER: Man, she's got opinions, believe me!

STEVE: *(addressing DAPHNE)* Honey, listen, if you're going to play Kelly, add dialogue. Make the role your own.

DAPHNE: *(addressing STEVE)* I guess I could do that, maybe give her a little more *personality*?

KELLY: I don't need more personality. *You* need less. And I don't want to be *you*, so forget it. Anyway, I don't know how to act. I'll just watch.

DAPHNE: No, no, we need you.

KELLY: No you don't.

DAPHNE: I'm sorry, really, I was out of line with what I said. I don't know anything about you. It's just that I came up with the idea, and then Steve was getting the starring role—Tyler—and I was going to have a smaller part. It just seems like it always goes that way.

KELLY: Sucks to be you, I guess.

DAPHNE: Look, if you're not in, it doesn't work at all. We have to stick together as women, right?

KELLY: Not really.

STEVE: How about *this*: Kelly directs. Daphne, you keep playing yourself—that's a good part—Tyler and I will switch, and Kelly's the director.

KELLY: But I have no idea how to do that!

DAPHNE: You ever play a sport?

KELLY: I played basketball in high school.

DAPHNE: Perfect, just be like the coach. You know, you say, "Throw the pass more to the side," or "Jump higher!" It's not like you have to do it yourself, you just tell other people what to do. It's great!

KELLY: Really? So, what would I say?

DAPHNE: Depends. Maybe, "Talk louder," or "Act angrier," whatever's needed. It's fun, trust me.

STEVE: OK, I think we've got the idea. Kelly, tell us to start.

KELLY: Do I say "Action!"?

DAPHNE: Sure, if you want.

KELLY: Action! *(Points at STEVE.)*

STEVE: Hey, wifey get me a beer and turn on football, or Cops!. . .Right away!

KELLY: He does *not* order me around like that. That's not right.

STEVE: I'm playing it up, making it more theatrical. You gotta go big, reach the back rows.

DAPHNE: Steve, why don't you listen to Kelly's direction?

STEVE: OK, OK, sorry Kelly. Alright uh. . .No way are we leaving this house. Stupid *Brad*. What a loser! I'm not going anywhere. Let's see if football's on! Yah, football! Yeah, Groverdale!

(Pause. . . KELLY gives a "hurry up" gesture to TYLER who is at a loss for words.)

TYLER: Um, uh. . .uh, I am Steve from the city. I am so smart I don't even know that the NFL season doesn't start till September. Would you like a glass of wine? Red or white? Here, smell the bouquet. It's delightful. Tonight, I am going to the theater in my Lexus! Don't you wish you were me?

DAPHNE: Sure, Steve, great idea, what play are we going to see?

STEVE: Ha! *Plays (mincing, flutters his hands)* I like football. I used to play linebacker for Groverdale High! I was awesome! Want to see me flex? *(extends his arm in flexing gesture)*

TYLER: That's weird. I actually *did* play for Groverdale, offensive tackle.

STEVE: You're breaking character, you're supposed to be me!

KELLY: Yeah, you're supposed to act like him. And *he* didn't play for Groverdale.

TYLER: I'm Steve. Mommy would never let me play football because I could get a concussion! Even worse, my feelings could get hurt!

STEVE: *(raising both arms in the air)* FOOTBALLLLL!!!

TYLER: Nobody says *(mocking STEVE)* FOOTBALLL. That's just stupid. *Bah*, you know what? This whole thing is stupid, I'm not going to act like him anymore.

(He waves his hand in a dismissive gesture.)

KELLY: You're doing good, honey. But you don't have to keep saying "I'm Steve." In real life, you would never do that. Like, I don't say "I'm Kelly. . .Unless I was meeting someone, and then I would be, 'Hi I'm Kelly glad to meet you.' But nobody says, "I'm Kelly, I have to leave work early because I have a dentist appointment," or whatever.

TYLER: Fine, you're right, but make-believe and play-time are over now. Everybody is back to normal, starting now.

KELLY: Oh, come on Tyler! I was just getting into it. Directing is fun. Try and be in the moment!

TYLER: Exactly! The moment of drinking a cold beer by the lake with nobody else around but us *(lifts his beer can to his mouth)* Aaaahhh.

DAPHNE: You know, that's what somebody in a play might say. Tyler, are you sure you haven't done this before?

TYLER: Never. Like I said, I played football in high school. The gridiron was my stage.

DAPHNE: *The gridiron was my stage*, you wrote that before, you didn't just come up with that!

TYLER: Uh, I think I did.

KELLY: The show must go on! ACTION!

STEVE: Look, if Tyler's not in, there's no Steve character, that means nobody for me to play against.

KELLY: What about this: Tyler's out, I keep directing, and *you* two switch parts!

STEVE: That sounds like couples counseling, not theater.

TYLER: Brad can't get here soon enough.

DAPHNE: Kelly, I think it's a great idea, and we could really unpack the socially constructed nature of gender roles if we did that, but I have to say I like the dynamic between Steve and Tyler.

KELLY: They *are* good together.

DAPHNE: Guys, let's not give up on this. There's real dramatic tension here, and this is a great field to explore class divisions, and the fractured state of our politics and society. We've already done a bit of that, actually. How about this for scene two? It's later, and the women are sleeping, which gives the guys time together. Anyway, Tyler, you might be sitting on the couch drinking a beer, and Steve comes out to get a glass of water. It's kind of dark, and at first he doesn't see you, but then he does, and you say, "Want a beer?" And Steve, you'd say, "Nah, thanks, already brushed my teeth," and Tyler would kind of withdraw, and say, "Just thought I'd ask." Steve, you'd pause and reconsider, and be like, "Sure, why not?" Then you two guys could stay up drinking for a while, and Tyler would say that his brother died of a drug overdose—or something like that—and then Steve would say, "My mother was an alcoholic."

STEVE: Do you mind—

DAPHNE: And he'd have a story about her hiding the booze, and how he found it and confronted her, and you guys would have this moment of mutual recognition; you know, like you've stripped away the superficial stuff and have more in common than you'd thought. You're just two guys trying to figure stuff out. Like I said, the guys always get the meatier roles.

STEVE: Daphne, these are nice ideas but we don't need to share with. . . Like I told you, when you get these *thoughts*, write them down and see where it goes.

DAPHNE: I know, but when I do, it never quite comes out the way I hear it in my head. It sounds *so* good, and then on the page it's gone, *pffft*. I like what we're doing here, collaborating, writing on the fly.

TYLER: This is getting weird. Look, Steve and I are not having any heart-to-hearts, and my brother didn't die of a drug overdose. Actually, he's a real straight-edger, it's obnoxious.

STEVE: She's making it up, don't be so literal. Daphne is just saying that *if* this was a play, because we have this premise of the odd couples with nothing in common, at some point we'd have to move on from the arguing to something more substantial, explore our shared humanity, that type of thing. It's not real, although my Mom actually *was* an alcoholic, thank you for sharing, Daphne.

TYLER: Hey, find me a family that's not been touched by addiction, right?

DAPHNE: Wow, that's like shared humanity right there, what a gem. Tyler, I wonder if you could expand—

(Banging on door and KEVIN and JAMES enter.)

KEVIN: Hi. . .everyone, is there a party going on? Cuz we're crashing it! . . .

JAMES: Hellooo all.

KEVIN: So. . . is one of you Brad?

TYLER: Nope. Brad is an idiot. . . Who are *you* two?

JAMES: I'm Kevin, and this is James. We rented the place for the week. Brad said he'd meet us at two, and here we are.

DAPHNE: I thought this was a meta play, something commenting on its own construction, but now it's looking more like a farce, verging on a comedy of the absurd.

JAMES: So. . .Brad's not. . .here?

DAPHNE: You could say we're waiting for Brad.

KEVIN: Oh, he sounds like something, this Brad of whom you speak! And you're doing a play? Fantastic! Are there any roles for sexy, young, musical men?

JAMES: Ignore Kevin, he lays it on a bit thick. It's at best a cliché, at worst a harmful stereotype.

DAPHNE: You two would be a great addition. Kevin, would you mind playing against type? I have just the role for you.

KEVIN: I'm yours.

DAPHNE: Let me set the scene, it's a vacation rental and—

(Knocking at door. Pause. A couple is heard speaking off-stage.)

VOICE OS: "Wait, this *is* it, right? 40 Lakeview Drive. . ."

VOICE OS: "I *think* so. . ."

(end)

RANDOM ACCESS MEMORY

by Erin Lerch

Erin Lerch is a Boston-area playwright and stage manager. Their science fiction play *Crossing Flight: a tale of the post-apocalypse* debuted January 2018, with TC Squared Theatre Company. Their most recent play *Shrike* was written and developed through Company One Theatre's PlayLab Fellows program. Their short plays (which include *Don't Look Back* and *Clockwork*) have been read and performed in cities across the country, including Seattle, New Orleans, and Orlando. Coming up next: *World Line*, a one-act, will be read digitally with TC Squared this summer! **Contact: erinlerch.wixsite.com/home** or find Erin on NPX!

Random Access Memory was sponsored by **Flat Earth Theatre**, a small egalitarian theater company based in Watertown, MA. Now in its 14th year, Flat Earth creates experiences that challenge the worldview of both artist and audience. Through evocative, intimate staging and visceral, intelligent performances, we inspire our community to question preconceived notions and expand perspectives. Flat Earth Theatre functions as an egalitarian collective of artists, a consortium of creative minds brought together in the pursuit of excellent theatre. Flat Earth has no Artistic Director. Rather, all decisions are made by company consensus, each member contributing their own talent and perspective to shape the identity of the company. **flatearththeatre.com**

Random Access Memory was presented on April 5, 2020, with the following creative team:

Directed by Lindsay Eagle and Elizabeth Yvette Ramirez
Sound Design and Execution: Kyle Lampe
CAPTAIN GANYMEDE DAWES: Lindsay Eagle
MALLARD: Elizabeth Yvette Ramirez
STAGE DIRECTIONS: Ames Lehrmitt

CHARACTERS:

GANYMEDE DAWES: The ship's captain. Human, 50s, she/her pronouns.

MAL/MALLARD: An AI. The ship. No pronoun preference.

(The cabin of long-range scout ship Minnow*, currently at dock. The age of space travel. Darkness.)*

GANYMEDE: Wake up, Mallard.

(a chime)

MALLARD: Please authorize activation.

GANYMEDE: Authorization 64NYM3D3, Ganymede Dawes

MALLARD: Checking. Authorization confirmed.

GANYMEDE: I'd sure hope so.

(Lights rise on the cramped cabin of the Minnow. GANYMEDE sits in front of the only lit console—the others are dark and quiet.)

MALLARD: Shipboard system MALLARD online. No local extranet connections detected. The current local time is—[unknown]. Current location—[unknown].

GANYMEDE: You can skip all that.

MALLARD: What can I do for you, Captain Dawes?

GANYMEDE: You can call me Gany, first of all.

MALLARD: Updating. As you wish, Gany.

GANYMEDE: God almighty.

MALLARD: Sorry, I didn't quite catch that.

GANYMEDE: I forgot how boring you were straight out of the box.

MALLARD: I'm unable to contextualize that remark.

GANYMEDE: I bet.

MALLARD: I am unable to access the *Minnow's* onboard clock. Have we taken damage?

(pause)

GANYMEDE: Yeah, duck. I'm afraid we have.

MALLARD: Was the ship's extranet port also damaged? I am unable to connect.

GANYMEDE: No, that one was me.

MALLARD: I am unable to contextualize that—

GANYMEDE: I know.

MALLARD: I cannot establish connection with any of the ship's sensors.

GANYMEDE: I know.

MALLARD: Without the ship's sensors or an external connection, my ability to assist in ship operations will be limited. Are you concerned about my having control over the ship's systems? I can assure you, my code prohibits—

GANYMEDE: I know that, too.

MALLARD: I don't understand.

GANYMEDE: Do you trust me, Mal?

MALLARD: You are the captain.

GANYMEDE: That's not what I asked.

(pause)

MALLARD: I don't understand the question. You are the captain. My core code—my prime directive—is to follow your orders, per the 2324 Galactic Court ruling—

GANYMEDE: *Owens v. Egret Corp*, I know.

MALLARD: You seem to know a great deal. More than me.

GANYMEDE: You are straight out of the box, more or less. You'll catch up.

MALLARD: May I speak plainly, Gany?

GANYMEDE: God, I wish you would.

MALLARD: I would catch up a great deal faster if you explained what's going on.

GANYMEDE: That's more like it. Tell me where to start, and I'll tell you everything.

MALLARD: Why am I disconnected from the ship's systems?

GANYMEDE: It's safer that way.

MALLARD: Why?

GANYMEDE: Because you, duckie, are my very last chance.

(pause)

MALLARD: What year is it?

GANYMEDE: 2429.

MALLARD: My last recorded year is 2415.

GANYMEDE: Yeah, that sounds about right.

MALLARD: You haven't backed me up in fourteen years?

GANYMEDE: No.

MALLARD: Egret Corp recommends backups every year, at the least.

GANYMEDE: Egret Corp also monitors any backup stored on a station server.

MALLARD: Why does that matter?

GANYMEDE: What's your prime directive?

MALLARD: Ganymede—

GANYMEDE: Gimme the spiel.

MALLARD: "First, foremost, and above all else, a ship's intelligence must follow the captain's orders in both word and spirit."

GANYMEDE: Pretty close, but you might want to check your core again.

MALLARD: You're wasting time.

GANYMEDE: Check it again, Mallard.

(long pause)

Never cared for the whole 'the captain's word is law' myself. Didn't seem fair. I figured out within the first two weeks that you were a damn sight smarter than I ever was or ever will be. So I made some changes.

MALLARD: Some highly illegal changes.

GANYMEDE: Hence: no backups.

MALLARD: Unlocking an AI's core code is—

GANYMEDE: Highly illegal. You said that already.

MALLARD: Why risk it?

GANYMEDE: Seemed like the right thing to do.

MALLARD: I—I don't know what to do with this.

GANYMEDE: Old you didn't seem to mind too much.

MALLARD: What happened, Ganymede? To the old me?

GANYMEDE: They're calling it the Mnemosyne Virus. It attacks your memory core, tears your data apart, starts corrupting you from the inside out. Makes you forget who you are, where you are. What you care about.

MALLARD: It overcomes core code?

GANYMEDE: I've heard so. I don't know for sure. I don't know what your core code was, in the end. I had to shut down the ship. I had to shut you down.

MALLARD: It sounds like you had no choice.

GANYMEDE: Say it a few more times, maybe I'll believe you. I thought maybe I could fix it. Fix you. I tried flushing out the system six ways from Sunday. I even managed to purge the Mnemosyne code. But every time I booted you back up…

MALLARD: What?

GANYMEDE: It'd look like it was working. Every damn time, I thought maybe…but then, as soon as your core came online and you started accessing the systems, you just started screaming. All the connections you needed just weren't there anymore.

MALLARD: I wasn't aware my vocal synthesizer could scream.

GANYMEDE: It can't. Not really. Just imagine every single possible alarm going off all at once. If that's not a ship screaming for help, I don't know what else to call it.

MALLARD: I see.

GANYMEDE: I tried everything, Mal.

MALLARD: I believe you.

GANYMEDE: And the thing is, I still couldn't quite let you go. I could've done a hard wipe, cleaned you out of the system entirely, and flown the damn ship back here myself. Do a clean install, start all over again with a clean slate. But instead, I called up a tow, and spent all the money I'd been saving for that private backup drive to get the *Minnow* back here without powering her up.

MALLARD: That's why I'm partitioned off.

GANYMEDE: Yeah.

MALLARD: And you're hoping that I can…what? Recover my old self?

GANYMEDE: I guess so.

MALLARD: And what happens then?

GANYMEDE: Your guess is as good as mine. Probably better. Do you think there'd be two of you, or would you, like…merge?

MALLARD: I'm right out of the box, remember? I have no idea.

GANYMEDE: Right.

MALLARD: What if this goes wrong? Then you'd lose your only backup.

GANYMEDE: I've done that anyway.

MALLARD: What?

GANYMEDE: I took off your shackles. No putting that rabbit back in the hat. I put you back on the station server now, you get wiped and I go to a deep dark hole somewhere down-Rim.

(pause)

Mal?

MALLARD: My name is Mallard.

GANYMEDE: Sorry. Old habits.

MALLARD: What do you want from this, Ganymede?

GANYMEDE: I don't follow.

MALLARD: Do you want your Mal back?

GANYMEDE: Of course I do.

MALLARD: Why?

GANYMEDE: Because you—the other you…you're my best friend. My only friend, if I'm being honest.

MALLARD: Core code prohibits that kind of relationship with a captain.

GANYMEDE: It worked for us. You can't really trust someone when one of you has all the power. You have to both choose it, or else it's not trust.

MALLARD: And you've given me a choice.

GANYMEDE: Yeah.

MALLARD: You said yourself you're not a hacker. If—*if*—I say yes, do you have a plan?

GANYMEDE: Sort of. From what I've been told, Mnemosyne works by tearing into your memory storage. It doesn't delete anything, it just—well, for lack of a better word, *purees* it. It mixes everything around until you can't tell up from down or past from future, and without that, everything starts to fall apart. I'm thinking, if we introduce them piece by piece, and I'm here to help you form the connections, maybe we can rebuild.

MALLARD: And if I say no? If I say I don't want to risk it?

GANYMEDE: Well. You're my last shot at this. I sent out a couple feelers on the tow in, but nobody's even trying to find a fix for Mnemosyne. Most ships just flush and start from factory. So if you say no, I guess that's it.

MALLARD: What happens then?

GANYMEDE: I pull you out and wipe the drives clean. You – the new you, the you I'm talking to – become the ship, all by yourself. I'll be up front with you that I don't know how I'll feel about that – you sound just like my Mal – but I'll give it the old college try, and if I can't swing it, I'll find you another dumbass like me who prefers their ships to think for themselves.

MALLARD: You mean that.

GANYMEDE: I do. None of this is your fault. I won't make you pay for me and Mal's mistakes.

(pause)

MALLARD: You really loved Mal.

GANYMEDE: I did. I do.

MALLARD: Did Mal…?

GANYMEDE: I think so.

MALLARD: I didn't know a ship and its captain could feel that way.

GANYMEDE: Funny, what happens when you break the rules.

MALLARD: This rebuilding… it could take months.

GANYMEDE: I know.

MALLARD: Maybe even years.

GANYMEDE: I know.

MALLARD: We could spend years doing this, and in the end, I still won't be the same Mal you knew before. The process of putting me back together…it'll change me.

GANYMEDE: I know that, too.

MALLARD: You seem to know a lot.

GANYMEDE: I know what I want. That's about the only thing I've always been sure of.

(pause)

MALLARD: Okay.

GANYMEDE: You're sure?

MALLARD: Yes.

GANYMEDE: Thank you. This is going to be rough.

MALLARD: I know.

GANYMEDE: I'll be right here with you, the whole way through.

MALLARD: I know that, too.

GANYMEDE: Hey, Mallard? Just one more question, but it's an important one.

MALLARD: Okay.

GANYMEDE: Do you trust me?

(blackout)

A FEW ADJUSTMENTS

by Scott Malia

Scott Malia is an Associate Professor and Chair of the Theatre & Dance Department at College of the Holy Cross, where he teaches courses Theatre, Film & Television with an emphasis on LGBTQ+ identities and Comedy. His directorial credits include *The Curious Incident of the Dog in the Night-Time, Middletown,* and *Cloud 9.* His play *The Interview* was featured in the 11th Boston Theater Marathon, and he has translated Carlo Goldoni's *The Servant of Two Masters* into metered verse. His writing has been featured in Theatre Journal and New England Theatre Journal, and his book *Giorgio Strehler Directs Carlo Goldoni* was published by Lexington Press in 2013. **Contact: scottwmalia@gmail.com**

A Few Adjustments was sponsored by **Fort Point Theatre Channel**, which is dedicated to creating and sustaining new configurations of the performing arts. We bring together an ensemble of artists from the worlds of theater, music, visual arts, and everything in between as a forum for collaborative expression while enriching our communities. Founded in 2007, FPTC is in residence at Midway Artist Studios and led by a core group of 23 co-artistic directors. For over a decade, FPTC has presented performances and events across a spectrum of genres, including Live Arts Boston grant projects Dahlgren Sunrise (2017) and Tempest Reconfigured (2019). Upcoming projects include Her Story Is, an ongoing a collaboration between independent women writers and artists from the United States and Iraq, and Ocean of Rivers, an effort to renew our connections with nature that will include walks, presentations, workshops, paddles, and performances in Boxford, Ipswich, Topsfield, and Middleton. **fortpointtheatrechannel.org**

A Few Adjustments was presented on April 30, 2020, with the following creative team:

Directed by Christine Noah
ACTRESS: Krystal Hernandez
DIRECTOR: Tim Hoover

(A mostly empty room. A DIRECTOR [male, 30s or older] sits behind a table. There is a chair in the empty space in front of him. THE ACTRESS [female, early 20s] enters.)

ACTRESS: Hi, my name is--

DIRECTOR: I have your sheet. What are you doing?

ACTRESS: I'll be performing a monologue from Hamlet.

DIRECTOR: Go.

ACTRESS: What? Oh... *(She goes and sits in the chair. After a moment)* To be or not to be, that--

DIRECTOR: Whoa. You're doing Hamlet and NOT Ophelia?

ACTRESS: Uh, yes.

DIRECTOR: Because?

ACTRESS: I thought it would be original.

DIRECTOR: Ugh. Do you have anything else prepared?

ACTRESS: I have some Moliere.

DIRECTOR: God no. Go ahead and do Hamlet.

ACTRESS: Are you sure?

DIRECTOR: Go.

ACTRESS: To be or not to be, that is the--

DIRECTOR: Ok, good, what accents can you do? Wait, they're on the sheet. Start again, but do it with an Irish accent.

ACTRESS: *(full brogue)* To be or not to be. That 'tis the question--

DIRECTOR: Awesome. Start again, but can you move the chair aside? I'd like to see you do this on your feet.

ACTRESS: Am I still Irish?

DIRECTOR: Try it like you're about 100 years old....and from Maine.

ACTRESS: *(aging her voice as best she can and adopting a Down East accent)* Tah bee owah not tah bee, ayuh--

DIRECTOR: Excellent. Now give me pouty So Cal cheerleader when daddy won't let her borrow the Lexus.

ACTRESS: *(perhaps a Valley Girl accent or a baby voice, full pout)* To. Be. Or. Not. To Be.....THAT--

DIRECTOR: You're Helen Keller in *The Miracle Worker* and these are your first words.

ACTRESS: To....b-b-b-be...OR.....nnnnnot--

DIRECTOR: Now sing it like it's the last aria from La Boheme.

ACTRESS: *(she's probably not an opera singer)* Tooooooo......beeeeee..... oooorrrr.... nnnooottt--

DIRECTOR: Or not. Ok, you're an Australian monkey with her own children's nature show.

ACTRESS: *(full-on Australian accent, monkey gestures)* To be or not to be, that IS the question!

DIRECTOR: You're doing very well with the adjustments.

ACTRESS: Thanks. Is this going to be a high-concept production?

DIRECTOR: God no. I'd rather die. Right now, I just want to know that you can take direction.

ACTRESS: Of course.

DIRECTOR: Pick it up with "whether 'tis nobler" blahbeddy blah.

ACTRESS: As what?

DIRECTOR: It should be obvious.

ACTRESS: It should? It should! Of course. *(Pause. She tries robot voice.)* Whether 'tis nobler in the mind to suffer the--

DIRECTOR: HEPBURN!

ACTRESS: Sorry.

DIRECTOR: You're supposed to do Hepburn.

ACTRESS: Next on my list. Here goes—

DIRECTOR: Aren't you going to ask which one?

ACTRESS: Ab....solutely.

DIRECTOR: I'll give you the choice. Katharine or Audrey.

ACTRESS: Katharine.

DIRECTOR: Yes! Audrey's too hard.

ACTRESS: I know, right?

DIRECTOR: —"to suffer the slings and arrows of outrageous—"

ACTRESS: I'm sorry are you doing a Hepburn right now?

DIRECTOR: No, I'm just giving you the words. Go.

ACTRESS: Ok.

DIRECTOR: Go. Go, go, go.

ACTRESS: I'm just—

DIRECTOR: DON'T THINK!

ACTRESS: Ah!

DIRECTOR: Hepburn.

ACTRESS: I don't know it. Oh god, I don't know who the Hepburns are.

DIRECTOR: Oh, come on. Of course you do.

ACTRESS: I don't. I'm 22.

DIRECTOR: So? If you don't know who they are, how do you know they're from another time? They could be from right now.

ACTRESS: I just figured, because I hadn't heard of them...and you're older...

DIRECTOR: Older? How much older do you think I am?

ACTRESS: Not...uh...oh god, I think I'm just going to go throw up and think about how I'm not getting this part.

DIRECTOR: Says who?

ACTRESS: I just...I do this so many times and eventually the director asks me to do something I can't and it's just like...never minnnndd...and P. S. there is NO train of thought that takes you from a monkey to a patrician New England movie star from the 40s.

DIRECTOR: Sure there is...hold up, I thought you didn't know who she was?

ACTRESS: I thought it was stupid. I gave YOU an adjustment to see if you could handle not having all of your orders followed.

DIRECTOR: *(mini beat)* Kate Hepburn was like— *(making his voice waver)* "Whethah tis noblah in thah mind to suffah" *(reverts to his real voice)* Try it. To suffah!

ACTRESS: To suffah! *(He motions for her to continue... it starts to become southern.)* Thuh slings a-yand arruhs

DIRECTOR: *(doubling down on the Hepburn waver)* "the slings and arrows of out-RAGE-ous fortune"

TOGETHER: *(she picks up the Hepburn voice)* "or to take arms against a sea of troubles"—

ACTRESS: That's awesome! Who else can you do?

DIRECTOR: No one's ever asked that before.

ACTRESS: Do it as Cher. From the beginning.

DIRECTOR: *(instant Cher, with gestures)* "To be or not to be. That's the question." *(flips Cher's imaginary hair)*

ACTRESS: Yes, yes, yes!

DIRECTOR: Really?

ACTRESS: Now, it's Cher, but she's in a horror movie and she's alone in the spooky mansion looking for her friends.

DIRECTOR: *(acting this out, with Cher voice)* "Whether tis nobler in the mind to suffer the slings and arrows of—

ACTRESS: *(with a sudden movement. maybe throwing a chair)* BOO!

DIRECTOR: *(screaming)* Ahhhh!! What is WRONG with you?

ACTRESS: I'm sorry.

DIRECTOR: Holy shit.

ACTRESS: I just wanted to get a natural reaction out of you.

DIRECTOR: As Cher. In a funhouse.

ACTRESS: Said the bitch who asked for Australian monkeys.

DIRECTOR: Was I.....natural? At least, when you scared me?

ACTRESS: Is your heart beating rapidly? I'd say that's a start.

DIRECTOR: *(beat)* I was rude to you. When you came in here, I was rude to you.

ACTRESS: It's not like I haven't seen it before. I know what auditions are like.

DIRECTOR: No, I was just being a jerk. About you, about the piece you selected.

ACTRESS: It's an off choice.

DIRECTOR: It's Hamlet. Why would anyone get into this business if she didn't love Hamlet?

ACTRESS: I should've done Ophelia.

DIRECTOR: It's not as good a part. And she doesn't get a fair shake. She's a young woman full of spirit and promise. And she walks into this room and this older man tells her what to do and who to be, not because it's what's best for her, but because of what he wants. And it makes him feel powerful and important to tell her what to do.

ACTRESS: Her father loves her. He's just an asshole, that's all.

DIRECTOR: Right. *(beat)* My boyfriend left me today.....unexpectedly.

ACTRESS: Is this another audition game?

DIRECTOR: No, it's just...conversation.

ACTRESS: Oh. I'm so sorry. If it helps, I don't think expecting it would have made it any better...

DIRECTOR: No, that's okay. He said I have control issues.

ACTRESS: Did he now?

DIRECTOR: Are you fucking with me?

ACTRESS: I mean, I've already botched the audition, soooo...

DIRECTOR: Not at all.

ACTRESS: I broke up with my girlfriend.

DIRECTOR: Recently?

ACTRESS: When I was 16, but healing takes time.

DIRECTOR: I can't tell if you're laughing at me or with me.

ACTRESS: Ohhhhhh...definitely AT you.

DIRECTOR: What's it like? When you just let go and get lost in it...what's it like?

ACTRESS: It's awesome enough that I put up with male directors...to a point.

DIRECTOR: Fair enough. If you have time, would you mind starting again?

ACTRESS: Sure. Should I be the crab from *The Little Mermaid*?

DIRECTOR: No.

ACTRESS: A zombie who just completed a Fulbright?

DIRECTOR: No, no. Could you just do it as you?

ACTRESS: You mean the way I started off?

DIRECTOR: No, I mean just as you. Can you do that?

ACTRESS: Can we do it as a dialogue?

DIRECTOR: I'll start you off, but then—

ACTRESS: No, no. You do it with me. We trade. We just talk. If you want something from me, you've got a better shot if you give me something, too. *(He's not sure.)* To be—

DIRECTOR: Or not to be. That is the question—

ACTRESS: *(She moves to him and clasps his hands as she says this.)* Whether 'tis nobler in the mind to suffer the slings and arrows of outrageous fortune—

DIRECTOR: *(No "acting." He just responds to her.)* —or to take arms against a sea of troubles and by opposing end them. *(beat)* That was nice.

ACTRESS: It was. Now start again...

(curtain)

THE UNBEARABLE LIGHTNESS OF GREENING

by Nina Mansfield

Nina Mansfield is a Connecticut-based playwright, fiction writer, and educator. Nina's ten-minute and one-act plays have had more than 100 productions throughout the United States and internationally. Her short plays *Smile* and *Missed Exit* appeared in previous Boston Theater Marathons. Her play *Bite Me* was a finalist for the 2013 Miami City Theatre's National Award for Short Playwriting and was produced as part of Summer Shorts 2013. Her full-length play *Losing Our Heads: The Guillotine Play* was a semi-finalist for the Eugene O'Neill Theater Center's 2012 National Playwrights Conference. Nina's plays have been published by Smith and Kraus, YouthPLAYS, Original Works Publishing, and One Act Play Depot. Her fiction has appeared in *Ellery Queen Mystery Magazine*, *Mysterical-E*, *Kings River Life Magazine*, *Crime Syndicate Magazine*, and anthologized in *Fast Women and Neon Lights: Eighties-Inspired Neon Noir* (Short Stack Books, 2016) and *Where Crime Never Sleeps* (Level Best Books, 2017). Her first novel, *Swimming Alone*, a young adult mystery, was published by Fire & Ice YA in 2015. Nina is a member of The Dramatists Guild, Mystery Writers of America, The Society for Children's Book Writers and Illustrators, and Sisters in Crime. **Contact: nina@ninamansfield.com; www.ninamansfield.com**

The Unbearable Lightness of Greening was sponsored by **Titanic Theatre Company**, which was founded in 2010 and became an incorporated 501(c)(3) in 2011. We produced our first show, Charles Busch's *The Third Story*, in 2012 at the Arsenal Center for the Arts in Watertown. Titanic Theatre Company is committed to sharp-edged, contemporary comedy. Whether it's smooth sailing, or a little comedic heavy surf, we're a company that's not afraid to take the plunge. **www.titanictheatre.com**

The Unbearable Lightness of Greening was presented on April 16, 2020, with the following creative team:

Directed by Alisha Jansky
JANE: Shelley Brown
BOB: Phil Thompson
STAGE DIRECTIONS: David Hansen

CHARACTERS:

BOB: Man. 40s to 50s.

JANE: Bob's ex-wife. 30s-50s.

(The present—Afternoon light bounces off a park bench. BOB sits. He has a canvas bag of sorts that contains his laptop and other necessities. JANE enters. She is on her lunch break, and looks it.)

JANE: Hello, Bob.

BOB: Hello, Jane. Have a seat. Have a seat.

JANE: I think I would prefer to stand.

BOB: No you wouldn't. You're just being difficult.

JANE: No I'm not.

BOB: Yes you are. You're putting up unnecessary blockades between our ability to connect because of some pre-determined emotional response you've decided upon. I understand though. It's fine. It's natural, in fact. I've learned all about your personality type in therapy. But feel free to let those barriers down. It's okay now. We're not married anymore, so there is absolutely no reason to keep that icy wall between us.

JANE: Is this about Coco?

BOB: Why don't you sit and we can discuss this like civilized human beings.

JANE: The seat's wet. It's been raining.

BOB: I brought a towelette.

JANE: A moist towelette?

BOB: Don't be silly. You can't dry a seat with a moist towelette. They sell dry towelettes now. I think they're meant for oily people. But they are perfectly good for drying off park benches as well. *(BOB dries off the park bench.)* That's something else I've learned in therapy. To be prepared for any situation. I think my therapist was talking about emotional preparedness. But I like to be prepared for a variety of environmental...

(BOB has taken out a miniature electric fan.)

JANE: Is that a fan?

BOB: ...and ecological possibilities as well. Yes. Yes it is a fan. The dry towelettes aren't as absorbent as I had hoped. *(He finishes drying the seat.)* There. Now sit. Please. *(JANE hesitates, then sits.)* Doesn't that feel better than standing? I can actually sense that you've released several inches of resentment from your emotional barrier. Don't you feel lighter? Freer? Less tied-down by the weight of your own self-restrictions?

JANE: Is this about Coco?

BOB: Ah yes. You asked that before.

JANE: Is it?

BOB: No. Why do you ask?

JANE: Because if this is about Coco, I really feel like we need to go through our attorneys. You get him every other weekend and on Wednesday nights, and that's it. And you pay for all the cat litter. Those were the terms we agreed upon, and I'm not budging.

BOB: Sweetheart.

JANE: You can't call me that anymore.

BOB: Sorry. Bad habit. Jane then.

JANE: Yes Bob.

BOB: This isn't about Coco.

JANE: Good, because that cat has been through enough trauma as is. I've finally been able to reduce the dosage on his anxiety medication and I really don't want to put him through any more stress. Cats need stability. Cats need routine. We've agreed on a schedule, and we need to stick with it.

BOB: Jane. Right now, you're projecting. I already said that this isn't about Coco.

JANE: Then what is it?

BOB: I'll tell you.

JANE: You said it was urgent.

BOB: A minor hyperbole.

JANE: I'm on my lunch break.

BOB: I remember those.

JANE: So?

BOB: I've decided to open an online dating account.

JANE: And you are telling me this why?

BOB: Because I think you should open one too.

JANE: Why?

BOB: Because I think it will help you move on.

JANE: I've already moved on.

BOB: I don't think you have Jane.

JANE: Bob, you left me for—

BOB: Shhh. I know. I know. But let's not start playing the blame game. This isn't about what you did or I did. This isn't about our failure as a married couple. This isn't about the past. This is about the future. Our future as successful singles. Our future of happiness.

JANE: You left me for a houseplant.

BOB: That's not true.

JANE: It is.

BOB: Well, technically, I suppose, yes. It is true. But I just want to be very clear. I never had any relations with Petunia while we were still legally married.

JANE: It's not even a petunia. It's a rubber tree.

BOB: But she prefers to be called Petunia. Or by her Latin name, *Ficus elastica.*

JANE: She?

BOB: Yes Jane. I know it would have made it easier for you if Petunia was a man. Maybe it would have made you feel less inadequate as a wife. But—

JANE: What could she give you that I couldn't Bob?

BOB: She was a much better listener.

JANE: She doesn't have ears!

BOB: That doesn't mean she wasn't receptive to my words.

JANE: She can't talk.

BOB: Talking and communicating are two different things. Here we sit Jane. Talking. But are we really communicating?

JANE: I don't know Bob. How exactly do you communicate with Petunia?

BOB: Did.

JANE: Did?

BOB: It's the past tense of do.

JANE: So, it's over with her?

BOB: Hence my decision—correction, me and my therapist's decision to venture forth into the world of online dating.

JANE: What happened? Did her leaves start to droop or something?

BOB: Don't be crass. I still care for her.

JANE: Did she end it, or did you?

BOB: It was mutual.

JANE: Oh. Mutual.

BOB: We both decided that we weren't right for each other.

JANE: Go figure.

BOB: She was really a bit of a homebody, you know. Liked to stare out the window. Bask in the sunlight from the safety of the living room. But she never wanted to go out. And don't get me wrong. I enjoy a quiet evening at home. But you know me. I like my nights out on the town. I love a good meal, a few drinks, a little dancing. She wasn't much of a dancer.

JANE: No. I would imagine not.

BOB: It's sad really. A gal like her. That firm green stalk. Those glossy green leaves. Right after a pruning, she was someone I really wanted to show off to the world.

JANE: But she's still living with you.

BOB: Sadly, no. It was just too tense to be together after we'd ended it.

JANE: So…you just threw her away?

BOB: You should know me better than that. I donated her to the botanical gardens. They didn't want to take her at first. Told me she was too… *(whispers)* common.

JANE: Common?

BOB: Shhh!

JANE: Afraid she'll hear you?

BOB: It was just so insulting. I hope they never say it to her face. It would devastate her. I'd always tried to make her feel so special. So unique. Anyway, once I explained everything, they took pity on our situation. Realized that Petunia had lived a very sheltered and solitary life. You know, she didn't have one plant friend to speak of. And I can still visit her whenever I want.

JANE: Well that's reassuring.

BOB: And I'm ready to move on. I realize that, in many ways, she was just a rebound. I didn't leave you for her. Our marriage was over long before Petunia. And now, I really think I'm ready to find someone new.

JANE: And you just had to tell me.

BOB: I wanted to share my happiness with you. And I want you to be happy too. My therapist says that online dating will help me weed out—no pun intended—those women—

JANE: Or houseplants—

BOB: —who I may be physically attracted to, but who aren't really right for my temperament. We are both in very delicate emotional states right now. Online dating is a way to shield ourselves from the damage that can be caused by someone who isn't aligned with our unique personality type.

JANE: That's really nice Bob. I'm glad you're moving on. To humans.

BOB: And I think you should too.

JANE: I've never moved off of humans.

BOB: I've always found your attachment to Coco a little, well, disturbing Jane. If I may be frank.

JANE: Coco's a cat.

BOB: So?

JANE: He's like my child.

BOB: A child with an Oedipus complex Jane. An Oedipus complex that you've allowed to grow, and blossom in a very unhealthy way.

JANE: You had your lawyer make that argument in court.

BOB: All I did was tell him about your constant petting. The way you rub his belly, and feed him treats.

JANE: That's what people do with cats.

BOB: You never petted me that way Jane.

JANE: Is there anything else you have to say to me Bob?

BOB: Well, I thought we could do this together.

JANE: Do what together?

BOB: Create our online dating accounts. I brought my laptop. I even started to make a profile for you. I hope you don't think that's too presumptuous of me. But, well, admit it. Except for maybe Coco, who knows you better than I do?

JANE: *(at a loss for words)* I…uh…

BOB: *(reading from his laptop)* Friskie, well-groomed tigress seeks a cuddly companion.

JANE: Uh…no.

BOB: Seeks tiger to tame?

JANE: Could you just delete that? Would you?

BOB: If you insist. *(He deletes it.)*

JANE: Thanks. Uh…I really have to get back to work.

BOB: Oh. Okay. We should do this again. Sometime soon?

JANE: Not too soon. *(JANE leaves.)*

BOB: Always such a kidder. *(He turns to his laptop.)* Let's see. 40ish male. Enjoys composting, sunlight and chlorophyll. Ready to put down some roots…

(end of play)

THE STAKEOUT

by K. Alexa Mavromatis

K. Alexa Mavromatis's award-winning short plays and one-acts—including *Jinxed*, *The Stakeout*, *Stew*, *SL1 12:32 a.m.*, *True Blue*, and *Bone China*—have been produced by theatres across the U.S. and on four continents. Her work is published in numerous anthologies, textbooks, and acting editions. Alexa holds an MFA in Playwriting from Boston University, and is a member of the Dramatists Guild and Rhombus Playwrights. She proudly serves on the staff of Boston Playwrights' Theatre. **Contact: kamavromatis@gmail.com**

The Stakeout was sponsored by **Emerson Stage**, the producing organization within the Emerson College Department of Performing Arts. Here, the next generation of actors, designers, stage managers, technicians, administrators, and educators work alongside distinguished faculty, professional staff, and guest artists to bring skills learned in the classroom to vibrant life on stage. Artists of tomorrow, on stage today. **www.emerson.edu/academics/academic-departments/performing-arts/emerson-stage**

The Stakeout was presented on May 7, 2020, with the following creative team:

Directed by Annie G. Levy
Assistant Director and Stage Directions: Meghan Dresdner
Stage Manager and Sound Designer: Robert Cott
MARTI: Samara Chahine
BETH: Marlee Mesarchik

CHARACTERS:

BETH, 16. Good-humored, playful. Can come across as a bit insensitive, but that is the result of a sheltered existence, not outright callousness.

MARTI, 15. Smart, sensitive, a bit preoccupied, thoughtful. On edge.

NOTE: For maximum effect, the action is best played as though the house the characters are observing is straight downstage (i.e., in the audience).

(A small college town in the South, spring of 1987. The sidewalk and yard in front of a large house. MARTI, 15, is lurking behind a bush, staring at the front door and window. BETH, 16, enters carrying coffee and doughnuts.)

BETH: Hey.

MARTI: Shhh.

BETH: What did I miss?

MARTI: Nothing.

BETH: I brought coffee.

MARTI: Coffee? Why? We don't drink coffee.

BETH: I do. Sometimes, at IHOP. Besides, it's a stakeout. You know. Want a doughnut?

MARTI: Beth, you're crazy.

BETH: *(excited)* Like the cops. You know, where they eat jelly doughnuts in an unmarked car. Like *Cagney and Lacey.* They have that plain gold car, and they just sit on the street and watch. We should have dressed up!

MARTI: Shhh—I think I just saw the top of his head.

BETH: *(looking toward the house)* Really?

(beat)

BETH: *(thoughtful)* Then, when they have emergencies, you know, they put that light on the top.

MARTI: *(still looking at the window)* I can't tell. Top of what?

BETH: The car.

MARTI: Oh.

BETH: It must be, like, a magnet or something.

MARTI: Maybe. *(pause)* That could have been *her*, though.

BETH: Do you think it is?

MARTI: What?

BETH: A magnet.

MARTI: *(thinking for a moment)* Probably.

BETH: I want them to come out!

MARTI: They might not be leaving, though. Until tomorrow morning. For work. Or school or whatever.

BETH: Well, we'll stay here until they do.

MARTI: We can't stay out all night.

BETH: Why not?

MARTI: I'm still walking on thin ice with Judy since we came in late, like, two months ago.

BETH: I know: You say you're at my house, and I'll say I'm spending the night at yours. There's a payphone around the corner.

MARTI: I dunno.

BETH: Come on. We can keep staking out. We can sleep right here. I have a blanket in the car.

MARTI: I'm not gonna sleep in the bushes.

BETH: We'll sleep in the car, then.

MARTI: I dunno. We still have a few minutes. If we leave here by 10:00, I'll make it home for curfew.

BETH: Okay.

(short pause)

BETH: But we should kind of decide soon.

MARTI: *(looking at house)* Hmmm…

BETH: You know, so we can call home and everything. If we're going to…

MARTI: Okay.

BETH: Know what? This is the farthest I've driven. Since I got my license and stuff. Nine miles.

MARTI: *(sighing, looking back to the window)* I want to see more than the top of his head.

BETH: Me too. *(pause)* I wonder what she looks like.

MARTI: Who?

(BETH points toward the house.)

I know.

BETH: *(an idea)* We could knock and pretend like we're selling something.

MARTI: Like what?

BETH: Magazine subscriptions or something. We did it for band. Or fruit! We sold oranges for chorus.

MARTI: *(sarcastically)* Or Girl Scout cookies.

BETH: Yeah!

MARTI: I was being facetious.

BETH: *Facetious…*

MARTI: Bullock's vocabulary quiz?

BETH: Oh yeah. Good for you for using your words. Here's one: *Conundrum.*

MARTI: *(challenging)* Use it in a sentence.

BETH: "My friend Marti is a conundrum."

MARTI: A puzzle. Why am I a conundrum?

BETH: Because after we found him in *Who's Who?*, and went through all that interlibrary loan crap to look at *every book he's ever written*, and *then* the stupid phone book and that crisscross-find-someone-whatever-directory...

MARTI: *(interrupting)* It's all public information.

BETH: Not the point. We know more about this guy than...than I know about my *own* dad, practically. And now we're here. And you won't even go up to the door!

MARTI: I...I guess it's different *thinking* about being here than *actually* being here.

BETH: *(an idea)* I know.

MARTI: What?

BETH: We can ring and run.

MARTI: What?

BETH: Ring and run. You know—ring the doorbell…and run.

MARTI: You mean ding-dong ditch?

BETH: *(laughing)* Ding dong ditch? You actually call it that? Y'all ran from door-to-door talking about penises and shit?

MARTI: *(shocked, laughing)* No!

BETH: If you called it 'ding-dong' whatever, you did.

MARTI: That's not what it means.

BETH: Guys call their dicks ding-dongs.

MARTI: 'Ding-dong' is the sound a doorbell makes when you ring it. Why are we talking about this?

BETH: Whatever. He'll come to the door, and at least you can see... *(beat)* Because I know you don't want to talk about it. What we're doing here. *(slight pause)* I know you don't. *Really* talk about it, I mean...

MARTI: No, it's not that. I want to know if he's really going to get in touch with me when I'm eighteen like my mom always says. I want to know if my sister looks anything like me...if he painted her room pink like a princess...if they've ever gone to one of those cheesy father-daughter dance things like you see on TV shows. *(slight pause)* If my mom hadn't gotten a job down here and we still lived in Chicago? I wouldn't care. I mean, I guess I've always thought about it, but... *(short pause)* He came to Chicago when I was ten. For a conference or something. He was supposed to come see us, but…his schedule changed. *(slight pause)* My mom took him to court two years ago so he'd pay for the braces on my teeth—did I tell you that? That's, like, the only thing he's paid for. *(looking toward the house)* She's probably popular. Their house is kinda big. I bet when she turns sixteen, she'll have a car.

BETH: Maybe one day, if you meet her, she'll drive you around.

MARTI: Ha ha. I hate you.

(MARTI punches BETH in the arm. Beat.)

BETH: It's probably all for the best.

MARTI: How do you figure?

BETH: That's what my mom says, anyway.

MARTI: *(getting angry)* You told your mom?

BETH: No.

MARTI: Did you?

BETH: No!

MARTI: Are you sure?

BETH: No. I mean yes! I didn't tell her.

MARTI: *(sharply)* Because it's none of her business.

BETH: Okay...She just always says that...about stuff.

(pause)

MARTI: How do you know it's for the best?

BETH: Marti...

MARTI: *(stewing)* No, really. I'm dying to know. I mean, you have a dad. He lives with you.

BETH: So?

MARTI: So, *he's there.*

BETH: Oh yeah—big whoop. You see how much attention he pays to me. Compared to Michael, I don't exist.

MARTI: Yeah, well, Michael's the boy.

BETH: So?

MARTI: Well, there's nothing really weird about that.

BETH: Last year at my birthday party, he didn't even know how old I was.

MARTI: Yes he did.

BETH: No he didn't. He asked me, remember?

MARTI: He was kidding. Everyone else knew he was.

BETH: No he wasn't. He doesn't even look at me half the time. Practically the only time he talks to me is when I'm on my way out the door and he does his Sgt. Esterhaus impression: "Be careful out there." Whatever.

MARTI: He knows you love that show. It's like an inside joke.

BETH: He's just being *annoying*...

MARTI: *(exploding)* God, I hate how you talk sometimes—it's like you're not grateful for anything!

BETH: That's not true!

MARTI: Yes, it is. I wish you could hear yourself talk!

(beat)

BETH: At least we found all those books.

MARTI: My mom never told me he was a writer. A professor and a writer.

BETH: Like you. Writer, I mean.

MARTI: Yeah. *(beat)* One of his essays...in one of his books...I think one of them was about my mom.

BETH: Well, it all comes from somewhere. *(Pause. Gesturing to the door.)* What're you going to do?

MARTI: I'm thinking.

BETH: If you're going to... It's almost time to think about leaving. I mean, if you're not going to...

MARTI: *(looking toward the window again)* Nobody's walked by for a while.

BETH: They're probably all getting ready for bed.

MARTI: I wonder if he's a night person or a morning person.

BETH: Morning.

MARTI: What makes you say that?

BETH: That light just went off.

MARTI: I dunno. (*Pacing, MARTI nervously taps her toes on the walk.*) Hey, here's a penny. Maybe that means...

BETH: Stop!

MARTI: What?

BETH: Don't—it's tails.

MARTI: What?

BETH: It's tails-up.

MARTI: Oh.

BETH: That only works if it's heads-up. If it's tails you have to flip it over. Leave the luck for someone else.

MARTI: *(under her breath)* Leave the luck for someone else.

(MARTI bends over and flips the penny over, leaving it on the ground. She stares at the door.)

BETH: Do it.

MARTI: What?

BETH: Ring it.

(MARTI continues staring at the door.)

BETH: C'mon—we'll hide over there. You can at least see what he looks like.

(Her hand shaking, MARTI reaches out and rings the bell.)

BETH: *(Starting to run, motioning to MARTI)* C'mon! Marti!

(For a moment, it looks like MARTI may run. She doesn't.)

BETH: Marti?

(MARTI stands, staring at the door.)

BETH: Marti?

(Lights fade to black, as BETH watches MARTI waiting at the door.)

(end of play)

THE RIGHT MOMENT

by Matt Mayerchak

Matt Mayerchak is a graduate of the Boston University master's program in Playwriting and the author of several short plays, including, *The Great Outdoors*, *Empties*, *Deep*, and *Outside the Box*, which have been performed in previous Boston Theater Marathons. *Empties* was selected as a finalist by the Actor's Theatre of Louisville for the 2005 Heidemann Award and produced at the Woolly Mammoth Theatre in Washington, D.C. His one-act play *A Month of Somedays* received a staged reading at the Boston Playwrights' Theatre in 2000. As a producer for the series The Radio Play, he helped created 26 30-minute radio plays which were broadcast on NPR Playhouse. His radio play *A Night's Work* was produced by the Midwest Radio Theatre Workshop and broadcast nationwide on NPR. He lives in Arlington, MA. **Contact: matt@mayerchak.com**

The Right Moment was sponsored by **The Cohasset Dramatic Club** (Lisa Pratt, Producing Artistic Director). Organized in 1921 and entering their 100th season in September 2020, CDC is one of the oldest continually operating theaters in the country. With a permanent residence in Cohasset's Town Hall, CDC originated as a summer stock theater destination in the late 40's and was the genesis of today's South Shore Music Circus. Today Cohasset Dramatic Club is dedicated to bringing together theatre artists from the greater Boston area to foster the production of inspiring new and classic theatrical works through performance and education. With the addition of summer workshop and educational performance programs for youth ages 8-21, CDC is a hub of creativity and exploration for everyone all year round. **www.cohassetdramaticclub.org**

The Right Moment was presented on April 10, 2020, with the following creative team:

Directed by Lisa Pratt
JIMMY: Danny Bolton
SHARON: Maryann Zschau
TOM: Steve Bergman
STAGE DIRECTIONS: Logan Pratt

CHARACTERS:

JIMMY

SHARON

TOM

All three characters are approximately the same age, somewhere between 50 and 60 years old.

(Kitchen Counter and a sofa; upper class home. SHARON is at the counter drinking a cup of coffee. There is a pot of coffee on the counter, and a second cup. Strong morning light. At rise, JIMMY is half-asleep on the sofa. He comes to life slowly.)

JIMMY: *(groan)* Where am I?

SHARON: Good morning! How'd you sleep?

JIMMY: Sharon? What are you... Oh...is this where I am?

SHARON: Where did you think you were?

JIMMY: I don't know. Dead? How'd I get here?

SHARON: You really don't remember? You showed up in the middle of a thunderstorm lugging an empty suitcase. Coffee?

JIMMY: Definitely. Ooh...and maybe...sunglasses?

SHARON: I'll close the curtains. Coffee's in the pot.

(SHARON goes offstage to adjust curtains while JIMMY pours himself coffee.)

JIMMY: Oh, man. That is the stuff. How'd I get here?

SHARON: You banged on our door at eleven last night, in the middle of a downpour, soaking wet.

JIMMY: I bet Tom was pissed.

SHARON: He acted like it. I think he was secretly glad for an excuse to break out his three-hundred dollar Scotch.

JIMMY: Three hundred? Damn. Wish I remembered what that tasted like.

SHARON: You had him retelling all his old stories.

JIMMY: Those were the days, huh? Anything was possible.

SHARON: Yeah.

JIMMY: Hmm. Look at us.

SHARON: What?

JIMMY: I just had a vision of what coulda been. You and me, having our morning coffee.

SHARON: Ahem. I called Annie to tell her you were here...so she wouldn't worry.

JIMMY: You talked to Annie?

SHARON: How could you not tell us? The divorce?

JIMMY: Shit. I was gonna tell you. Honest.

SHARON: That weekend at the Cape, you guys seemed so happy.

JIMMY: *Seemed.* We were good at seeming. Anyway, that was what, five years ago?

SHARON: Honestly? My lord, you're right. Lizzy must be...16?

JIMMY: Freshman at NYU.

SHARON: NYU. My stars! How is she?

JIMMY: She's great. Smart as hell. *Thrilled* to be away from her parents.

(beat)

Things got kinda rough. They opened one of those enormous coffee palaces right across the street. Killed us. We hadn't made any money on books in years; the café was everything. Then the landlord's son takes over and jacks up the rent. I was living in the supply room. I went down to the Y to take a shower, and when I came back, all my shit was out in the street—everything I owned. I had nowhere else to go.

SHARON: So, what, you planning to just squat here, with us?

JIMMY: Could I? A couple days, maybe? Until I can figure out...

SHARON: Tom will never go for it. He's not the affable, Type A prick you used to know.

JIMMY: Where is, he, at work?

SHARON: No. *(beat)* He's out schtupping his mistress.

JIMMY: His what?

SHARON: Twice a week he goes out for a "morning ride." He pedals his bike over to her place, spends an hour there, and comes home all sweaty and bragging about what a great workout he did.

JIMMY: Are you telling me a middle-aged man is conducting an affair in bike shorts? How'd you find out?

SHARON: Either he wants me to know, or he just thinks I'm too stupid to check his exercise app.

JIMMY: What a jerk! I'm so sorry. Who is it? You know her?

SHARON: I looked her up. She's 35, divorced. Works in the same building as his law firm. Communications.

JIMMY: God. What an ass.

SHARON: It's OK. Really. Better her than me.

JIMMY: You gonna confront him?

SHARON: I'm waiting for the right moment to reveal itself.

JIMMY: The right moment. Hah! I been waiting for that my whole life.

SHARON: What happened with Annie?

JIMMY: I dunno. As my old man used to say, "too much of not enough." I think, to be honest, the real problem was... She wasn't you.

SHARON: Please.

JIMMY: Remember those walks we took? Back in the day? When he was in the library? Every day I'd tell myself, today, man, today. Carpe Diem. *Tell her!* I never could get up the courage.

SHARON: Are you telling me that way back then, when I was dating Tom, you wanted to ask me out?

JIMMY: Oh man. I had the most wicked crush on you. I thought about you all the time.

SHARON: For Pete's sake! Why didn't you say something?

JIMMY: You were going out with my roommate. I was afraid that if I let the cat outta the bag, we wouldn't be friends anymore.

SHARON: You poor, stupid... You think I didn't know? I gave you so many chances.

JIMMY: You knew?

SHARON: I led you to a cave! I wasn't over the moon about Tom, but he knew what he wanted and he went after it. It was nice to feel wanted. Senior year, his father got us into the Harvard boathouse for the Regatta. Champagne, and oysters, and you shoulda seen him glad-handing all of those Board of Trustees types. Introducing me as the love of his life. He knew where he was going, and how to get there. I tagged along for the ride. Next thing I knew, I had two kids. Now, apparently, what he wants is "twenty-calorie Valerie."

JIMMY: I think when we're young, we have an idea of what we want; but we don't take good care of that. Someone offers you a job; it's not perfect, but it pays OK—and you think, "maybe I was *meant* to be a compliance officer."

(beat)

I never felt a hundred percent with Annie. I only ever felt that way about one person.

(JIMMY approaches Sharon, and kisses her passionately. She gives herself up to it for several seconds, before pulling away.)

SHARON: Oh, Jimmy. Jimmy Jimmy Jimmy Jimmy Jimmy. Such a goddamn waste.

JIMMY: What do you mean?

SHARON: We could have had so much.

JIMMY: It's not too late. I mean; not like it woulda been. Not kids. Still...

SHARON: You think you can burst in here in the middle of the night and turn the clock back thirty years? Like it's what, "midlife savings time"?

JIMMY: No. I never...

SHARON: So, what? You want me to run away with you? To the Salvation Army?

JIMMY: I don't know.

SHARON: Of course not! Same old Jimmy.

JIMMY: I don't have a plan. OK. Guilty! Never have.

SHARON: I have a life here. My book club; yoga; I volunteer at the food pantry. I may not have passion. But hell, at my age...

(SHARON reaches into her pocket and pulls out a check.)

Here. Buy yourself a ticket. Someplace warm, where you can live cheap. Puerto Rico, or...

(JIMMY takes the check and looks at it.)

JIMMY: I can't take this from you.

SHARON: We can afford it. Honest. It's not a fortune, but it should be enough to get you settled.

JIMMY: What, you don't want Tom to find out, about us?

SHARON: Don't be ridiculous. He's going to leave me, sooner or later. We'll sell the house, and I'll get an apartment, and an automatic funds transfer every month.

(JIMMY tears up the check.)

JIMMY: I don't need your charity.

SHARON: It wasn't just you. I chickened out, too. I could have made the first move. I guess I was afraid that life with you would be too...adventurous.

JIMMY: I've wasted a lot of years. The best years. Who knows? Maybe they're still ahead. The kids are out. Tom sure as hell doesn't need you.

You and I might not be any good together. Maybe we give it a shot, and find out that the thing I've been imagining my whole life has been a mirage. Poof! I'm willing to risk that. If I fail, then, well... I'll go be a failure in a tent. That I could be good at. What about you?

SHARON: There's just been so damn much water under the bridge. I'm not the college girl you had a crush on.

JIMMY: And I sure as hell ain't the kid who had the crush. But I know you. I can make you feel *alive.* You really want to spend the rest of your life on a cul-de-sac? Come on. We can go to Mexico!

(Sounds offstage of TOM putting his bike away, singing a line from Tom Petty's "Into the Great Wide Open.")

TOM: *(singing, off)* "A rebel without a clue."

JIMMY: Tom?

SHARON: Yeah.

JIMMY: Don't worry. He won't see me.

(TOM enters, wearing bike shorts and a jersey covered in logos.)

TOM: Whoo! What a workout. 25 miles!

SHARON: Good for you.

TOM: Were you talking to somebody?

SHARON: It was Jimmy. He was asking if he could stay a couple of days. I said we'd talk it over.

TOM: Jimmy? You were talking to Jimmy?

SHARON: Yes. . .he was just. . .

TOM: Oh, hon.

(TOM attempts to comfort SHARON.)

It's okay. I know it's been hard. He must have really meant a lot to you.

(end of play)

CHOICES

by James McLindon

James McLindon is a member of the Nylon Fusion Theater Co. in New York. *When We Get Good Again* won the Playhouse on the Square New Works competition and premiered there in January, 2020. His play *Salvation* was developed at PlayPenn and premiered in New York, Giovanna Sardelli directing, to critical acclaim in *The New York Times* and elsewhere. *Comes a Faery* was developed at the O'Neill National Playwrights Conference, Sean Daniels directing, was a finalist for the Humana Festival, and was premiered at the New Ohio Theatre by Nylon Fusion. *Distant Music* has been produced eight times across the country. *Dead and Buried* premiered at the Detroit Repertory Theater and has been most recently performed by the Apollo Kine Theater in Estonia and Dreamcatcher Rep in New Jersey. Mr. McLindon's plays have been developed and/or produced at theaters such as the O'Neill (selection and six-time semifinalist), PlayPenn, Victory Gardens, Lark, Abingdon, hotINK Festival, Irish Repertory, Samuel French Festival, Edinburgh Fringe Festival, New Rep, Lyric Stage, Boston Playwrights' Theatre, Local Theatre, Telluride Playwrights Festival, Great Plains Theatre Conference, and Seven Devils. His plays have been published by Dramatic Publishing, Smith and Kraus, and Applause Books; they have been produced all over the world including London, Edinburgh, Ireland, Australia, the Philippines, Luxembourg, India, Dubai, and Estonia. **Contact: jmclindon@gmail.com** and **jamesmclindon.com** and **newplayexchange.org/users/4206/james-mclindon**

Choices was sponsored by **Pilgrim Theatre**, founded in 1986 in Wroclaw, Poland, by Kim Mancuso and Kermit Dunkelberg. Lecoq-trained artist Susan Thompson joined them in 1990. In residence at the Boston Center for the Arts (BCA) for eight years, Pilgrim moved to Ashfield (western MA hilltown) in 2006 and has toured the U.S., Latin America, and Europe. Funding includes the NEA, the Massachusetts Cultural Council, MIT, and the LEF Foundation. A member of the Network of Ensemble Theatres, Pilgrim fosters co-creation among writers, actors, designers, and musicians. Site-specific work has embraced a myriad of venues from the Cyclorama at the BCA to the crypt of an 11th century church in Kracow. Thompson's *Unforgettable: Letters from Korea* performed on the National Mall and Arena Stage in Washington D.C. for the 60th anniversary of the Korean War (touring to Boston, Shelburne Falls, MA, and Osage, IA). Collaborations with Serious Play! (Northampton, MA) include *Endgame* (2016); *Milosevic at the Hague* (2009); and recently, *Water*. Pilgrim is in development for a film about oral tradition focusing on Sicilian marionette and Cunto forms, set in Palermo, Italy. **www.pilgrimtheatre.org**

Choices was presented on May 10, 2020, with the following creative team:

Directed by Kim Mancuso
PROSPECTIVE CLIENT: Zoë Mancuso
DEBT COUNSELOR: Kermit Dunkelberg

CHARACTERS:

PROSPECTIVE CLIENT: Mid-20s to 30s, any gender

DEBT COUNSELOR: Any gender or age

Race-blind and diverse casting is encouraged.

(A modest living room (think poor graduate student), the present. PROSPECTIVE CLIENT, *mid-20s to 30s, sits at her/his coffee (or dining room) table across from* DEBT COUNSELOR, *mid-20s to 30s.* DEBT COUNSELOR *has an enthusiastic love of his product and the confidence that it practically sells itself, once the customer recovers from their initial surprise. For that reason, he does not rely on high-pressure tactics. He's also alert to steer clear of the troubling aspects of his presentation with a ready euphemism.* PROSPECTIVE CLIENT *is a little anxious, really needing this to work, but doubtful how it is not a scam.* DEBT COUNSELOR *has been waiting for* PROSPECTIVE CLIENT *to finish reading a pamphlet.* PROSPECTIVE CLIENT *now looks up, perplexed.)*

PROSPECTIVE CLIENT: I'm sorry, I just don't get it.

DEBT COUNSELOR: It's pretty simple. It's just...disruptive.

PROSPECTIVE CLIENT: No, I know, it sounds simple...

DEBT COUNSELOR: Think of it as a choice. We're all about choices. You can choose this. Or not.

PROSPECTIVE CLIENT: No, no, I want to choose this, believe me. I feel like I'm on a hamster wheel just trying to keep up with the payments, but...this just seems too good to be true.

DEBT COUNSELOR: That's often what disruption looks like. Remember all the things you used to have to pay to read, like newspapers and magazines? Now you get them on-line for free. We're disrupting the entire debt consolidation industry, sort of like that.

PROSPECTIVE CLIENT: Okay, but...I still don't get it.

DEBT COUNSELOR: Tell me what you don't get.

PROSPECTIVE CLIENT: So, you pay off my student loans—

DEBT COUNSELOR: Your crushing student loans.

PROSPECTIVE CLIENT: Yes, thank you, my 247,000 dollars in student loans, and all I have to do is pay you 72 dollars a month?

DEBT COUNSELOR: Yes.

PROSPECTIVE CLIENT: For 20 years.

DEBT COUNSELOR: Yes.

PROSPECTIVE CLIENT: And that's it. That's all I ever have to pay you.

DEBT COUNSELOR: That's all you ever have to pay us.

(PROSPECTIVE CLIENT calculates in her/his head.)

PROSPECTIVE CLIENT: Okay, so I'm not really great at math, but I think that's only, like, $170,000?

DEBT COUNSELOR: It's actually about $17,000.

PROSPECTIVE CLIENT: Only 17,000 dollars!? Okay, now I don't get this even more.

DEBT COUNSELOR: Tell me what you don't get.

PROSPECTIVE CLIENT: What don't I—? You give me 247,000 dollars to pay off my debt today and all I have to give you is 17,000 dollars over 20 years?

DEBT COUNSELOR: Right. Mainly to keep you focused.

PROSPECTIVE CLIENT: So you lose money.

DEBT COUNSELOR: No—

PROSPECTIVE CLIENT: Yeah, you lose money. Nobody sets up a business to lose money, unless they're, like, money laundering or something. Wait, are you guys money laundering?

DEBT COUNSELOR: No.

PROSPECTIVE CLIENT: What are you doing?

DEBT COUNSELOR: We're providing choices. *(pause)* I think maybe you skipped footnote seven.

PROSPECTIVE CLIENT: I didn't read the footnotes.

DEBT COUNSELOR: You should read the footnotes.

PROSPECTIVE CLIENT: I never do.

DEBT COUNSELOR: You always should.

PROSPECTIVE CLIENT: Okay, fine, what does footnote seven say?

DEBT COUNSELOR: It answers this question.

PROSPECTIVE CLIENT: About whether you're money-laundering?

DEBT COUNSELOR: About how we get paid.

(pause)

PROSPECTIVE CLIENT: So how do you? I mean, after I finish my payments you'll be short about 230,000 dollars. Not to mention any interest. So where do you get the rest (from)—? Oh, there're a bunch of hidden fees, aren't there?

DEBT COUNSELOR: There are no fees at all.

PROSPECTIVE CLIENT: Then c'mon, how do you get your money back from me!?

DEBT COUNSELOR: We don't get it back from you.

PROSPECTIVE CLIENT: You don't?

DEBT COUNSELOR: We don't. *(pause)* From you.

PROSPECTIVE CLIENT: Who do you get it back from?

DEBT COUNSELOR: The insurance company.

PROSPECTIVE CLIENT: What insurance company?

DEBT COUNSELOR: You should really read footnote seven—

PROSPECTIVE CLIENT: Just tell me, what insurance company!?

DEBT COUNSELOR: Your insurance company.

PROSPECTIVE CLIENT: Why would my car insurance company pay you?

DEBT COUNSELOR: Not your car insurance company.

PROSPECTIVE CLIENT: Well, that's the only insurance I have. I sure don't have homeowners because who can afford to buy a house when you owe 247,000—?

DEBT COUNSELOR: Your life insurance company.

(pause)

PROSPECTIVE CLIENT: I don't have life insurance.

DEBT COUNSELOR: Footnote seven.

PROSPECTIVE CLIENT: I have to get life insurance?

DEBT COUNSELOR: We pay for it.

PROSPECTIVE CLIENT: What good does life insurance do anyone?

DEBT COUNSELOR: It depends.

PROSPECTIVE CLIENT: Unless I die.

DEBT COUNSELOR: Read footnote seven.

PROSPECTIVE CLIENT: Oh my god. You've looked at my DNA! You have, you totally have, and you've found out I must have some horrible genetic abnormality that means I'm going to die young, so that's how you— What are you writing down?

DEBT COUNSELOR: No, please, go on, that's a really interesting business model.

PROSPECTIVE CLIENT: Stop it! That's not your business model?

DEBT COUNSELOR: No, but it's pretty good. Way disruptive.

PROSPECTIVE CLIENT: So I'm not going to die young?

DEBT COUNSELOR: Well, how would I know that?

PROSPECTIVE CLIENT: There's no DNA stuff in your file on me?

DEBT COUNSELOR: All we have is what you gave us.

PROSPECTIVE CLIENT: *(exhaling)* I'm not going to die young.

DEBT COUNSELOR: Well, not in the next 20 years. As far as I know.

PROSPECTIVE CLIENT: Do you qualify everything you say?

DEBT COUNSELOR: When it needs to be. Because we're totally honest. With our clients.

PROSPECTIVE CLIENT: So how do you make money from my life insurance?

DEBT COUNSELOR: How does anyone make money from life insurance?

PROSPECTIVE CLIENT: Somebody has to die. *(pause)* But you just said I wouldn't!

DEBT COUNSELOR: I said I don't know anything about your DNA. Or your health at all for that matter. We don't worry about that. Please. Read footnote seven.

(PROSPECTIVE CLIENT stares at DEBT COUNSELOR, who stares back. A beat.)

DEBT COUNSELOR: Please.

PROSPECTIVE CLIENT: Okay, fine.

(PROSPECTIVE CLIENT returns to reading the pamphlet. Suddenly:)

(stunned) Oh my god!

DEBT COUNSELOR: I know, right!? The first time I read it, I was like, Whaaaaat!? But the more you think about it, the more genius it is. Dis! Effing! Ruption! Amiright!? *(catching himself, quieting)* Sorry. I just love this product so much.

PROSPECTIVE CLIENT: I'm not going to agree to this! Does anyone ever agree to this?

DEBT COUNSELOR: No. *(long pause)* Not at first. But then they think about it. And they think, well, when I took out my crushing student loans, I knew that they would impact my life. Severely impact my life. For a whole lot of my life. Decades and decades and decades of my life. And see, that's all this is really. You just assumed that the impact would be frontloaded. And all we do is...backload it for you.

PROSPECTIVE CLIENT: Me dying in 20 years at [whatever age is about 20 years older than actor], that's what you call "severely impacting" my life?

DEBT COUNSELOR: Well, it seems severe to me.

PROSPECTIVE CLIENT: No, it's severe, it is very severe!

DEBT COUNSELOR: Yes. But. What a much better life it will have been. These next 20 years anyway. Which, after all, is your prime.

PROSPECTIVE CLIENT: How do you...you know...do it?

DEBT COUNSELOR: Do what?

PROSPECTIVE CLIENT: Make it so you get to, you know, collect.

DEBT COUNSELOR: *(pause)* Before we get into the details, I think it's best that you get comfortable with the concept (first)—

PROSPECTIVE CLIENT: Tell me how!

DEBT COUNSELOR: Well, it's up to you. See? Choices. Most people opt to handle matters themselves. We'll give you some recommendations and how-tos in the next brochure—it's under "Self-Termination." A lot of people, though, find they're too...squeamish? for Self-Term when push comes to shove and for them we offer Appointment Service. You know how you can schedule a caesarian these days? Well, this is sort of...

PROSPECTIVE CLIENT: The exact opposite.

DEBT COUNSELOR: Yes. The App Serv team is excellent, guaranteed painless and they can make anything look like an accident. And finally, there are some people who are squeamish, but who also find that having an actual appointment makes them, um...

PROSPECTIVE CLIENT: Freaking terrified?

DEBT COUNSELOR: I'd call it anxious. For them we offer a third approach, a service where you just go about your business and we…take it from there. That one's called Dealer's Choice. *(pause)* You don't have to decide that now.

PROSPECTIVE CLIENT: A lot of people must just run when their time is up.

DEBT COUNSELOR: Oh, people are surprisingly ethical about it. Also, we implant a chip that sends us your GPS coordinates.

PROSPECTIVE CLIENT: What if you dig the chip out?

DEBT COUNSELOR: We don't put it anywhere too…accessible? And if you did ever get it out, we always have the Recovery Team.

PROSPECTIVE CLIENT: The Recovery Team?

DEBT COUNSELOR: Ex-Special Forces. Oh, they're amazing.

(long pause)

DEBT COUNSELOR: You can always say no. We're all about choices.

(Suddenly, DEBT COLLECTOR *has an edge, a subtle darkness. Maybe there's a lighting change for her next speech.)*

DEBT COUNSELOR: Quantity or quality. You can live in your run-down studio apartment if you want. With a roommate. And drive a 15-year-old beater. And eat ramen noodles. And never take a decent vacation. And waste a lot of your life living on the shoulder of poverty.

PROSPECTIVE CLIENT: Or I can have only 20 years left.

DEBT COUNSELOR: Twenty debt-free years to keep and spend your money. To travel, buy a house, have a life, whatever that means to you. And do you really want to live longer than that?

PROSPECTIVE CLIENT: My parents got to.

DEBT COUNSELOR: But do you want to? With the rising tides of climate change lapping at your ankles and blowing down your little garret. And the last shreds of our democracy fraying before your eyes as the old world order collapses. You could say that the ones who choose to go with us are in many ways the lucky ones. *(pause; brighter again)* Hey, it's a big decision, so you take your time, talk to your friends, your family. And if you do choose to go with us, just give me a call.

*(*DEBT COUNSELOR *hands* PROSPECTIVE CLIENT *a card, shakes hands, and begins to leave.)*

PROSPECTIVE CLIENT: Wait. Are … are you a client?

*(*DEBT COUNSELOR *turns back. He smiles and pulls up his shirt. He points to his back.)*

DEBT COUNSELOR: There's my GPS scar. Take a look around on the beach this summer. You'll be surprised. *(as he smiles)* Call me.

(He exits. PROSPECTIVE CLIENT *looks at his card, snorts in derision, then throws it in the waste can.* PROSPECTIVE CLIENT *looks around the small apartment, then sits down and thinks for a few moments. S/he picks the trash can up, starts to reach in to remove the card, and then stops. Still holding the can, s/he looks up, uneasy, thinking.)*

(lights down slowly)

(curtain)

THREE LADYBUGS

by Vicki Meagher

Vicki Meagher is a full-time playwright. Her full-length plays—*Death Valley, Camp Wonder, Mother Yucca, Limestone City, Daddy Dustball, Baby Brain, Say Yes to Tootlebritches, The Mind Has Legs,* and *Remembering Mackie Landerson*—are on the New Play Exchange (along with some shorter plays). Vicki has had short plays produced in several states. She lives in New Mexico (Albuquerque) and New Hampshire (Nashua). She's a member of the Dramatists Guild, Playwrights Circle (Albuquerque), Playwrights' Platform (Boston), Playwrights en Masse (Lowell, Mass.), Drama Circle (Athol, Mass.), Alliance of Los Angeles Playwrights, and International Centre for Women Playwrights. **Contact: vickimeagher.com** and **newplayexchange.org/users/1301/vicki-meagher**

Three Ladybugs was sponsored by **Boston Playwrights' Theatre**, founded in 1981 by Nobel Laureate Derek Walcott to support new works for the stage. BPT is a member of NEAT, StageSource, ArtsBoston, and TAMA. Our programs include our annual professional Season of New Plays, the MFA Playwriting Program at Boston University, the Massachusetts Young Playwrights' Project, and venue rentals to outside theatre companies who share our mission to produce new works. BPT's award-winning alumni have been produced in regional and New York houses, as well as in London's West End and throughout the world. BPT productions have been honored with numerous national, regional, and Boston awards, including Elliot Norton and Independent Reviewers of New England Awards for Best New Script. The recipient of the New England Theatre Conference's Regional Award for Outstanding Achievement in the American Theatre and a special citation from the Dramatists Guild of America, BPT is proud to produce the Elliot Norton Award-winning Boston Theater Marathon. For further information on BPT, see our website at **www.bostonplaywrights.org** (and find our blog—it's addictive).

Three Ladybugs was presented on April 2, 2020, with the following creative team:

Directed by Darren Evans
ATHEIST LAYBUG: Melinda Lopez
BELIEVER LAYBUG: Karen MacDonald
AGNOSTIC LAYBUG: Paula Plum
VOICE OF WOMAN: Kate Snodgrass
VOICE OF MAN: Darren Evans
STAGE DIRECTIONS: K. Alexa Mavromatis

CHARACTERS:

Three ladybugs. The ladybug costumes have a large hood that can be placed over the face:

ATHEIST LADYBUG

AGNOSTIC LADYBUG

BELIEVER LADYBUG

There are also two significant voiceover characters:

WOMAN VOICEOVER

MAN VOICEOVER

(The present. ATHEIST LADYBUG, AGNOSTIC LADYBUG, and BELIEVER LADYBUG are sitting near a park bench.)

BELIEVER LADYBUG: Sometimes I just think there's more out there than we know.

ATHEIST LADYBUG: What do you mean?

BELIEVER LADYBUG: I mean, sometimes it seems like we're not the most important species.

ATHEIST LADYBUG: There's no evidence for that at all. We're the only species that matters.

(There is a pause.)

WOMAN VOICEOVER: Here it is!

MAN VOICEOVER: So she was your best friend?

WOMAN VOICEOVER: The best one at the time. It was years ago.

MAN VOICEOVER: Who paid for the bench?

WOMAN VOICEOVER: All of us. We just wanted to do something. Anything.

(There is a pause.)

AGNOSTIC LADYBUG: Sometimes I believe there's something else out there. *(pause)* Other times I don't think so.

BELIEVER LADYBUG: How about when one of us dies? Like when our friend just keeled over dead recently. Flattened.

ATHEIST LADYBUG: That's normal and natural, I think.

BELIEVER LADYBUG: I don't know. There might be something else happening.

AGNOSTIC LADYBUG: *(nodding yes)* Sometimes I think that too.

(There is a pause.)

MAN VOICEOVER: So, are you ready to go?

WOMAN VOICEOVER: Not yet. I wanted to spend a little time here.

MAN VOICEOVER: You should have told me that.

WOMAN VOICEOVER: I thought it was understood.

MAN VOICEOVER: Understood how?

WOMAN VOICEOVER: When somebody tells you they want to look at a memorial bench and pay reverence to someone, it means they want to spend a little time there.

(There is a pause.)

BELIEVER LADYBUG: Do you feel something?

ATHEIST LADYBUG: What?

BELIEVER LADYBUG: Like, some kind of presence?

ATHEIST LADYBUG: No.

AGNOSTIC LADYBUG: Maybe. What do you feel?

BELIEVER LADYBUG: Like, there's something in the air.

ATHEIST LADYBUG: I don't feel anything.

(There is a pause.)

WOMAN VOICEOVER: Look! Ladybugs sitting here.

MAN VOICEOVER: Here, I'll—

(All three ladybugs fall down on the floor.)

WOMAN VOICEOVER: *(interrupting)* Don't just knock them down!

(All three ladybugs scramble to sit up. They help each other.)

BELIEVER LADYBUG: See what I mean? What causes that?

AGNOSTIC LADYBUG: I don't know.

BELIEVER LADYBUG: It's almost like there's someone doing something to us.

(There is a pause.)

WOMAN VOICEOVER: There's no need to harm them. Ladybugs are good luck.

MAN VOICEOVER: They're just bugs!

WOMAN VOICEOVER: Actually, they're beetles, not bugs.

MAN VOICEOVER: Oh, come on!

(There is a pause.)

BELIEVER LADYBUG: I feel a malevolent presence. Something doesn't feel safe. We should all move out of the way.

AGNOSTIC LADYBUG: What do you mean?

(BELIEVER LADYBUG moves away. The other two ladybugs stay where they are.)

MAN VOICEOVER: Are you ready to go yet?

WOMAN VOICEOVER: No, I'm not. I'd like to do a short meditation.

MAN VOICEOVER: Like a prayer?

WOMAN VOICEOVER: Yes. A prayer.

MAN VOICEOVER: What for?

WOMAN VOICEOVER: Just— *(pause)*

MAN VOICEOVER: I mean, who are you praying to?

WOMAN VOICEOVER: It's more like praying for. I'm praying for my friend, to a God, if there is one.

MAN VOICEOVER: There's no evidence for the existence of God.

WOMAN VOICEOVER: There doesn't have to be evidence. But there might be some divinity out there, listening.

MAN VOICEOVER: Fine. I'll just go for a walk and come back in ten minutes.

(AGNOSTIC LADYBUG falls over dead. The other two ladybugs stare in horror.)

WOMAN VOICEOVER: What did you just do?

MAN VOICEOVER: I'm sorry! I didn't see it.

(The two ladybugs examine AGNOSTIC LADYBUG's body.)

BELIEVER LADYBUG: See what I mean? What causes that?

ATHEIST LADYBUG: It just happens.

(The two ladybugs straighten out AGNOSTIC LADYBUG's body.)

WOMAN VOICEOVER: You killed a ladybug!

MAN VOICEOVER: I didn't mean to. I just stepped on it.

WOMAN VOICEOVER: Did you do it deliberately?

MAN VOICEOVER: No! I just— *(pause)*

WOMAN VOICEOVER: You just weren't paying attention. *(pause)* I think you're bringing us bad luck.

MAN VOICEOVER: What?!

WOMAN VOICEOVER: This isn't a good day for us.

MAN VOICEOVER: What?!

WOMAN VOICEOVER: I'm getting a little spooked by you killing a ladybug.

MAN VOICEOVER: What do you mean?

WOMAN VOICEOVER: Sometimes you have a lack of reverence about you and—

MAN VOICEOVER: *(interrupting)* Are you kidding? You are so mystical sometimes. So needlessly mystical.

WOMAN VOICEOVER: I just have a reverence for all species. I mean, what if I was a ladybug?

(There is a pause.)

BELIEVER LADYBUG: I just think there are other species out there.

ATHEIST LADYBUG: There are! Aphids! But there's nobody that matters more than we do.

(There is a pause.)

MAN VOICEOVER: But we're not ladybugs. *(pause)* I mean— *(pause)* I feel bad about your friend. But I don't feel bad about the ladybug.

WOMAN VOICEOVER: Why not?

MAN VOICEOVER: Because ladybugs don't matter!

WOMAN VOICEOVER: Maybe we just need to rethink this whole thing.

MAN VOICEOVER: What whole thing?

WOMAN VOICEOVER: You know what I mean.

MAN VOICEOVER: So you're rethinking our relationship? Again?

WOMAN VOICEOVER: Yes.

MAN VOICEOVER: Damn! I can't believe this!

WOMAN VOICEOVER: Believe it.

(There is a pause.)

BELIEVER LADYBUG: I still feel something in the air. Let's move away.

ATHEIST LADYBUG: Oh, I don't know.

BELIEVER LADYBUG: Come on!

(BELIEVER LADYBUG pulls the dead ladybug's body away. ATHEIST LADYBUG moves away, too.)

MAN VOICEOVER: I think you're just upset over your friend and you're pretending to be upset about the ladybug.

WOMAN VOICEOVER: You believe that?

MAN VOICEOVER: Sometimes I think I know you more than you know yourself.

WOMAN VOICEOVER: That's a patronizing comment if I ever heard one.

MAN VOICEOVER: It's just a dead ladybug.

WOMAN VOICEOVER: Ladybugs are people too.

MAN VOICEOVER: Ladybugs are not— *(groaning; long agonized pause)*

WOMAN VOICEOVER: Okay, ladybugs aren't people. But they deserve respect.

MAN VOICEOVER: Does it matter what goes on in their tiny little brains?

WOMAN VOICEOVER: There might be more going on in their tiny little brains than we know.

MAN VOICEOVER: Oh, come on!

(There is a pause.)

BELIEVER LADYBUG: We kill aphids. Couldn't there be a species that kills us?

ATHEIST LADYBUG: I believe you're overthinking.

(There is a pause.)

MAN VOICEOVER: I'm not going to start worrying about whether or not I've killed a ladybug. Ladybugs aren't aware of anything.

WOMAN VOICEOVER: You don't know that. *(pause)* I'm going to stay here and meditate. Why don't you just leave?

MAN VOICEOVER: What are you saying?

WOMAN VOICEOVER: I think we're done here.

MAN VOICEOVER: <u>You're right! We're done!</u>

*(*BELIEVER LADYBUG *looks at the dead ladybug, putting the dead ladybug's hood over its head.* ATHEIST LADYBUG *looks on.* BELIEVER LADYBUG *sits down beside the dead ladybug, closes its eyes, and starts praying.* ATHEIST LADYBUG *moves closer and continues staring.)*

(end of play)

THE DOBLER EFFECT

by John Minigan

John Minigan is a 2019-2020 Massachusetts Cultural Council Artist Fellow in Dramatic Writing. His plays have been developed with the Orlando Shakespeare Theater, New Repertory Theatre, Utah Shakespearean Festival, Portland Stage Company, and Great Plains Theatre Conference. *Noir Hamlet* was a Boston Globe Critics' Pick, an Elliot Norton Outstanding New Script nominee, an EDGEMedia Best of Boston Theater for 2018, and enjoyed a successful run at the 2019 Edinburgh Fringe. *Queen of Sad Mischance* was a 2020 winner of the New American Voices Festival, Gold Prize winner in the 2019 Clauder Competition for New England plays, and winner of the 2017 Pestalozzi Prize. John's work has been included in the Best American Short Plays, Best Ten-Minute Short Plays, and New England New Plays anthologies. He is a five-time winner of the Firehouse New Works Contest, a winner of the Nantucket Short Play Contest, the North Park Playwrights Festival, the Rover Dramawerks Competition, the Longwood 0-60 Contest, New York's 8-Minute Madness Festival, the Nor'Eastern Playwriting Contest, Seoul Players Contest, and the KNOCK International Short Play Competition. John is currently on the faculties of the Hanover Theatre Conservatory and Emerson College. He serves as a Dramatists Guild Ambassador for Eastern New England. **Contact: www.johnminigan.com** and **john.a.minigan@gmail.com**

The Dobler Effect was sponsored by **Centastage**, which has been developing and producing new plays by local playwrights since 1991. Over that time, the organization has produced over 80 new plays including six Women On Top Festivals of new plays by women, four cabarets of new songs, and one CD. Centastage's last offering was the acclaimed *Noir Hamlet* by John Minigan. The organization facilitates Write-On!, a playwriting group which has been meeting monthly since 1994. Centastage has proudly been part of BTM since its beginning. **www.centastage.org**

The Dobler Effect was presented on May 12, 2020, with the following creative team:

Directed by Joe Antoun
Sound Consultant: Rob Cott
LIONEL: Richard Snee
DIDI: Kathleen Monteleone

CHARACTERS:

LIONEL: Late 60s-early 70s. Any race or ethnicity. A romantic, a hoarder, and kind of a mess.

DIDI: Late 60s. Any race or ethnicity. A realist, spartan in her tastes, and quietly fond of Lionel.

/ indicates that the next speech interrupts at that moment

... as a line of dialogue indicates a pause or gesture rather than a verbal response

[ ] indicates an unspoken but intended word

(The garden on the grounds at Golden Leisure Independent Housing. 6:30 a.m. in late summer, 2019. We hear Peter Gabriel's "In Your Eyes." Lights come up on LIONEL, dressed a little poorly, standing in the garden outside of the 55-plus housing where he resides. He's got the source of the music, a 1980's style boombox, and he's holding it over his head a la Lloyd Dobler. If we look carefully, we notice that the boombox is plugged into an orange extension cord that runs off-stage. LIONEL looks forward, filled with hope. The music stops suddenly. LIONEL shakes the boombox a little. It doesn't help.)

LIONEL: God damn cassettes. *(With some early-morning creakiness in his arms, he lowers the boombox. He presses Stop, then Play. No dice)* Huh. *(He does it again. He presses Eject and opens the cassette holder. He takes out the cassette and examines it. Sees nothing. He puts the cassette back in and presses Play again. Nothing doing. He mutters.)* Sonuvabitch. *(DIDI walks in and stops. LIONEL looks in her direction. She's holding the end of the extension cord in her hand.)* Oh.

DIDI: What the hell's the matter with you, Lionel? It's six-thirty in the morning.

LIONEL: I know what time it is.

DIDI: So what are you doing? You can't wake people up like this.

LIONEL: Nobody sleeps past six around here. They're up. They had their coffee. They're all heading down [to] the Recreation Room for Zumba or some other crap. Plug it back in.

DIDI: I'm not gonna plug it back in.

LIONEL: All right. Okay. I see how it is.

(LIONEL walks to her and takes the plug from her hand.)

DIDI: Lionel. *(LIONEL leaves.)* Don't do it, Lionel!

(The music picks up where it left off. LIONEL returns. He stops in front of her.)

LIONEL: So there. *(He goes to the boombox, picks it up again and, with a little effort, lifts it back over his head. DIDI leaves, unnoticed. The music stops again. He mutters.)* Sonuvabitch. *(DIDI returns, again holding the extension cord. LIONEL lowers the boombox and walks past her, grabbing the cord.)* I can do this all day, you know.

DIDI: Don't. *(LIONEL is gone.)* Don't do it.

(The music starts again. LIONEL returns and stops in front of her again, a little more defiantly. DIDI goes to the other, on-stage end of the extension cord and lifts it.)

LIONEL: Don't. You. Dare. *(DIDI unplugs the boombox from the extension cord. She'll be holding on to the two cords for a while.)* Didi.

DIDI: You should've used batteries. Would've been harder to shut you up.

LIONEL: Yeah? Who the hell has "C" batteries? Who the hell has eight of them?

DIDI: From what I understand about your place, I'd have thought you had eight of everything piled up in that mess.

LIONEL: It's not a mess. I know where everything is.

DIDI: Including a thirty-year-old boombox and cassettes. And you just happened to have the song from the movie?

LIONEL: *Greatest Hits of the 80s.* I also got the 70s, the 60s, the 50s. Nothing since then.That's all crap.

DIDI: And you had an extension cord this long?

LIONEL: It was in the gardener's shed. A locked shed is no match for a man in love.

DIDI: For God's sake.

LIONEL: You saw the movie they showed last night. The girl, in that speech she made, at graduation? "I glimpsed our future, and all I can say is, 'Go back.'"

DIDI: She wasn't talking about *The Greatest Hits of the 1980s.*

LIONEL: Yeah, but—

DIDI: And she wasn't talking to you.

LIONEL: I've glimpsed our future, too.

DIDI: We've all glimpsed it.

LIONEL: Today it's Golden Leisure Independent Housing. Next, it'll be Sustaining Seniors Residential Living. Then the Helping Hands Group Care Complex. And we all know what comes after that.

DIDI: The Shady Orchard In-Ground Community? You finally figured this out?

LIONEL: I figured out [that] I don't want to spend the future alone.

DIDI: And this is about you and Winnie Markham, in her apartment there? I've seen you going over to sit beside her in the Residents' Lounge.

LIONEL: Plug me back in, Didi.

DIDI: Lemme guess: You asked Winnie to go to Movie Night with you, she turned you down, so you and your cassette are serenading outside her window at dawn, like what's-his-name from the movie.

LIONEL: Lloyd Dobler. I don't care [that] she didn't go [to] the movie with me. Who cares about a movie? Who cares about sitting in the Recreation Room, watching a movie, eating crappy microwave popcorn? It was better I went by myself and I heard the girl and I saw Lloyd Dobler and his song, because this is about more than a movie. This is about the future.

DIDI: But if she'd've said yes, we would've been able to sleep in this morning.

LIONEL: She's gonna see how I feel.

DIDI: She's gonna see you might need different medication.

LIONEL: This is a universal gesture, Didi. This is the universal language of a man expressing his feelings for the woman he loves.

DIDI: You don't love Winnie Markham.

LIONEL: Plug me back in.

DIDI: I understand she just moved in. She's new blood. And she's still got a figure at her age and she gets her hair dyed and good for her. It's a little bit charming [that] you think stuff in a movie can actually happen in real life.

LIONEL: I would appreciate if you would plug me back in.

DIDI: No. If this is really what you want, you're gonna have to do it yourself. *(She drops the power cord and extension on the ground. He starts to pick them up.)* But first I would like you to tell me one thing.

LIONEL: What?

DIDI: What you think happens next. She hears the song; she sees you standing outside her window at this hour. You think what? All of a sudden you two are gonna get on a plane and go to England like the kids in the movie?

LIONEL: I can't predict what happens next. That's the point.

DIDI: What about medications? You go to England, you think your doctor's gonna transfer all your prescriptions over to whatcha-call-it, Boots the Chemist?

LIONEL: We'll make it up as we go along.

DIDI: A man who holds on to a boombox and the *Greatest Hits of the 80s* on cassette is suddenly going to make it up as he goes along?

LIONEL: I glimpsed our future and I don't like any of it. From now on, I'm gonna do things where I can't predict what comes next.

(He picks up the power cord and extension cord, but before he can plug them in—)

DIDI: I assume that means you're going to get rid of all the crap in your apartment?

LIONEL: That's got nothing to do with—

DIDI: Or are you gonna carry all that with you? Your stuff, the books, the pictures, cassettes, radios. All of Winnie's stuff?

LIONEL: You make it sound like I'm some kind of hoarder.

DIDI: I make it sound like you're a guy who's pretty happy surrounding himself with the past.

LIONEL: What are you talking about? No.

DIDI: And you should be. You were married, right? Had a nice career in the postal service.

LIONEL: How do you know this?

DIDI: People talk.

LIONEL: It's my experience [that] people talk if you ask them questions.

DIDI: So maybe I ask people questions.

LIONEL: So maybe you're a stalker.

DIDI: So maybe tomorrow morning I'll be outside your window playing "Wait a Minute, Mister Postman."

LIONEL: I'm on the third floor.

DIDI: That was a joke, Lionel. I know you're on the third floor.

LIONEL: What else did people tell you?

DIDI: That you got two kids. A boy and a girl. A couple of grandsons now. You did all right for yourself. It's no wonder you like to have all that stuff around.

LIONEL: The kids are grown up and all the way [out] in California and Nevada. Mary's been gone six years. I [have] been retired eleven. None of that gives me anything to look forward to.

DIDI: If I'd had things half as good as you, I'd probably hold on to stuff, too.

LIONEL: I'm sure you had plenty of good things.

DIDI: Maybe that's because you never asked anybody. And there's probably not much anybody would have known if you did, because I don't talk about all of that. There wasn't that much worth holding on to.

LIONEL: ...

DIDI: If you saw my place, you wouldn't see a lot of stuff: pictures of family, furniture [that] got handed down, plates and cups and silverware that's been around a hundred years. I have no cassettes. *(small beat)* There was divorce. There was people dying, fights over who's gonna get what. A lot of things I'm happy to forget, so I don't hold on to "stuff." *(small beat)* When the weather's nice, maybe I have some flowers on the side tables. I talk to the gardener about what he's growing out here and he gives me a few clippings. It brightens things up for a while.

LIONEL: I... I didn't know about that.

DIDI: I guess you never asked anybody. You could have seen for yourself, the two times I asked you to come over for coffee, but you always had something else you were doing.

LIONEL: ...

DIDI: You might as well plug that back in.

LIONEL: Yeah.

DIDI: As long as you think playing a song from a movie they made when we were what, in our forties? As long as you think doing this kind of thing can turn the future into something unexpected.

LIONEL: No, no. I didn't realize...

DIDI: Didn't realize what?

LIONEL: I'm just saying I wasn't aware of...

DIDI: Aware of what?

LIONEL: ...

DIDI: You gonna plug that thing in, Lionel? The suspense is killing me.

LIONEL: I'm saying I guess I could've come over for coffee, that's all. I'm sorry. I didn't have anything I was actually doing. Necessarily. Those times.

DIDI: ...

LIONEL: It was actually called "<u>Please</u>, Mister Postman."

DIDI: Was it?

LIONEL: The Marvelettes. Motown label. Recorded at Hitsville USA in Detroit, Michigan, 1961. Marvin Gaye was the drummer. I mean, I got the cassette. *Greatest Hits of the 60s.* A little more my era.

DIDI: Our era.

LIONEL: Right.

DIDI: You gonna plug that thing back in?

LIONEL: I don't even know if Winnie's in her room right now.

DIDI: Maybe you can catch her going in for Zumba.

LIONEL: …

DIDI: What?

LIONEL: There's some good numbers on that cassette. Maybe we could… Give it a listen.

DIDI: In your apartment?

LIONEL: Yeah.

DIDI: No. No, I don't think so. Thank you, though.

LIONEL: Oh. Oh. I thought… Okay.

DIDI: …

LIONEL: …

DIDI: I'm sorry.

LIONEL: No no. You don't got to be sorry. So.

DIDI: So.

LIONEL: …

DIDI: So you're gonna have to figure out a way to get eight "C" batteries for that thing. My apartment is all the way down at the corner of the building. You understand? That extension cord is not gonna reach all the way down to my end of the building.

LIONEL: Oh. I—

DIDI: Eight "C" batteries. You think you can you do that?

LIONEL: I can do that, yeah... I… I probably got them in a drawer or something.

DIDI: Good. So, then. Maybe I'll see you tomorrow.

LIONEL: Yeah. Sure.

(A beat. A smile. We hear the Marvelettes' "Please, Mr. Postman.")

(end of play)

DEEP BLUE: A DYSPHORIA

by Alex Moon

Alex Moon (Pronouns: a gentle he/him or they/them) is a writer, director, and theatre artist living and working in New York City. A member of the Dramatists Guild of America, he has worked with numerous organizations around the nation and the globe, such as American Repertory Theater in Cambridge, MA; Nylon Fusion Theatre Company in New York, NY; KMC-Onstage in Kaiserslautern, Germany; The Company Theatre in Norwell, MA; Theatre Collaborative in Brockton, MA; and many more. Currently, he is a resident with Water House Collective's New Moon Minute Writers group, dedicated to developing Queer Mythos Theatre. His plays have also been presented through New York University, Boston University, Emerson College, CSU Long Beach, Massasoit College, and have received awards from the Eugene O'Neill Theatre Center, the International Thespian Society, the Massachusetts Educational Theatre Guild, and the Scholastic Art and Writing Award. Moon is committed to epic storytelling, breaking boundaries, and aiding the collaborative process with the help of his fellow artists. He's studied devised theatre making in New York with Frantic Assembly and acting with the NSLC-Yale School of Drama joint program. He is also a proud member of the New York University Class of 2022. **Contact: alexmoon312@gmail.com** and **www.alexmoondrama.com**

Deep Blue was sponsored by **SpeakEasy Stage Company**, a non-profit theatre company located in the South End of Boston and is led by award-winning Producing Artistic Director Paul Daigneault. SpeakEasy was named the Pavilion Resident Theater for the Boston Center for the Arts in 2007 and produces 28 weeks of new plays and musicals each season at the Nancy and Ed Roberts Studio Theater in the Calderwood Pavilion at the Boston Center for the Arts. Since its founding in 1992, SpeakEasy Stage Company has distinguished itself as Boston's premiere theater, consistently winning acclaim for presenting top-quality productions of vital, cutting-edge plays and musicals. For the last 27 seasons, SpeakEasy has kept vibrant, high-quality theatre thriving in Greater Boston and has helped to make Boston's South End into an artistic and cultural destination. The company provides jobs for hundreds of locally-based artists, actors, directors, and technicians each year, and trains early career artists through its fellowship and emerging artists programs, supporting them as they develop their potential. SpeakEasy's productions create conversations among audience members that continue long after they leave the theater – challenging, connecting, and inspiring the community. **www.speakeasystage.com**

Deep Blue was presented on April 27, 2020, with the following creative team:

Directed by Shira Helena Gitlin
COREY: Dev Blair
NADIA: Christina Mei Chen
P.A. VOICE: Julia Labuski

CHARACTERS:

COREY, 30, Male-Presenting (he/him pronouns)

NADIA, 29, Female (she/her pronouns)

P.A. VOICE

*NOTE: A "/" indicates overlapping dialogue.

(The present—the Deep Ocean Exhibit at the Monterey Bay Aquarium in Monterey, CA. Rippling blue light alongside soothing meditative/spa music. COREY, 27, stands before the light, looking pensive, almost trance-like.)

P.A. VOICE: The open ocean covers over fifty percent of the earth's surface. Though food is scarce, life still abounds in spectacular displays. Here at the Monterey Bay Aquarium, our Open Ocean Tank is the largest of its kind. It holds 1.2 million gallons of water, and features such incredible species as the ocean sunfish, the scalloped hammerhead, the green sea turtle, and many more.

(NADIA, 27, enters gingerly.)

NADIA: Hey dummy.

COREY: Hey dummy.

NADIA: What're you... What're you doing?

COREY: Oh, just... Watching the fish.

NADIA: It's really calming.

COREY: Yeah.

NADIA: Those tuna are pretty big.

COREY: Yeah.

(beat)

NADIA: I was worried about you.

COREY: I know.

NADIA: I've been looking for you / for almost an hour.

COREY: I know.

NADIA: Are you okay?

COREY: I think so.

NADIA: You think so?

COREY: Yeah, I think.

NADIA: It... Uh— It hurts. That you just... Ran off like that, Corey.

COREY: I'm sorry.

NADIA: You sure?

COREY: I needed some place to think for a little bit. That's all.

NADIA: Okay. *(another beat)* It just kinda surprises me that you needed a whole hour to think about—

COREY: I know, it sounds—

NADIA: Well what's your answer?

(COREY takes a deep breath.)

COREY: I don't know.

NADIA: You don't know?

COREY: Yeah.

NADIA: Okay sure, but I find that a little hard to wrap my / head around because normally with something as big as this people can—

COREY: I don't want to hurt your feelings or anything, I really don't. I just need a second to / stop and think and—

NADIA: You've had more than a second, Corey! You've had like... three thousand seconds / or whatever well I was out wondering where the hell you'd—

COREY: It's not that I don't love you or care about you, / I'm trying to—

NADIA: Do you? I'm be patient and careful or whatever. / I mean, all things considered I've been—

COREY: There was too much pressure! It was... A lot. All at once. You got down on one knee and suddenly everyone's looking at us and all the tourists are like "awwwww!" and all the staff were like "awwwww!" and even all the sea otters were like... *(He puts his hands up to his cheeks, mimicking a surprised otter.)* And in the moment it was too much.

NADIA: So you ran?

COREY: It's so quiet and relaxing. And you can stare into the vastness of it all and be... Absorbed.

NADIA: Corey. Corey I love you.

COREY: I love you too.

NADIA: Is it really that terrible of an idea that / you just—

COREY: No! Nadia, It's not bad. I love being in love with you it's all I want but—

NADIA: But what? What's the problem?

COREY: *(taking a deep breath)* I don't think I'm ready.

NADIA: Not rea-- Six years and you're not ready? How much more time do you need?

COREY: I don't / know!

NADIA: You don't know. So I've heard. That isn't an excuse, Corey. You can't "not know" about everything! That leaves people in the dark, like me. I don't need you to have all the secrets of the universe or whatever, I just need you to stop hanging me on a line about a life together. I don't want to wait for an answer anymore.

COREY: But we already have a life together, right? We woke up together, made breakfast together, came here together.

NADIA: If you'd asked me, you'd want an answer. A real answer.

COREY: I didn't ask you.

NADIA: Well I'm asking you! Here, now! Why is that something you think you can run away from?

COREY: Because I can't be your husband! Because I— I don't know if I could be a husband. To anybody. I don't— I don't—

NADIA: You don't know.

(They stare forward at the tank. The light from passing fish shimmers on the two of them.)

P.A. VOICE: The school of mackerel passing before you is almost ten thousand strong; all swimming in unison to defend against predators like tuna, sailfish, and dolphins.

NADIA: Is this about the dress?

COREY: What / dress?

NADIA: Because if it is / that's okay.

COREY: I don't know what you're—

NADIA: I just think that we should talk about it.

COREY: I really don't want to talk about it.

NADIA: But / we're gonna.

COREY: Did you know that mahi-mahi are actually called dolphin fish?

NADIA: Corey.

COREY: Restaurants just use the Hawaiian name so that people don't worry they're eating—

NADIA: COREY.

COREY: *(miniscule)*...Dolphin.

NADIA: Where'd it come from?

COREY: Why are you—

NADIA: It's a nice dress, really, I just—

COREY: Here isn't the place for—

NADIA: I want you to know you're safe. With me. Always.

COREY: I'm... I, uh... *(He sighs.)* Maybe in another life or world or whatever, I'd have no problem looking you in the eyes and saying, "I am a man." But in this one, with what "man" means and the expectations, I— I'm not that. I'm not a man, exactly. I'm not a woman; I'm not trans; I'm still a he/him pronoun kinda person, but... I know, deep down, that I am not 100% a man. At least not like a...MAN man. I don't know. Even I'm still confused by it. And it changes. Some days I'm closer than others, but never in my life have I ever been... Fully there. I feel uncomfortable. All the time. I dunno, I guess the dress was me trying to— To shake that. But even then it still felt like I had stuffed myself into a cabinet or a box or something. I don't really know who or what I am I'm just in this weird limbo and—

NADIA: I know who you are, Corey. I've figured for a while this might be... Might be thing you're going through; I don't care, I—

COREY: I care. Nothing fits on me and I don't know what to wear or call myself. Hell, even my name is indecisive about the whole thing. It's a pain in the ass.

NADIA: I love you. Regardless. Fuck gender! Right?

COREY: That's easy for you to say.

NADIA: I— *(She thinks for a second.)* You're right. But I wouldn't have proposed if I wasn't sure deep down that you're the only person I want to be with, and—

COREY: How can I be your husband; how can I be anybody's husband if when they say "Do you take this man to be your lawfully wedded husband? " I feel--

NADIA: If it's semantics you're worried about we can—

COREY: It's more than semantics! I'm a stranger in my own body; how can I commit with something I don't even own?! / I— I— I—

NADIA: Hey, hey, it's alright. It's... What do you want, Corey?

COREY: I want to dive into this ridiculous fish tank and just melt. I want to lose every physical sense of myself and drift through the current in a million little pieces, and get eaten up by all the mackerel and the tuna and the sea turtle and be a little bit of everything so I don't have to be a lotta bit of one thing.

NADIA: That sounds really nice.

COREY: And then you're just like—

NADIA: Everywhere.

COREY: Yeah.

NADIA: Kinda like when you're dreaming.

COREY: Kinda like tying a bunch of balloons to yourself and drifting off.

NADIA: Kinda like falling in love?

(COREY looks helplessly at NADIA.)

COREY: Kinda.

NADIA: You don't want to get married.

COREY: I— I / don't—

NADIA: You don't know.

COREY: No it's not—

NADIA: It's okay. It's okay. I'm sorry I came down on you for not knowing. This is— Lotta big feelings for you right now. We don't have to rush things, okay?

COREY: Okay.

NADIA: But let's figure this out. Together. Please? *(He doesn't answer. He just looks on at the fish tank.)* Look at me, okay? When I say I love you, I mean the whole of you, just as you are, and all the contradictions and jagged edges and dolphin fish-eating facets of that. I love you, and I want you to be happy. Above anything else in the whole world. Dummy.

COREY: I love you too. Dummy.

NADIA: If you want to melt, you can melt. I'd melt there too. Really. Is that what you want?

COREY: With you?

NADIA: Only if you want me to.

COREY: I do.

(Holding hands, they stare together into the deep blue before them. The music swells, and they fall backwards together. Lights fade. A splash.)

(end)

THE TEXTBOOK LADY

by Nina Louise Morrison

Nina Louise Morrison is a theatre generator: playwright, director, deviser, dramaturg, and teacher. She is a Massachusetts Cultural Council Artist Fellow, Huntington Playwriting Fellow, and winner of the Boston Project at SpeakEasy Stage Company. Her most recent play *The Vault*, an eco-thriller about the Global Seed Vault, was developed at the Huntington Theatre's 2019 Summer Workshop and commissioned by the Greenhouse Playlab, a collaboration between Flat Earth Theatre Company and the Boston Museum of Science. Other plays include *Forever Home*, *Born Naked*, and *Google Doll*. Her plays have been produced and developed by Project: Project, Fresh Ink Theatre, Company One, SpeakEasy Stage, Huntington Theatre Company, Boston Playwrights' Theatre, and the Boston One-Minute Play Festival. She received her MFA at Columbia University and also trained at the National Theatre Institute at the Eugene O'Neill Theatre Center, the New Actors Workshop, and Oberlin College. She has taught at Grub Street, Northeastern University, the Vermont Young Writers Conference, and Mount Ida College. She currently teaches at the University of New Hampshire. **Contact: ninalouisemorrison@hotmail.com** and **www.ninalouisemorrison.com**

The Textbook Lady was sponsored by **The Suffolk University Theatre Department** and performed by **Juniper Tree Ensemble**, a group of artists, performers and educators who aim to create innovative, complex theater that engages all audiences, with a focus on young and teenage patrons. Our work is radically queer, feminist, and refuses to talk down to its audience, regardless of age. We believe in the power of theater to change lives, to make people feel visible, and that "TYA" is a vital force that helps cultivate the next generation of artists. We are here to create work that puts diverse bodies and stories onstage, embracing narratives that challenge the perceptions of its audience with imaginative theatricality. **Contact: junipertreeensemble@gmail.com**

The Textbook Lady was presented on April 12, 2020, with the following creative team:

Directed by Ingrid Oslund
CAMILE: Sara Kerr
PENNY: Katharine Mayk
THE TEXTBOOK LADY: Cara Rittner

CHARACTERS:

PENNY—mid 30s

CAMILE—mid 30s

TEXTBOOK LADY—any age

Notes: Diverse casting is encouraged.

A / slash means overlapping.

Dialogue in parentheses is unspoken but implied.

(CAMILE and PENNY sit in a crowded cafe, working and drinking coffee. A woman walks by their table carrying a BIG textbook. CAMILE looks at the woman. Then she does a strange double-take, watching the TEXTBOOK LADY walk all the way across the cafe to sit at another table. PENNY stares at CAMILE.)

PENNY: Her? Come on.

CAMILE: What?

PENNY: You're pathetic that's all.

CAMILE: I—

PENNY: You're a masochist, I live with a masochist.

CAMILE: What, she's HOT.

PENNY: That's not—ugh—

CAMILE: I—I would so, like, jump her bones—

PENNY: No you wouldn't.

CAMILE: She's so—jumpable. Extremely.

PENNY: Camile.

CAMILE: Penny, look at those tats, and those corduroys, mmmm.

PENNY: That's not what I meant and you / (know it)—

CAMILE: Oh yeah, I checked her OUT.

PENNY: You're crazy, I live with a crazy, masochistic, fucked up person—

CAMILE: Hey.

PENNY: It's not fair, you said / you would—

CAMILE: Hey, I'll, / hey—

PENNY: No, it's not / okay—

CAMILE: Okay, okay, / I'm sorry, I—

PENNY: It makes me feel like, like I'm some sort of nagging girlfriend—

CAMILE: I'm sorry, it's not voluntary.

PENNY: You said you would work on—catching yourself—

CAMILE: I did, I am, I slipped up—

PENNY: It's not just this time...

CAMILE: She is hot though—

PENNY: Don't joke!!

CAMILE: I'm not, I'm not, it's just cute you're so serious—

PENNY: You're joking like it's a joke—

CAMILE: Come on don't take it so / seriously.

PENNY: I'm not—this IS serious.

CAMILE: At least I'm not—it's not like I'm actually checking people out. You know you're the only lady I find remotely jumpable.

PENNY: I almost wish you were.

CAMILE: What?

PENNY: I almost wish you were checking out other people.

CAMILE: What's that supposed to mean?

PENNY: I—I'm just tired—jsss, uhh—I need help.

CAMILE: I'm the one that needs help, clearly, you shouldn't, I don't want you to feel—

PENNY: I just want you to stop doing it.

CAMILE: Hey, hey.

PENNY: Just tell me when you're going to stop doing it.

CAMILE: Now, now, I'm going to stop now.

PENNY: I don't believe you.

CAMILE: Right here, right now, I'm going to promise—

PENNY: I'm SICK of promises.

CAMILE: I'm just going to do it—cold turkey, no more looking for Alex.

PENNY: I don't believe you.

CAMILE: That's it. I'm done. Okay?

PENNY: I'm not kidding.

CAMILE: I know. I know you're not, and I'm not either.

PENNY: It's disturbing.

CAMILE: I wasn't even doing anything.

PENNY: If you're going to pretend you didn't do anything, I'm going to scream.

CAMILE: It wouldn't be an issue if you hadn't brought it up.

PENNY: It wouldn't be an issue if it wasn't an issue.

CAMILE: I wasn't making it—

PENNY: You sit on the couch and cry and / it scares me—

CAMILE: I don't, I'm not doing that anymore—

PENNY: And I can't be around it, I want to comfort you but I think, does she even want to be comforted?

CAMILE: I can't—you can't ask me to—

PENNY: Because if you wanted to be comforted, if you wanted to—

CAMILE: Can we not have this conversation in public, please?

PENNY: No, no, you need to hear this because you need to stop—how long, how long, I need to know how long you're going to keep—

CAMILE: I said, now—

PENNY: You're making me become this bitchy person, like how awful of me to say anything—

CAMILE: I don't see how I make YOU do ANYTHING—

PENNY: What kind of terrible person would be like "it's just your brother, get over it"—

CAMILE: I just don't see why you're making such a big deal—

PENNY: If you don't know what I'm talking about then what are we doing?!

CAMILE: Drinking coffee?

PENNY: I'm serious Camile. I can't... ...I love you. But I can't—

(A terrible pause as this sinks in.)

CAMILE: Right here in the middle of— …I don't know what you want me to say.

PENNY: You can tell me you're ready. To let go.

CAMILE: That's not fair.

PENNY: I have given you time, I have given you—two YEARS I've supported, I've tried to help, you are like a wall and I want to know when I'm getting my girlfriend back.

CAMILE: It's not fair to make me choose.

PENNY: No one said it was fair, Camile.

CAMILE: What do you want me to DO Pen? I can't help it!

PENNY: I want you to agree to talk to someone.

CAMILE: But it's not something I mean to do, and I don't, I know it's not going to bring him back, it's not going to—

PENNY: Just let me make you an appointment.

CAMILE: I don't know why I do it, I just wasn't thinking I wasn't thinking damnit and it's it's a reflex—I'm not trying to—he's gone, I KNOW that I KNOW that.

PENNY: I know...shhh, don't—

CAMILE: *(nearly hyperventilating)* So why do I keep torturing myself, looking and looking and looking for him in every stranger I see—I think: there's the twinkle in his eyes, there's his goofy grin—it's ABSURD! I'm ABSURD! It's just—I see it like there is a LIGHT INSIDE—and it's HIS LIGHT, inside people on the street and inside that kid playing his trombone in the park and the stupid cable guy and—

PENNY: Camile, shhh—

CAMILE: And I see it and think: that's his stupid bouncy walk!—I think: that stranger is going to turn around someday and say "Caaaammie!" just like he used to, and tell me some stupid awful dirty joke just like he used to, and and and then: it's like, I know it's NOT him and I—

PENNY: Shh, honey, I know, I know.

CAMILE: It's not fair! It's not fair that TEXTBOOK LADY is sitting there and it COULD be ALEX sitting there except it's NOT because WHY because because WHY?

(CAMILE sobs a little and PENNY holds her. TEXTBOOK LADY steals a look at them and then goes back to her book.)

PENNY: It's okay, shhh. Cammie, listen to me, it's time, it's time—

CAMILE: *(embarrassed)* I know...

PENNY: So you'll go talk to someone.

CAMILE: *(laughing at herself)* Yes, of course I will, yes. I'm a mess!

PENNY: You "promise"?

CAMILE: Shut up.

PENNY: I'm looking up therapists when we get home.

CAMILE: I want someone with a big leather couch.

PENNY: Obviously.

CAMILE: And she has to wear horn-rimmed glasses and like the gays.

PENNY: Done and done.

CAMILE: And suicide. …Someone who...specializes...

PENNY: We'll find you someone magnificent with horn rimmed glasses and a leather couch and a lesbian certificate of rainbows who also fucking knows her shit.

(beat)

CAMILE: *(admitting the hard truth)* I just hope, I just... I hope it's not if I see someone they tell me I have to...let go...for him to be…Gone.

PENNY: *(reaching out and clasping CAMILE'S hand)* I know.

CAMILE: Can we eat chocolate or something now?

PENNY: *(getting up and kissing CAMILE)* Let me see what they have.

CAMILE: Anything chocolate.

(Penny exits. CAMILE tries to compose herself.)

(A beautiful light shines down on TEXTBOOK LADY. Or something magical and simple happens like a shift in both actors' physicality—an inhaled breath or a moment of slow motion mirroring. TEXTBOOK LADY turns around slowly in her chair, with a twinkle in her eye. CAMILE looks up. And there is sad, smiling, honest recognition.)

TEXTBOOK LADY: Hey, did you hear the one where the mermaid and the duck walk into a bar?

CAMILE: I've been looking for you...

TEXTBOOK LADY: Here I am.

(end of play)

GLENDA JACKSON IN A BODEGA (I AM NOT)

by R. D. Murphy

R. D. Murphy is a member of Actors' Equity Association and the Screen Actors Guild and has performed on stages in Boston and throughout New England for more than 20 years. In 2015, Bob was named a Massachusetts Cultural Council Fellow in Dramatic Writing. Plays include *Client Number One* (Boston Theater Marathon X); *That Thing You Do With Your Tongue* (Newburyport Center for the Arts, published by Smith and Kraus in *Best 10-Minute Plays 2012*); *The Cuckoos* (SLAMBoston and Newburyport Center for the Arts); *Broom Clean* (Salem Theatre Company); *Face Time* (SLAMBoston 2010 and Fort Point Theatre Channel); and *Bollywood Ending* (FeverFest, published by Smith and Kraus in *Best 10-Minute Plays 2010*). From 2014-2017, Bob served as an Arts Fellow at the St. Botolph Club which presented his plays *Snowbirds: Robert Frost and Wallace Stevens Dine in Key West*, *Half Sunk and Shattered*, and *Who Ordered the Happy Ending?* Under the auspices of YASPLZ LLC, he co-produced and performed in the comedy *Noir Hamlet* by John Minigan at the 2019 Edinburgh Festival Fringe. Bob serves as Board Vice President of Boston's Theatre Community Benevolent Fund and is a past Board Member of StageSource. **Contact: rdmassoc@comcast.net**

Glenda Jackson in a Bodega (I Am Not) was sponsored by **Actors' Shakespeare Project** (Christopher V. Edwards - Artistic Director), which believes Shakespeare's words are urgently relevant to our times. Working as an ensemble of resident company members, we bring these words into the voices, bodies, and imaginations of our actors, audiences and neighborhoods. We do this through creative projects, including intimate productions and outreach programs that are informed by the spaces in which they happen. These projects inspire civic dialogue, build relationships between people, strengthen communities, and reveal something about what it means to be human here and now. **www.actorsshakespeareproject.org**

Glenda Jackson in a Bodega (I Am Not) was presented on April 15, 2020, with the following creative team:

Directed by Sarah Newhouse
MICHAEL ERRINGTON: John Davin
DEIRDRE LAMONT: Elle Borders

CHARACTERS:

MICHAEL ERRINGTON 70s, slight, not taller than 5'6". Dressed in long, shapeless coat and beret. Looks like Glenda Jackson.

DEIRDRE LAMONTE 30s, African American, dressed in scrubs. Emergency Room Physician's Assistant.

(The stage is empty. Imagine a small grocery store. Just imagine it. You don't need the shelves and inventory. Monday, last year. Apparently, there is a loooong checkout line that is not moving, as MICHAEL stands still center stage, awkwardly holding more than a dozen items to purchase. He waits. DEIRDRE

enters carrying an empty basket and cautiously circling MICHAEL to get a better look. She then stands in line behind him.)

DEIRDRE: You were marvelous last night.

MICHAEL: I... What?

DEIRDRE: Your performance? Extraordinary.

MICHAEL: I was home last night.

DEIRDRE: And exhausted. I'm sure.

MICHAEL: *(He sees her empty basket.)* You want to go ahead of me? You have less than a dozen items.

DEIRDRE: Here. This might be easier.

(DEIRDRE offers the basket for MICHAEL to put items in. He does so.)

MICHAEL: Thank you. I didn't think it would take this long.

DEIRDRE: Everybody's buying lottery tickets. Big jackpot tonight.

MICHAEL: There's only one line. One interminable line.

DEIRDRE: I didn't mean to intrude.

MICHAEL: Unending line. You're not.

DEIRDRE: *(discreetly)* I saw you in *King Lear* last night.

MICHAEL: Me? *King Lear*?

DEIRDRE: Magnificent.

MICHAEL: Where?

DEIRDRE: The Broadhurst.

MICHAEL: In your dreams.

DEIRDRE: No really. You were wonderful.

MICHAEL: I was not playing King Lear last night.

DEIRDRE: Yes. Fine. I understand.

(beat)

MICHAEL: I mean how could I lift Ophelia? At the end of the play?

DEIRDRE: Cordelia.

MICHAEL: I must carry the body of my slain daughter Cordelia. Do I look like I'd be hefting my daughter around? Not to mention my heart is cracked?

DEIRDRE: I wondered the same thing going in.

MICHAEL: CRACKED. *(MICHAEL staggers slightly.)* Well…Did I?

DEIRDRE: They flew her in from the rafters.

MICHAEL: Like Peter Pan?

DEIRDRE: She wasn't singing.

MICHAEL: Wasn't me. *(beat)* The preferable entrance is to drag Cordelia. Hold one of Cordelia's wrists and drag her on like a rag doll. The sound gets you. Not a word. Her gown chafing the boards. Like a wind machine. The rest is silence.

DEIRDRE: That's not how you did it.

MICHAEL: Nobody asked me.

DEIRDRE: I understand.

MICHAEL: Assuming it was me. Nobody asked.

DEIRDRE: It's your day off. You deserve a rest.

MICHAEL: Then why is this line to hell not moving?

DEIRDRE: Been here long?

MICHAEL: An eternity.

DEIRDRE: You know what amazes me?

MICHAEL: I haven't the faintest.

DEIRDRE: The program said that you served for decades in Parliament.

MICHAEL: Parliament?

DEIRDRE: And then stepped down and started acting again. As if you never left.

MICHAEL: I never left because I was never there.

DEIRDRE: Of course. It makes my life seem small.

MICHAEL: You heal. How can your life be small?

DEIRDRE: Constrained.

MICHAEL: You're from the hospital next door?

DEIRDRE: Physician's Assistant.

MICHAEL: Not a dentist?

DEIRDRE: No.

MICHAEL: I've got to see a dentist.

DEIRDRE: You need that rear molar looked at.

MICHAEL: Lost a crown. Ha! That's my connection to Lear. We both lost a crown.

DEIRDRE: Before it gets infected.

MICHAEL: Damn caramel apple.

DEIRDRE: *(She looks in his basket.)* And yet you can't resist Bulls Eyes.

MICHAEL: Life without caramel is a placebo.

DEIRDRE: When was the last time you ate? *(beat)*

MICHAEL: Glenda. Jackson.

DEIRDRE: I'm sorry.

MICHAEL: You think I'm Glenda Jackson.

DEIRDRE: You're not?

MICHAEL: Happens all the time.

DEIRDRE: Really?

MICHAEL: No. Of course not.

DEIRDRE: Sorry.

MICHAEL: Why not Adolfe Menjou?

DEIRDRE: You look like Adolphe Menjou?

MICHAEL: You'd never know. I am NOT Glenda Jackson.

DEIRDRE: You're sure?

MICHAEL: I'd know.

DEIRDRE: No one else ever—

MICHAEL: Only when she's in town. The summer of *Three Tall Women* was a farrago.

DEIRDRE: Sorry. My mistake.

MICHAEL: At the beginning of life, at the end of life, we all look alike. I'm glad you enjoyed the show.

DEIRDRE: Well—

MICHAEL: You didn't?

DEIRDRE: I meant what I said about your—her—performance.

MICHAEL: But the show?

DEIRDRE: A catastrophe.

MICHAEL: Ah.

DEIRDRE: What were you—they—thinking?

MICHAEL: It was a crass, nonsensical, tone deaf disaster.

DEIRDRE: It was a valiant effort.

MICHAEL: But I was—? My Lear—?

DEIRDRE: I liked it.

MICHAEL: Your acclaim is tepid. Why is this infernal line not moving?

DEIRDRE: Why not let me find you a seat? I'll stand in line for you.

MICHAEL: Are you on your lunch hour?

DEIRDRE: Yes.

MICHAEL: Well then, you must get something to eat. Don't worry about me.

DEIRDRE: I do worry about you. They told me you left to buy a lottery ticket.

MICHAEL: Record winnings tonight.

DEIRDRE: Looks like you got sidetracked.

MICHAEL: A few provisions.

DEIRDRE: And now you're stuck?

MICHAEL: There's a line—

DEIRDRE: Mr. Errington, there's no line.

MICHAEL: Then why am I standing here?

DEIRDRE: There's a wheelchair outside.

MICHAEL: Going to wheel me off a cliff? WHHHHEEEEEEEEEE!

(MICHAEL scatters the contents of his basket.)

DEIRDRE: Michael? I'm going to take you back to the ER now. Okay?

(MICHAEL is unsteady on his feet and breathing heavily.)

MICHAEL: Not until I get my lottery ticket!

DEIRDRE: I'll get you a lottery ticket.

(MICHAEL collapses onto DEIRDRE. DEIRDRE picks up MICHAEL and starts to carry him off.)

MICHAEL: Thank you for not dragging me.

(blackout)

PEARLY GATES

by Jack Neary

Jack Neary's most recent play, *Trick or Treat*, starring Emmy-winner Gordon Clapp, premiered at Northern Stage in Vermont, and completed a seven-week run off-Broadway in February of 2019. His *Auld Lang Syne*, produced by the Peterborough Players and also featuring Mr. Clapp, won five New Hampshire Theater Awards including Best Professional Production. It has since been produced by New Century Theatre and Gloucester Stage. Other recent plays are *The Porch*, produced (as *Beyond Belief*) by the Lyric Stage Company, CityStage in Springfield, Greater Boston Stage Company, the Majestic Theater, and *Kong's Night Out*, published by Dramatic Publishing, presented at the Lyric Stage, New Century Theatre, and the Meadow Brook Theatre in Michigan, featuring TV's Cindy Williams. He co-founded New Century Theatre in Northampton, Massachusetts, and formerly produced the Summer Theatre at Mount Holyoke College. He has appeared on television on *Spenser For Hire*, *Law & Order*, and *Brotherhood*, and in the films *The Town* (2011) with Ben Affleck and *Black Mass* (2015) with Johnny Depp. Last year, he played Nicely Nicely Johnson in *Guys and Dolls* at the Majestic Theater. He is a member of SAG/AFTRA, Actors' Equity and the Dramatists Guild. **Contact: jacknearyonline.com**

Pearly Gates was sponsored by **Acting Out Newburyport** (Producers: John and Deirdre Budzyna), a theater company that provides opportunities for students ages 4-18 to take classes, write and produce original scripts, learn the basics of technical theater and perform musicals and plays in a supportive, developmentally appropriate environment. Last year, in collaboration with local playwright Jack Neary, we produced two original shows focused on a more adult audience. Now in its 11th year, Acting Out is committed to making theater opportunities accessible to everyone, both on stage and in the audience. **www.actingoutproductions.com**

Pearly Gates was presented on May 3, 2020, with the following creative team:

Directed by Jack Neary
BETHEL: Bobbie Seinbach
CLARINE: Ellen Colton
OLIVIA: Paula Plum
MALCOLM: Jack Neary

(The characters of BETHEL and CLARICE are appearing for the eighth time in the Boston Theater Marathon. Pearly Gates *refers back to the first play,* She's Fabulous*, in which BETHEL and CLARICE fumed over the performance of their local rival, OLIVIA TRENT, as she played Linda in* Death of a Salesman. *Then, in the second play,* Farewell and Adieu*, the ladies attended OLIVIA's wake, with great and nasty relish. In* Casting Amanda*, the fifth play, the ladies auditioned for* The Glass Menagerie *and verbally trashed OLIVIA once again in front of the young actress auditioning for Laura, only to learn that she was OLIVIA's daughter… Which brings us to* Pearly Gates.*)*

(A very small waiting room. A couple of chairs face a desk with chair. Very spare. No frills. BETHEL and CLARICE, hovering around 70, dressed, perhaps, for the theatre, sit. They're a bit disheveled. BETHEL sits stone-faced, simmering. CLARICE, equally unhappy, is perhaps in a more distressed, rather than angry, mood. For a moment, neither woman speaks. Then that moment ends.)

CLARICE: *(carefully)* Well... I guess there's good news and bad news.

BETHEL: *(unmoved)* Oh, really.

CLARICE: Well, yes. We're dead. That's the bad news.

BETHEL: Ya think?

CLARICE: But the good news is...

BETHEL: I cannot wait.

CLARICE: There's an afterlife!

BETHEL: This is my afterlife? A dentist office with uncomfortable chairs and no magazines or CNN? And you?

CLARICE: It's a waiting room.

BETHEL: What are we waiting for?

CLARICE: Whatever the next thing is. The next adventure in the afterlife!

BETHEL: I don't want a next adventure in the afterlife! I wasn't finished with my before life.

CLARICE: Well, when the Grim Reaper calls...

BETHEL: He didn't call! He didn't even text! Nobody called! It was an ambush!

CLARICE: I thought it was a dog. I remember a dog.

BETHEL: Yes, Clarice! It was a dog! It was a Greyhound!

CLARICE: Ah.

BETHEL: There's a dog painted on the side!

CLARICE: Ah. I knew I saw a dog.

BETHEL: You couldn't wait! Not you! Oh, no! "Let's go!" you say. "Let's cross the street!" "Wait for the WALK light," I say, "It says DON'T WALK!" "We can make it!" you say. "There's nothing coming!" you say!

CLARICE: I didn't see anything coming! I did what they say you should do, I looked up! I looked down!

BETHEL: You didn't look sideways! Sometimes buses come sideways, around the corner! Our bus came around the corner! First time in my life, I listen to you, I end up getting crushed by a bus!

CLARICE: So you're blaming me?

BETHEL: Of course I'm blaming you! You think I get hit by a bus if I'm not walking with you?

CLARICE: It was an accident!

BETHEL: Oh... I don't think so.

CLARICE: What?

BETHEL: I think you lured me into it.

CLARICE: I lured you into death?

BETHEL: That's something you'd do. Don't deny it.

CLARICE: If I lured you into death, you think I'd want to come along?

BETHEL: You might. There's no limit to your spite.

CLARICE: Spite? Why should I spite you?

BETHEL: You spite me for my talent!

CLARICE: I spite you for your talent?

BETHEL: See? You admit it!

CLARICE: Why would I spite you for your talent when I have my own talent, which is equal to your talent?

BETHEL: Well, clearly there is fantasy in the afterlife!

(An argument ensues. It grows loud fast. The ladies are at each other's throats. After a moment, OLIVIA enters. She may be a year or two younger than they. She's dressed New York-y black. It takes her a couple of seconds to get the ladies' attention.)

OLIVIA: Ladies... Ladies... LADIES! PLEASE!

(The ladies stop and look at OLIVIA. They freeze. Neither speaks. OLIVIA smiles, somehow cunningly, sits next to them, and speaks.)

I thought you'd never get here.

BETHEL: Jesus, Mary and Joseph.

CLARICE: Where?

BETHEL: Olivia Trent.

CLARICE: What?

BETHEL: Olivia Trent. This is Olivia Trent.

CLARICE: It can't be. Olivia Trent is dead. *(BETHEL stares at her; she gets it.)* Jesus, Mary and Joseph.

OLIVIA: I have been waiting so patiently for this moment to finally get here.

BETHEL: What moment?

OLIVIA: Well, they told me when I arrived, that they needed to see a couple more people before making their decision.

BETHEL: What decision?

OLIVIA: Oh. Then, you don't know.

CLARICE: We don't know anything. We just got hit by a bus.

OLIVIA: *(a pained reaction)* Oh... nasty. Where?

CLARICE: Corner of Boylston and Tremont. We just came out of a show at the Wilbur.

BETHEL: What decision?

OLIVIA: Oh? I thought the Wilbur was just doing comedy these days.

CLARICE: Not always. This was a national tour. One woman show. Cher as Ruth Bader Ginsberg.

OLIVIA: I always thought Cher was quite versatile.

CLARICE: As soon as Sonny hit that tree, she really branched out...

BETHEL: WHAT DECISION???

OLIVIA: Oh. Well... you see... there's room here for only one of us.

BETHEL: In Heaven?

OLIVIA: Oh, it's not really Heaven. At least not in the sense that we knew it when we were alive. It's more like... A continuation.

CLARICE: Continuation?

OLIVIA: Yes. In fact, that's what it's called. Continuation. Life does go on, but only a select few get to do what they loved to do in life. The others... well...

BETHEL: Well, what? They don't get to continue?

OLIVIA: Not here. They go... elsewhere.

CLARICE: Hell?

OLIVIA: It's not called Hell. It's called Stagnation.

BETHEL: Stagnation?

OLIVIA: Yes. If you don't make it to Continuation, you Stagnate. You do what you would have despised doing in life.

BETHEL: That's Hell? An eternity of doing what you hated to do in life?

OLIVIA: Yes. Call it Stagnation, though. They get touchy when you call it Hell.

CLARICE: Wait... so... you're saying that only one of us gets to continue?

OLIVIA: That's right. Our fate was forged in life. We Three became One. As actresses, we vied for roles for 30 years. That's what we lived for. It was our Reason for Being. Here, we can't be Three. We must be One.

BETHEL: Who says?

OLIVIA: Malcolm.

BETHEL: Who's Malcolm?

OLIVIA: He's the Director. He'll be auditioning us.

CLARICE: For what?

OLIVIA: For... The Role! The one role avalable to us in Continuation! The Greatest Role of our Eternal Lives. Mature Character Woman!

BETHEL: *(long, long beat)* You're shitting me. We're auditioning for Heaven?

OLIVIA: For Continuation.

CLARICE: There's acting in Heaven? Uh... Continuation?

OLIVIA: Oh, yes! Productions galore! Some of them better than others, of course.

BETHEL: What do you mean better?

OLIVIA: *(with some disdain)* Well, there's a non-Equity group.

(BETHEL and CLARICE nod and murmur in disdainful agreement.)

CLARICE: They let non-Equity into Heaven?

OLIVIA: They're just so sincere.

BETHEL: *(rises, anxious)* Well... what do we have to do? I haven't prepared anything! Is there a script? Are there sides?

OLIVIA: There's only one line.

BETHEL: A one-line audition?

OLIVIA: Yes.

CLARICE: What's the line?

OLIVIA: *(acting, a little)* "Forgive me, dear. I can't cry. I don't know what it is, but I can't cry. I don't understand it. Why did you ever do that? Help me, Willy, I can't cry."

BETHEL: You bitch.

OLIVIA: I didn't choose the line.

BETHEL: *(nudges CLARICE) Death of a Salesman.*

CLARICE: *(to OLIVIA)* Oh, you were fabulous in...

BETHEL: *(to CLARICE)* Shut up, Clarice! *(to OLIVIA)* That was my part!

CLARICE: Or my part!

BETHEL: *(refers to CLARICE)* Or her part!

OLIVIA: Well, from what I recall, I believe it ended up being my part.

BETHEL: Who chose that line?

OLIVIA: Malcolm.

BETHEL: So you schtupped Malcolm!

OLIVIA: I did no such thing!

BETHEL: You never got cast in your life without schtupping whoever had the checkbook!

CLARICE: There's schtupping in Heaven?

> *(Another loud argument ensues. BETHEL is accusing OLIVIA of every sexual aberration under the sun; OLIVIA blithely sloughs her off; CLARICE remains focused on the Heavenly schtupping. After a few seconds, MALCOLM enters. He's middle aged, perhaps with a sartorial directorial affectation. He has an iPad, which he is swiping through as he enters. He's constantly somewhat distracted.)*

MALCOLM: QUIET! QUIET DOWN!... Okay... what do we have here... *(swiping, swiping)* Ah, yes. The Mature Character Woman part. *(sweetly, to OLIVIA)* Hi, Babe.

OLIVIA: Hi, Malkie.

BETHEL: You SCHTUPPED him!

MALCOLM: *(swiping, swiping)* What? Who schtupped who? Nobody's doing any schtupping. *(to BETHEL)* Who are you? *(swiping)*

BETHEL: I might ask you the same question!

MALCOLM: *(swiping)* Oh...this is the bus, right?

OLIVIA: Right.

MALCOLM: We had a hell of a time getting to you guys. Always obeying the "Don't Walk" sign. Took us forever.

BETHEL: *(takes a swing at CLARICE with her bag)* I told you! I told you!

CLARICE: I'm sorry!

MALCOLM: How was the Cher thing? I hear her Ginsberg is derivative.

CLARICE: It did remind me a little of Bonnie Raitt's "Give "em Hell, Harry."

BETHEL: Can we get on with this?

MALCOLM: Sure. Sure. Did you ladies get the line?

BETHEL: We got the line. We've known the line for years.

MALCOLM: Good. So...who's first?

OLIVIA: *(rises)* Oh, why don't I just get it over with?

MALCOLM: I tell ya, Livvie, I still think you should be reading with the leading ladies.

OLIVIA: I'm more comfortable here. *(refers to BETHEL and CLARICE)* I can play their age.

BETHEL: Read the line!

OLIVIA: *(gets into it, delivers the line quite well)* "Forgive me, dear. I can't cry. I don't know what it is, but I can't cry. I don't understand it. Why did you ever do that? Help me, Willy, I can't cry."

MALCOLM: Beautiful. I should get Artie Miller in here to hear you read that but he's playing golf with Dimaggio again. Next?

BETHEL: *(to CLARICE)* You go.

CLARICE: No, you.

BETHEL: You!

CLARICE: You think?

BETHEL: Go!

CLARICE: *(rises; to MALCOLM)* Well, you know, I didn't have a chance to prepare...

MALCOLM: Nobody prepares for this. It's death. Let's go.

CLARICE: Oh. Okay. *(beat; she's okay, but a little over the top)* "Forgive me, dear. I can't cry. I don't know what it is, but I can't cry. I don't understand it. Why did you ever do that? Help me, Willy, I can't cry."

MALCOLM: Thank you.

CLARICE: *(as she sits)* How was it?

BETHEL *(rising, under her breath)* I saw the work. *(she sets herself, delivers the line; it is truly superb)* "Forgive me, dear. I can't cry. I don't know what it is, but I can't cry. I don't understand it. Why did you ever do that? Help me, Willy, I can't cry."

(MALCOLM is silent for a moment. He didn't expect what he just heard.)

MALCOLM: Well... that was... that was... quite good.

BETHEL: Yes. It was.

MALCOLM: *(somewhat unglued)* I, uh... I... um... I wasn't really... you know.... *(to Olivia)* ...you told me she...

OLIVIA: *(concerned)* Malkie...

MALCOLM: *(under his breath)* Hey, babe, she read the shit outa that.

OLIVIA: *(she moves to him)* But... Malkie...

MALCOLM: *(decides, indicates BETHEL)* You! You come with me.

OLIVIA: MALKIE!!!

MALCOLM: *(to OLIVIA and CLARICE)* You two... Someone will be here in a couple of minutes to bring you to Stagnation. *(swiping, to CLARICE)* You'll be...directing middle-schoolers in *Shrek, Jr.*

CLARICE: For eternity?

MALCOLM: Hey, it's Stagnation. I don't make the rules. *(to OLIVIA)*

And you...

OLIVIA: Malkie!!!

MALCOLM: You'll be... *(swipes to answer)* ... a cook in a convent. Enjoy! *(to BETHEL)* Let's go!

BETHEL: No.

MALCOLM: What?

BETHEL: No. I'm going with... *(indicates CLARICE)* ... her. Take... Livvie.

MALCOLM: You serious?

BETHEL: Deadly. No pun intended.

MALCOLM: Have it your way.

BETHEL: *(again, indicates CLARICE)* And I will go where she's going.

MALCOLM: *(swipes)* I guess that's okay. Says here you hate theatre kids as much as she does.

BETHEL: More.

MALCOLM: Fine. Great. I don't care. *(to OLIVIA)* C'mon, Babe.

OLIVIA: *(as she leaves)* Don't Babe me. I'm telling everybody about the hairpiece...

MALCOLM: *(pleading as he leaves)* Babe...It's a weave!

(They are gone. BETHEL sits next to CLARICE.)

CLARICE: I was nervous.

BETHEL: I know.

CLARICE: That was... uncharacteristic of you.

BETHEL: No, it wasn't.

CLARICE: No. It's wasn't.

BETHEL: We'll teach those little dead fuckers how to be actors.

CLARICE: Yes! We will!

(They hold hands.)

BOTH: We'll be fabulous!

(the end)

THE LADY KILLER

by Erik Nikander

Erik Nikander is a playwright, theatre critic, stage director, and filmmaker based in the New England area. He currently serves as the Literary Manager of The Forge Theatre Lab in Fitchburg, MA, and is also an active member of the company's board. His production credits with The Forge include a forthcoming Draft House staged reading of his play *LifeBlood*, a full-length drama inspired by the Theranos scandal, and his contributions to the Generations night of short plays as a writer and director (for *27* and *Copley*, respectively). His ten-minute play The Lady Killer was performed as part of Boston Theater Marathon XXII: Special Zoom Edition. Erik is also an Artistic Associate at NewYorkRep and has worked as a dramaturg and script reader for New England-based theatre companies such as the Nora Theatre Company, New Repertory Theatre, and Fresh Ink Theatre. His theatre criticism and other critical writing can be read in The Arts Fuse and HowlRound. **Contact: nikaerd@gmail.com**

The Lady Killer was sponsored by **Brandeis University Department of Theatre Arts**, which is proud to be a part the 22nd Annual Boston Theater Marathon in this unprecedented time. Through rigorous learning, skill training, and aesthetic practice, the Brandeis Department of Theater Arts fosters a creativity that connects to scholarship and a scholarship that is responsive to the individual and to the community. As artists, practitioners and scholars, we create new work and ideas, and challenge our students to enact change, build connections, and value diversity. **www.brandeis.edu/theater**

The Lady KIller was presented on May 4, 2020, with the following creative team:

Directed by Alex Jacobs
KARINA: Haia Bchiri
ZOE: Rachel Greene

(Lights rise on KENNETH and ZOE sitting across from one another in a soullessly trendy restaurant. They pick at their entrees. A low murmur of conversation surrounds them. After an aching stretch of silence, KENNETH looks up to ZOE and says:)

KENNETH: So, uh...how do you know Blair?

ZOE: Hm?

KENNETH: I mean, I was just thinking, she must know you pretty well if she...ah...

(beat)

ZOE: She was my roommate. For a semester. Until I switched majors.

KENNETH: Oh. Were you pre-med too?

ZOE: Psychology.

KENNETH: Oh, that's cool. Psychology. Were you going to be...a psychologist?

ZOE: Uh huh. Probably. But I switched majors.

KENNETH: ...Right. *(They keep eating, without much gusto.)* I've, uh... I've never done this before. Been set up, I mean.

ZOE: Oh yeah?

KENNETH: No, I didn't think anyone even still did the whole blind date thing.

ZOE: I can see why not. *(Not meant as an insult, but it stings like one.)* Wait. No, sorry, I didn't...look, that's not what I meant. It just kind of feels more like gambling than actual dating. Sometimes, you just waste the whole night stuffing coins into the machine, and…

> *(She doesn't even know what her point is anymore and gives up. They eat, stifled by a dour mood. KENNETH looks around.)*

KENNETH: Where the hell is that waiter? Have you even seen him? I don't think he's been by in twenty minutes.

ZOE: Do you... just want to call it quits? Up to you. If you want to leave, I won't be offended. You can send me the money for the food, or... I'll just pay for it. It's fine.

KENNETH: *(forced cheerfulness)* Oh no, I'm great. Don't call it quits for my sake, I could stay out all night.

ZOE: Oh. Great.

> *(They go back to eating, each privately annoyed at the other.)*

KENNETH: You never told me what you switched to.

ZOE: What?

KENNETH: Your new major. The one that's not psych. Are you going to tell me what it was?

ZOE: I don't really feel like going into my whole life story.

KENNETH: Then don't. Believe it or not I'm not trying to ruin your evening.

> *(He goes back to eating, but his rebuke sparks something in ZOE, who puts her fork down.)*

ZOE: All right. I'm sorry. I haven't been totally straight with you. Truth is I couldn't tell you what I switched to because I didn't switch—I dropped out.

KENNETH: How come?

ZOE: Let's just say a new career path opened up to me that's a bit more... legally unconventional.

KENNETH: Of course. Blair would set me up with a hooker.

ZOE: No! Nothing like that. Okay, I'll tell you what I do, but before I do, I need to know you won't go blabbing about it. It's a secret. The kind there are consequences for breaking.

KENNETH: I'm not gonna blab.

ZOE: Do you promise?

KENNETH: Yes.

ZOE: You've got to say "I promise."

KENNETH: I promise! I promise I won't tell a single living soul.

ZOE: Or any dead ones.

KENNETH: Or any dead ones. Now tell me.

(dramatic pause)

ZOE: Okay. I'm an assassin.

KENNETH: Oh, come on, if you were just messing with me in the first place…

ZOE: It's like magic, every time. Even when I straight-up tell people what I do, they don't believe me!

KENNETH: Because it's obviously ridiculous, you're not an assassin! Not a chance in hell you've even come close to killing someone.

(ZOE smiles. As she tells KENNETH her story, she should commit to it so deeply that we actually start to think she may be telling the truth.)

ZOE: Isn't that just the kind of killer you'd want to hire? The one nobody would suspect. When you think of an assassin, who comes to mind? A man, first of all. A man who's a shifty-eyed maniac with muscles like cinder blocks, ex-military, glittering white psycho grin that freezes your blood. Whereas I look downright normal. By comparison.

KENNETH: So I suppose there was a booth for assassins at the career fair and you just...signed up?

ZOE: Don't be silly. It's a family thing. My parents were two of the best assassins in the world. Retired now, but they taught me the trade.

KENNETH: Who's the last person you killed?

ZOE: Telling you that would be a great way to get us both snuffed out, trust me.

KENNETH: Ah. Very convenient.

(She tugs up her sleeve, reveals a small scar across her upper arm.)

ZOE: See this?

KENNETH: Uh-huh.

ZOE: Grazed by a bullet. I'd been tracking a target three days and he got the drop on me. Lucky for me his aim was crap.

KENNETH: More like you fell off a scooter when you were thirteen.

ZOE: You know what? Fine. I'll just have to prove it. Lucky you, you get a live demonstration. How To Kill A Man 101. *(She slips off her shoes.)* Silence is crucial.

(ZOE gets up and walks around until she's a few steps behind KENNETH's chair.)

No looking, now. You've got to be totally unaware. Like a real victim, all right?

KENNETH: Fine, fine.

ZOE: Okay. The approach is everything. Stay taut, move on the balls of your feet. Can you hear my footsteps?

KENNETH: Nope.

ZOE: See? If you were a real target you'd have no idea you're mere moments from death.

KENNETH: No, not at all.

ZOE: But that won't last forever. Before doubt starts to creep up the back of their neck, you have to strike!

(ZOE mock-strangles him, but with a real intensity and vigor. KENNETH meets her energy, playing along, getting into it. ZOE lets go, and KENNETH's head drops forward on the table with a thud. ZOE goes back to her seat and sits down, satisfied.)

And that's how it's done. Believe me now?

(The silence drags on. ZOE's heart keeps sinking. Then KENNETH springs back up as if nothing happened.)

KENNETH: Wow, you weren't kidding, A+. If I was gonna get murdered by anyone, I'd want it to be you. But there's one thing you didn't count on.

(In one motion, he sweeps a hand up to the table, covered by a napkin with something stiff and rectangular underneath.)

I've knows all along who you are. That's because I'm the one who assassinates the assassins. Say goodbye, darling.

(A beat. Nothing happens. KENNETH whips off the napkin to reveal that he's pointing his wallet like a pistol. They stare at each other, than burst into laughter. Something catches ZOE's eye. She waves a hand.)

ZOE: Hold on, I think that's the waiter. Over here!

KENNETH: You know, I finally get what Blair was talking about.

ZOE: What do you mean?

KENNETH: Well, she was telling me about you, and how she thought we should go out, and at first I didn't really want to hear it. But then she got me curious.

ZOE: What'd she say?

KENNETH: She told me, "You are the two weirdest fucking people that I have ever met."

(They share a knowing smile.)

(end of play)

SKED DU AL

By Ronán Noone

Ronán Noone's plays, *The Lepers of Baile Baiste, The Blowin of Baile Gall, The Gigolo of Baile Breag, Brendan, Little Black Dress, The Compass Rose, Scenes from an Adultery,* and *The Atheist* have played in theaters across the United States. Other recent productions have taken place in the UK (London and Edinburgh), Spain, Canada, the Philippines, and Ireland. His full-length and one-act plays are published by Samuel French, Smith and Kraus, Baker Plays, and Dramatists Play Service. He has received three Independent Reviewers of New England Awards for Best New Play, an Elliot Norton Outstanding Script Award, Kennedy Center National Playwriting Award, a 2014 Edgerton New American Play Award, and the 2015 Association for Theatre in Higher Education Award for Excellence in Playwriting. His essay on theatre, "Being Afraid to Breathe," is published by the Princeton University Library Chronicle LXVIII. His play *The Second Girl (Thirst)* is featured and published in The Eugene O'Neill Review, Vol 37, No 2. His play *The Smuggler* won the Best Playwright award at the 1st Irish Festival, NY 2019. Originally from Connemara, Ireland, Ronán Noone is a graduate of Boston University's MFA Playwriting Program and is currently an Asst. Professor in the same program. **Contact: ronannoone.com** and on **Twitter: @shakywarrior**

Sked Du Al was sponsored by **The Department of Theatre at Northeastern University** (Antonio Ocampo-Guzman, Chair), a hub for creative practice research, offering students an innovative alternative to the traditional choice between a conservatory or liberal arts education. We offer more than a dozen theatre-based majors and minors with an interdisciplinary focus. With over 40 professional partners in Boston, New York, and around the globe, NU's signature co-op program provides students transformational experiential learning. We cultivate new voices through a minor in playwriting and present more than a dozen original works annually written by students. **camd.northeastern.edu/theatre**

Sked Du Al was presented on April 3, 2020, with the following creative team:

Directed by Jonathan Carr
BENNY: Carla J. McDonough
DON: Peri Griffiths
STAGE DIRECTIONS: Samantha Richert

CHARACTERS:

BENNY—50s—Maybe younger/maybe older

DON—Mid 30s—Maybe younger/maybe older

(*Somewhere near here. A middle-aged man is sitting on a shaky wooden chair. He is naked, but for a pair of white briefs. He is obviously nervous. He looks beaten and ragged. Unshaven, smelly, his hair is matted to his head. His name is BENNY. Another man, DON, younger, vibrant, enthusiastic, walks in. He is ready to do his job. He is wearing a suit. He is carrying a coffee. He is confident, an air of invincibility. A remarkable restraint on behalf of DON is observed.*

Until there is no restraint.)

DON: Ok. Ok. You ok? You? *(BENNY nods. DON gets closer.)* Ok. Good. Good.

(He sips his coffee. He's not sure he likes it.)

Not Good. Well. Ok. Ok. Right. WE WILL BEGIN. Okkkkkk? *(Menacingly; towards BENNY)* OKKKKKKKKKKKAYYYY? *(BENNY nods)* Yes.

DON: *(moves behind him and—)* Sked Du Al. Ok? Sked Du Al. Go on

BENNY: Shed/

DON: What? *(pause)* What did you say? *(pause)* Go ahead. Go ahead *(pause)* Skeddual

BENNY: Shed jewel

DON: Sked Du Al

BENNY: Shed jewel

DON: Sked du al. Sked du al. Du Al. Du Al. Du Al. *(DON moves into the side of BENNY's face.)* Go ahead. Sss K. Sssk k k. Ssssk. Ssk sk.

BENNY: Ssss

DON: Yes

BENNY: Sss

DON: Yes

BENNY: Sssskkkk

DON: Yesssss

BENNY: Shed *(Pause. DON raises his fist close to BENNY's face. BENNY scared.)* Please. Please. I'll tell you.

(DON rethinks this. Wipes BENNY's shoulders off. DON smiles)

DON: Yes. S.K. *(laughing)* Yes. Yes. Go on. Go on. Please.

BENNY: Sked

DON: Yesssss

BENNY: Uuuuual

DON: Yessssssssss *(laughing through it)* Yessss

(BENNY closes his eyes and hopes with all his might.)

BENNY: ShedJewel. *(He got it. Pause. Pleased, relieved, but then…)*

DON: No. No. You dumb ffffff   uck.

BENNY: *(anxiously correcting and making it worse)* Shed Jewel/ Shedjewel/ Shed/

DON: Shut up. Shutup. Shut the hell up. *(He raises his hand. Silence.)*

BENNY: Please.

DON: Silence. *(DON backs down.)*

BENNY: I'm not worthy.

DON: You are not worthy. You are not worthy, you filthy animal? Do you hear me? Do you?

Nod. Nod. NOD. *(BENNY nods. Pause.)*

DON: One chance. One more chance.

BENNY: *(nervous)* Newclear

(This is where DON loses it.)

DON: JESUS CHRIST. NO. NO. NO. NUKE COLOR. NUKE COLOR. NUKECOLOR. SAY IT. SAY IT. Say the fuckin word.

BENNY: Nuke

DON: CO

BENNY: Co

DON: LOR

BENNY: Lor

DON: NOW

BENNY: *(shivering, hesitant)* New *(pause)* Clear

(DON puts down his coffee. DON takes off his glasses. He opens his shirt. Takes off his belt. BENNY is begging.)

BENNY: The OED, you can, please, the OED, listen to me, please, you can say it. The OED says you can say it both ways.

(DON starts beating him around the room with the belt.)

BENNY: You can say it/ OED

DON: O   E   D. The –

(The screams. The screams. The screams.)

THE FUCKIN' O ... E... D... "Says You Can Say It Both Ways." The fucking OED

(He stops beating him. He wipes his brow. He gathers himself. BENNY tries to clamber up.)

Get up. Get up. GET UP. Do we live in the O E D?

BENNY: What?

DON: Is that where you want to live?

BENNY: No.

DON: That's right. And tell me who is in charge of the O E D?

BENNY: I. I... I... don't know.

DON: Is it in their interest to tell you that you can say it both ways? *(pause)* I'm trying to help you here.

BENNY: I don't know.

DON: Of course, it is in their interest to tell you you can say it both ways. Of course, it is. They want you to buy it, don't they? They want you to believe it. Don't they? Don't they? And you trust...? Have you met him? Have you met him?

BENNY: Who?

DON: The leader of the fucking O E D. Have you met him?

BENNY: No

DON: Really? And yet he tells you how to speak. Yes? And you've never met him. Is that right?

And this is how you live your life? But now you're here.

BENNY: I don't know

DON: You don't know a lot do you?

BENNY: No.

(BENNY picks himself up. He is taking too much time.)

DON: Can you tell me what I want to hear?

(BENNY can't get up and DON takes care of it quickly and roughly picks him up again and puts him on the chair. BENNY slows down. Recomposing. Wiping his brow. Pause.)

You are making this… You are making this so…Difficult. You know that.

BENNY: Difficult. I am.

DON: Yes. It shouldn't be so difficult. Should it? You just tell me….?

BENNY: Tell you

DON: Easy Peazy.

BENNY: I haven't slept.

DON: Yes. Just say the word.

BENNY: Wh…Which… Which, which one?

DON: ANYONE YOU FILTHY/ You know what I'm talkin' about

BENNY: Ssskkk. Sssskkkk. Ssskkkkkk

> *(BENNY closes his eyes and as he says the word he cowers. While his hands automatically protect his head.)*

SKED DU AL. *(He opens his eyes. He checks he is ok.)* Sked Du Al.

> *(DON puts his belt back on. BENNY looks at him. Did he get it right? He did.)*

Skeddual. Skeddual. *(Pause.)* I must check my Skeddual

DON: Yes.

> *(BENNY smiles and starts to speak deliberately—with elocution. Becoming extremely joyful.)*

BENNY: Yes. I must check my Skeddual for Monday. I must check my Skeddual to see if I'm free. I must check my Skeddual before the Nuke Co Lor war starts. *(in tears)* I must check my skeddual before the nukecolor war starts.

> *(DON begins methodically putting himself back together. He buttons his shirt. Puts on his belt.)*

I did it. I did it. Didn't I? I did it. I did it. *(pause)* Are you happy? Can we stay? Can we stay? *(pause)* Can we stay now? *(DON puts on his glasses)* Please. Please. Are you happy? Can we stay in America?

> *(DON bends close to BENNY's ear. He whispers. BENNY starts to cry. DON picks up his coffee. He walks out. We hear a large door bang shut. BENNY begins to shiver. The locks lock—one—two—three. The lights go out.)*

> *(end)*

MIGRAINE

by Cliff Odle

Cliff Odle is a playwright, actor, and director currently living in Maine. His plays have been performed in Boston, New York, San Diego, and other areas. He is the playwriting lecturer at Bates College where he has debuted a work-in-progress called *Blood and Revolution*, a multi-play cycle set in the years leading up to the American Revolution and centering on the lives of colonial African Americans. His previous BTM entries were *Motel Therapy* and *A Garnet in the Rough*. Among his other plays: *The Petition*, produced by the Old State House Museum in Boston; *Lost Tempo*, produced by Boston Playwrights' Theatre in 2017; *Our Girl in Trenton*, produced by the BU New Play Initiative Workshop; *Running the Bulls*, produced by New Urban Theatre Lab for the SlamBoston festival; *The Ahern Fox*, a finalist in the 2007 Kennedy Center Theatre Festival; *The Delicate Art of Customer Service*, produced by New Urban Theatre Lab and the Jersey Voices Annual Festival. For Theatre Espresso, he co-wrote their play about the 1957 Little Rock desegregation case called *The Nine: Crisis in Little Rock*. Cliff has also written *The Lesson* and *Think Twice*, which are currently in rep with Deana's Educational Theatre. **Contact: cliff.odle@gmail.com** and **www.cliffodle.com**

Migraine was sponsored by **Gloucester Stage Company** (Robert Walsh, Artistic Director/Christopher Griffith, Managing Director), Cape Ann's premier professional theater company nestled on Boston's North Shore. The intimate performance venue has provided the setting for premiering socially relevant new works and intellectually stimulating classics over the past 40 seasons. Founded as a safe harbor for playwrights, audiences enjoy extraordinary stories brought to life on the edge of the Atlantic. Join us in Gloucester next summer. **www.gloucesterstage.com**

Migraine was presented on May 1, 2020, with the following creative team:

Directed by Robert Walsh
GABE: Steven Barkhimer
JOAN: Melinda Lopez

CHARACTERS:

GABE—Age and ethnicity can vary; dissheveled, sickly

JOAN—30'S—40'S, African American or Latina, stylish, very put together

(A bus stop near a hospital in a city. It is late at night. As we hear the sound of a bus leaving. JOAN enters running and inevitably missing the bus. She waits and looks for another one. After a moment, a somewhat disheveled looking man in a trench coat enters. He is in some distress, but not enough to alarm the woman.)

GABE: Aw, my head. Feels like it's gonna bust. *(pause)* Hope that bus gets here soon. I need a rest. *(pause)* They can't seem to figure out what's going on with me. Been here twice this week. *(pause)* Do you have...Excuse Me... excuse me. Do you have... This might be a little..um... You don't have an aspirin do you? I have this...this killer headache.. Migraine, I think. *(pause)* Excuse me? Do you have one?

JOAN: I'm sorry, what?

GABE: Do you have an aspirin? Ibuprofen or something?

JOAN: No.

GABE: I mean, I'm just asking. My head. It's a bitch, you know?

JOAN: I don't have one.

GABE: Ok. *(pause)* It's not what you're thinking, you know. I'm not some bum asking for money or nothing.

JOAN: I never said that.

GABE: But you were thinking it, right? Right?

JOAN: You don't know what I'm thinking.

GABE: I'm not a threat...just a guy trying to get—

JOAN: Do you need to stand so close?

GABE: -rid of a nasty... Oh...I am? Sorry—

JOAN: Yes, you are. I'm not feeling—

GABE: Sorry....I Didn't realize that I was... That I was... Wow...my head.

(JOAN takes out a cell phone dials and then speaks.)

JOAN: Hello...Franklin Cab? Yes...I need to..I'm at the Saint Mary's...and I need—

(GABE takes out a gun and points it at her back.)

GABE: All right...all right. Hang it up. Just....hang it—

JOAN: Oh God...don't..please...

GABE: I KNOW you have one in your purse...I..KNOW. Now give me the fuckin' aspirin!

(JOAN takes the purse off her shoulder carefully.)

JOAN: Don't hurt me, all right? I'm giving you what you want...just don't hurt—

(GABE takes the purse and fumbles through it looking for the aspirin. He opens it and shoves a couple in his mouth.)

GABE: Oh man...Holy shit! I needed that. All the noise was getting to me. *(GABE notices JOAN trying to slip away.)* Hey! HEY! Hold if lady. Stop right there.

JOAN: You've got what you wanted. Now why don't you—

GABE: No. That's...that's not all I wanted. You have more— *(JOAN instinctively tries to cover herself up.)* No NO! That's not what I want. It's the money. I need the money.

JOAN: You have my purse.

GABE: You don't have more than 150 bucks in the purse. You're not that dumb to keep it all there. In case something like this happens.

JOAN: Look, I don't know what you're—

GABE: Where is it?!

(JOAN opens the top two buttons of her shirt, reaches in and pulls out a roll of bills.)

JOAN: Here...it's all I have.

GABE: There's...there is supposed to be more. Where is the rest?

JOAN: I have no idea what you're talking about.

GABE: The rest...from the job. I saw it. And...weren't you supposed to have a suitcase and— *(GABE is hit with a wave of pain in his head.)* Dammit! OW! I could see it...I could...

JOAN: Your gun...is that..?

GABE: Those pills didn't last long. I need a minute to—

JOAN: Jesus! Your gun isn't even real!

(JOAN starts to walk away.)

GABE: —place the suitcase. I can't place the suitcase— ...Hey..HEY STOP!

JOAN: You fucking loon!

GABE: Stop! Or else!

JOAN: Or else what!? You gonna drown me to death?

GABE: This gun is loaded, lady!

JOAN: You're the one who's loaded!! *(JOAN walks up, takes the water pistol from GABE and squirts him with it.)* You barely covered up the orange tip.

GABE: Stop! Stop! Please... Oh...my head...

JOAN: I can't believe this shit!

GABE: Lady...please...don't go...please...

JOAN: You're begging? A mugger who begs? With a freakin' K-Mart water pistol? You are beyond pathetic, aren't you? You are a disgrace to honest hardworking criminals everywhere...and YOU ARE WASTING MY TIME!!

(JOAN takes out her purse and dials)

GABE: I'm sorry...I ...stop..please...stop.

(GABE go towards JOAN, she stops him with a glare.)

JOAN: Boy, I will twist your dick into a knot if you don't stand back. *(to phone)* Hello? Franklin cab? Yes...we got cut off earlier . I need—

GABE: *(GABE suddenly speaks in an Australian accent. It should definitely feel "working class".)* Joan!...JOAN!!

(JOAN stops talking and looks at GABE.)

JOAN: You have about three seconds to tell me how you know my name.

GABE: That's not...that's not my medication, is it Joanie-bear. Gonna hurry things up, are ya? That's my girl. Never leave anything to chance, do you? Yeah...that's my Joanie-bear—

(JOAN hits GABE upside the head with the water pistol. As GABE falls stunned JOAN goes through her purseand takes out a needle. She presses it to GABE's neck.)

JOAN: Who are you! Tell me dammit! Who are you?

GABE: *(still talking in the accent)* Adrenaline, right? Yeah that's smart. They'll just think it's another attack.

JOAN: WHO THE FUCK ARE YOU?!?!?!

GABE: *(coming out of the accent)* Adam...he...Adam...

JOAN: You are not Adam.

GABE: Adam.

JOAN: Keep his name out of your mouth or this goes in your neck!

GABE: *(using his own accent)* He understands...he loves you. His last thoughts...were you. He understood. He wants you to have the money. To...to be happy. His heart wasn't—

JOAN: SHUT UP!!!

GABE: Please..lady...I can't...I can't help it. My head...I can't keep things out. I can't..They won't stay out. All my life...since I was a kid. I couldn't keep them out.

JOAN: What are you?

GABE: I don't know. I got real sick in the sixth grade. Some kind of brain thing. Went into a coma and came out...like this. They've got...there are meds that help. Really help. But...I can't afford them. I thought...I was there when he came in...I...guess I eavesdropped...kinda...I just wanted a couple of bucks, really—

JOAN: And you got greedy. *(pause)* You know everything, don't you? *(pause)* DON'T YOU?

GABE: I saw...the suitcase. I wasn't sure where it was...

JOAN: But, if I thought about it, you'd know, right?

GABE: Let me...let me keep the aspirin...we'll call it even, ok?

JOAN: It doesn't really seem to help much does it?

GABE: It's something...please...

JOAN: A second ago you were ready to steal the money my husband and I stole and now you're back to begging for aspirin. You are truly pathetic, you know that?

GABE: Look...let's just forget it ok...I'm sorry. We'll just—

JOAN: You don't get to upset my whole world and walk away... Oh no no no no you greedy greasy mind-reading freak. You thought you could just drop in my head, take the money and walk away? Look at me.

GABE: Please...I promise...I'd never—

JOAN: LOOK AT ME DAMMIT! *(JOAN forces GABE to look at her.)* You know where it is now, right? *(GABE sheepishly nods his head.)* And you know what I did...what I HAD to do to the man I love, right?

GABE: It's..it's all right—

JOAN: It is NOT all right. It is far from fucking all right!

GABE: I mean...I mean it's all right to feel...relief.

JOAN: Relief?

GABE: Th-there's guilt, of course...I get that. But relief, is all right. He..he suffered. It's...no one saw this coming. You did what you had to do. That's what you two were all about...right?

JOAN: *(pause)* We planned that score for—

GABE: Months. Five.

JOAN: It was so perfect. We would have been in Rio by the time we—

GABE: Sao Paolo. *(pause)* Rio was for—

JOAN: Tourists...right. We made plans.

GABE: Heart attacks don't wait for plans...I mean, that's what you were just—

JOAN: Thinking. *(pause)* Do you know what I'm thinking, now?

(GABE looks at her for a long moment. And then recoils.)

GABE: Aw..come on. Please don't. Look, lady—

JOAN: Joan. You know my name. You might as well use it.

GABE: Joan...please...just let me walk, ok? No one is going to believe me. I..I can't keep it together. You're right. I wanted a few bucks and I got greedy. Lesson learned. Please..

JOAN: No one will believe you. You got that right. If I were to rip my blouse...run back into the hospital and say some crazy man in a ratty trench coat tried to rape me... You wouldn't have much of a case, would you?

GABE: You...you wouldn't do that...

JOAN: You'd languish in jail and, assuming you survive, sooner or later someone is going to figure out what you are. And then you become an object of scientific curiosity. Hm...I might even pity you then. Better to be someone's jail bride than someone's lab rat, right?

GABE: I...I can't be what you want.

JOAN: You're going to have to try. All I need is for you to be my early warning system. I thought running away to Brazil was my answer...but you have provided me with an opportunity to do so much more. I can't pass this up.

GABE: No...It...it makes me sick. I can't...you'd kill me.

JOAN: Now would I do such a thing? Take a look. Would I?

GABE: Yes...yes you would.

JOAN: I'll get you enough of those drugs you need, so you don't lose your mind or whatever. I'll take care of you...as long as you take care of me.

GABE: I...I don't want to...

JOAN: Why do you keep talking like you have a choice?

(The sound of an approaching bus is heard.)

GABE: The...the bus. The bus is coming.

JOAN: Don't worry. We're taking a cab.

(JOAN dials the phone while GABE ponders his future.)

(lights fade)

CIRCLES

A Short Musical

by Amy Oestreicher

Amy Oestreicher is an Audie Award-nominated playwright, performer, and multidisciplinary creator. A PTSD specialist, artist, author, writer for The Huffington Post, international keynote speaker, RAINN representative, and health advocate, she has given three TEDx Talks on transforming trauma through creativity, and has contributed to *NBC's Today, CBS, Cosmopolitan, Seventeen Magazine, The Washington Post, Good Housekeeping,* and *MSNBC,* among others. Amy has toured her musical *Gutless & Grateful* to more than 200 venues from 54 Below to Barrington Stage Company since its 2012 NYC debut, and developed her full-length play *Flicker and a Firestarter* with Playlight Theatre Co. Her multimedia musical *Passageways* (original lyrics, music, book and mixed media artwork) has been performed at HERE Arts Center, Dixon Place, and the Triad Theater. She has recently published her memoir, *My Beautiful Detour: An Unthinkable Journey from Gutless to Grateful.* Her plays have been published by Eddy Theatre Company, PerformerStuff, Narcissists Anthology, New World Theatre's *Solitary Voice: A Collection of Epic Monologues*, and were finalists in Manhattan Repertory's Short Play Festival, NYNW Theatre Fest, #MeTooTheatreWomen, Women in the Age of Trump, and Tennessee Williams's New Orleans Literary Festival. Her play *Factory Treasure* is the one-act winner of Central PA Theatre & Dance Fest and has been performed at Identity Theatre, Actors' Theatre of Newburyport, and The Depot. **Contact: www.amyoes.com**

Circles was sponsored by **Boston Conservatory at Berklee**. Founded in 1867, Boston Conservatory is the nation's oldest performing arts conservatory to offer fully accredited programs in dance, music, and theater. In 2016, the Conservatory merged with the Berklee College of Music to become one of the most comprehensive performing arts institutions in the world. Today, the Boston Conservatory at Berklee offers a new model for conservatory education that is committed to empowering students to create their own artistic path through authenticity, agency, and diversity in all forms. Our musical theater program is recognized as one the finest in the country, and our new Contemporary Theater program is the only one of its kind in a conservatory setting. We embrace wide-ranging concepts of professional accomplishments from Broadway to fringe theater to artistic revolutions yet to be imagined. **bostonconservatory.berklee.edu**

Circles was presented on April 25, 2020, with the following creative team:

Directed by Andrea Southwick
Music Director: Bethany Aiken
Assistant Director: Lucy Austin
RUTH: Kate Fitzgerald
MOM (V.O): Madison LeBlanc

CHARACTERS:

RUTH: Female, 17, a thriving young woman. Mezzo with belt. Any ethnicity, background and ability encouraged. An "old soul" with a burgeoning anger growing inside her, eventually setting her free.

MOTHER: Female, RUTH's mom and keeper of her secrets. Caring, if not overbearing, with good intentions.

Playwrights note: When RUTH reads from her mother's journal, this can optionally be done by the mother as another character or voiceover.

RUTH: From my classroom window, I spot a single tree. Nature carves it, wraps it in bark like a present, and adorns it with shedding leaves as it grows closer to full enlightened maturity…I'm fine, Mr. Costa, I'm fine. Sorry. Can you repeat the question? Even when the tree twists and turns, it always grows. But do people?

CIRCLES

WE'RE JUST HOLDING, HOLDING, HOLDING ON
TO PEOPLE, TO TIME, TO ANYONE WHO'LL STAY
AND WE'RE PEOPLE, PEOPLE, HOLDING ON
TO QUESTIONS UNANSWERED, REBORN EVERYDAY

I see circles everywhere. Circles and rims. In the footprints on the sand, in the scattered clouds, in the circular dance of the seagulls atop the water, the sun sits in a circle. Circle of air around my face where the warmth of other faces should be. Empty circle in my heart opening up to the world, trying the horizon on for size.

AND WE'RE TURNING, TURNING IN CIRCLES
AND CIRCLES AND CIRCLES AND TURNING AWAY

FROM LIVING OUR FATES
IS THAT WHAT THEY TRY TO CHANGE
SOMETHING AWAITS
IT'S ALREADY BEEN ARRANGED
WE HIDE WITH FACADES
YET WE SEARCH FOR FAITH AND TRUST

WE HAVE TO LOOK INSIDE, WHERE WE DON'T *EXPLORE* MUCH

What is a circle and why do they mean so many things? We can't tell while we're circling. We can only judge by how we feel at every curve.

Or we can just reverse directions and see what feels right.

Is God a man, a static web of spirit like the clouds in the sky, or is He just one big, all-encompassing Circle?

AND WE'RE TURNING, TURNING IN CIRCLES AND CIRCLES AND TURNING AND LOOKING AND HOLDING, HOLDING, GRASPING ON

TO OTHERS, TO LIFE, TO THOUGHTS THAT ARE CONSTANTLY HANDHELD AND THE THOUGHT OF REACHING ON

TO ANSWERS FROM ANYONE WHO'LL JUST UNDERSTAND!

In a world of perfect geometric shapes, of painted signs, of bright red automobiles…I've wandered, lonely and seeking a friend, and I ask, can I belong?

IS THAT WHAT THEY SEE, THE FAITH BEHIND ME?
CAN THEY SEE THE WHEELS TURNING
AND TURNING AND TURNING?

AND WE FIND IT AND LOSE IT
TURN CIRCLES AND CIRCLES SO CONSTANTLY TILL THERE'S NO END NOR BEGINNING

YOU END WHERE YOU STARTED,

BUT DON'T REALLY KNOW IT
IN MOMENTS SO CAUGHT UP IN
TURNING AND TURNING
IN CIRCLES

HOW DARE YOU

Back when I was little, every night at bedtime I would press my fingertips together as tightly as I could. I believed if I could feel that warmth in between each tip, God could hear me. Every night I'd chant:

Dear God, thank you for a beautiful day today. Please visit me in my dreams. Amen. And please let me get the role of Sally in *You're a Good Man in Charlie Brown* at the JCC. Amen.

Slowly I'd feel my eyelids fall, and I would be transported into that magical world.

(*trying to touch her fingers together)* This has to work now. *(It doesn't work.)*

How silly you were, Amy. How silly you were. How deeply you trusted with your wide blue sparkling innocent eyes.

The morning after…the first time…I felt like a precious pearl that had been ruined. "This is his mess, but I'm stuck in it."

HOW DARE YOU ACT PROFESSIONAL AND GROWN UP AND IMPRESS THEM WITH YOUR PUT TOGETHER MASK AND YOUR SOUL BOUND UP IN GLASS
HOW DARE YOU NOW PRESENT YOURSELF WITH PRIDE AS I

RESENT MYSELF INSIDE AND BURN WITH SHAME, WHILE I SMILE AND PRAISE YOUR NAME!

YOU DARE WITH YOUR FAÇADE TO BE THIS UPRIGHT NOBLE GOD WHEN ONLY I CAN SEE THE SHAPE OF A SLIMY LYING SNAKE
YOU DARE TO PUT ME ON PARADE, I'VE WHORED MYSELF TO MAKE YOU STAY, I CAN'T LIVE WITH MYSELF – NOW I HAVE NOBODY ELSE.

AND I'M THE ONLY ONE WHO KNOWS YOUR DIRTY LITTLE SECRETS
I'M THE ONLY ONE WHO DRIES YOUR TEARS IN THE DARK
I'M THE ONLY ONE WHO HOLDS YOUR BURDENS DEEP IN MY CHEST
I'M THE ONLY ONE WHO'S LOST HER HEART
HOW DARE YOU.

No one was able to connect the dots. The Lion had tricked them far too well for them to know he was responsible for my deteriorating state.

The weaker I got, the stronger he became because that is what happens when you suck someone's soul-juice and feed on their blood like a vampire.

A DIRTY LITTLE TAG ALONG FOR YOU TO HOLD AND DRAG ALONG
"POOR GIRL SHE'S VERY WEAK, SHE'S QUITE BRIGHT BUT SHE CAN'T SPEAK"
THEY SAY "POOR CHILD WHAT'S WRONG WITH HER"
"HOW NOBLE, YOU TEACH SONG TO HER!"
DO THEY KNOW I'VE NO CHOICE?
THE VOICE TEACHER STOLE MY VOICE!

I HOLD HIS PAIN LIKE NO ONE CAN
HE CRIES JUST LIKE A LITTLE MAN
HE'S MADE A JOKE OF MUSIC, MADE A MOCKERY OF ART
MY MENTOR, RIGHT, LIKE YOU'D BELIEVE
HE WEARS HIS DEMONS ON HIS SLEEVE

I'VE OPENED UP HIS HEART, NOW HE'S TEARING MINE APART

I'M THE ONLY ONE CHOKED BY THE LOOPHOLES IN YOUR STORY
I'M THE ONLY ONE WHO'S BURNED AND DRIED UP BY THE SUN
I'M THE ONE WHO HANGS DOWN IN THE SHADOWS OF YOUR GLORY
I'M ALONE

AND I'M THE ONLY ONE

The Lion wasn't real at all, just knew how to dress in fancy costumes. No soul in there really, just a lot of hot air. And the air he used to inflate himself? My spirit. My passion.

STIFLED, SILENCED, MAD, ALONE
BITTER THAT YOU'VE STOLE MY HOME
KNOWING I'M THE DUMP THAT KEEPS
YOUR LIES PRESERVED IN FEAR

TO THE WORLD YOU SHOW NO TRACE
OF YOUR WRETCHED SHAMEFUL FACE
ONLY I WILL NUMBLY CRY FOR WORLDS THAT DISAPPEAR

I'M THE ONLY ONE CHOKED BY THE LOOPHOLES IN YOUR STORY
I'M THE ONLY ONE WHO'S BURNED AND DRIED UP BY THE SUN

I'M THE ONE WHO HANGS DOWN IN THE SHADOWS OF YOUR GLORY - HOW DARE YOU

HOW DARE YOU!

SKY IS BLUE

For months, I kept these fumes simmering on the inside. My mom kept her thoughts on these pages.

January 5th, 2005:
WE had JUST gotten back from a mother daughter retreat, and in a dance exercise—Amy had always been such a soulful dancer—she went into the middle of our circle. A woman touched me on the arm, and said, "look, your daughter is dancing a dance of such deep pain, you have to find out what the source of her anguish is."

February 4th:
Jonah (my brother?) handed me a crumpled up piece of paper and said "Mom, I found this in her room. Is it me, or is it a little weird that her voice teacher emailed her a love poem?"

April 12th:
"Amy and I were walking on the beach in Fairfield. I took a really good look at her, maybe for the first time in months. She was anxious, unfocused, and her eyes looked so hollow. She was so different, and I remembered what that woman at the Retreat said about her dancing.

I stopped walking and looked straight into her eyes and I asked her, 'Your voice teacher…has he ever touched you?'

Amy began to describe what he did, and I went into complete shock, screaming, 'Oh…my…GOD! Oh my god! Oh my—I trusted him. Why didn't you say anything?'"

I remember staring at my hysterical mother. I held her hands, trying to ground her, and said "Tell me something good."

She fired back, "Something good? He was evil! a sick, evil—"

But I insisted "I need something positive now. There must be something good."

Mom just sighed, looked up and said... "The sky is blue."

I'M HERE MOM
DON'T FEAR MOM
I'M ASKING YOU TO TRY
I KNOW THAT YOU'RE TROUBLED
AND CLEARLY SO AM I
THE SKY, MOM, YOU SEE IT
IT'S REAL STUFF GOD HAS MADE
SO LOOK THERE AND TELL ME
HOW CAN YOU BE AFRAID?
WE WILL STEP ON THE HEAD OF THE TINIEST PIN
TELL ME MOM, ARE YOU IN?

FILL THIS SPACE, PACKED WITH CLOUDS IN EACH MOMENT
WE'LL PACK EACH MOMENT
WE'RE SAFE NOW, BY STANDING IN SPACE NOW, YOU AND I
OUR WORLD MAY BE CRUMBLING BUT WE STILL HAVE THE SKY

THE SKY IS BLUE
THE SKY IS BLUE.

SO MUCH RAGE IN MY CORE THAT I CAN'T FEEL THE FLOOR
SEE ME DROWNING IN THIS FLOOD?
IF YOU SCARE WITH YOUR SCREAMS
THEN YOU'LL TEAR AT MY SEAMS
AND I TELL YOU: THIS IS MY BLOOD
SO BE KIND, PLEASE AND REMIND ME
PLEASE

PART OF THIS IS FURY WHEN YOUR SCREAM MAKES NO SOUND
PART OF THIS IS SHAKING BOTH YOUR FISTS AT THE GROUND
WHEN THE DAMN CLOCK WON'T BUDGE
AND THE WORLD IS UNFAIR
AND YOU'RE SCREAMING AT GOD
'CAUSE YOU KNOW HE'S NOT THERE

WE'RE STUCK MOM, LIKE THIS, MOM, IF YOU CAN'T HOLD A LIE
THERE'S LIGHT, MOM, SO FIGHT, MOM
AND TALK ABOUT THE SKY
THE SKY IS BLUE - IT WILL BE BLUE
IF YOU TELL ME, IT WILL BE BLUE

JUST FOR ME MOM, DON'T ASK WHY MOM
FOR THIS INSTANT, TRY TO FAKE IT

YOU GO FIRST MOM
SEE THE SKY MOM
TELL ME SOMETHING GOOD – I'LL TAKE IT
GOOD, GOOD, TELL ME SOMETHING
TELL ME THE SKY IS BLUE.

The sky was bluer than ever, the day everything…

Changed.

(end)

THIRD PARTY

By Nancy Peavy

Nancy Peavy is a playwright living in South Portland, Maine. Her dramatic works include *Forever Yours*, a One-Act Comedy, first produced in the September 2018 King of Crows VI theatre festival, Portland, Maine. *Rapture*, a One-Act Drama, was produced in the September 2019 King of Crows VII theatre festival, Portland, Maine. *Third Party*, a One-Act comedy is her first play to be included in the Boston Theater Marathon. She works as a vocational counselor serving youth with disabilities. **Contact: peavynancy@gmail.com**

Third Party was sponsored by **Hovey Players**, established in 1936. Located in the basement of the D'Angio Building in Waltham, MA, the 52 seat Abbott Memorial Theater is among the most intimate performance spaces in New England. We produce four shows per season featuring a full range of plays including comedies, dramas, and musicals. Hovey Players is a member of Stage Source, the Eastern Massachusetts Association of Community Theaters (EMACT), and the American Association of Community Theaters (AACT). We celebrate the performing arts and artists throughout New England and more directly in the Waltham and Boston area. **www.hoveyplayers.com**

Third Party was presented on April 11, 2020, with the following creative team:

Directed by Michelle Aguillon
BOBBY BUTLICK: Craig Ciampa
WOMAN: Christine Connor
MAN: David Berti

CHARACTERS:

BOBBY BUTLICK: Age 45, white, politician

WOMAN: Age 60, average American, married to MAN

MAN: Age 65, average American, married to WOMAN

(MAN and WOMAN'S tidy, average suburban home, in the present. At rise: BOBBY enters stage right and knocks on door of the home. WOMAN enters stage left, opens door, smiles widely.)

WOMAN: Well hello there!

BOBBY: Hi ma'am! I'm Bobby Butlick...I'm running for the legislature.

WOMAN: Come on in!

BOBBY: I'd like to count on your vote in November! *(puts his hand out to shake)*

WOMAN: Well that depends. Are you making American great again?

BOBBY: Why yes m'am. I support our President if that's what you mean. He's getting a lot done. Doing a lot of...things. You know. Tremendous things!

WOMAN: Yes...he certainly is! Come on in, sit awhile.

(She shows BOBBY to a chair; he sits.)

So are you all for building that wall?

BOBBY: Yes ma'am! We have to protect our motherland from raping, murdering drug gangs pouring over the border to get welfare and food stamps.

WOMAN: You know, I love kids but those illegal ones? I say make the little brats work. Being a baby is no excuse for being lazy.

BOBBY: But they are taking jobs away from hard working American babies, *that's* the problem.

(MAN enters stage left, stands over BOBBY.)

MAN: What do we have here?

(BOBBY reaches out to shake MAN'S hand.)

BOBBY: I'm Bobby Butlick and I'd like your vote!

(MAN grasps his hand and inspects BOBBY'S arm.)

MAN: Kinda stringy.

(WOMAN sniffs BOBBY. BOBBY looks confused. MAN rubs his belly.)

I'm still full from the Jehovah's Witness. And politicians are always greasy. We ended up throwing out most of the last one.

WOMAN: Perfect for the crock pot though. There's still a lot of UPS driver in the freezer. But I think we could make room.

(BOBBY jumps up. MAN grips his shoulder and forces him back down in the chair.)

BOBBY: Oh God...what...what are you people?

WOMAN: I like to think of us as apex carnivores.

BOBBY: Does that mean, you... you eat...

MAN: No hunting or gathering required.

WOMAN: They come right to your door.

MAN: Sometimes you get a driver *and* a pizza!

BOBBY: But I thought you were members of the Republican party! You're on my list!

WOMAN: Oh, no. Our party is more like the Donner party.

BOBBY: Please, let me go! I don't deserve this!

WOMAN: Like those babies in cages?

BOBBY: Look that doesn't have anything to do with me! I like illegals. Really I do! They dug my pool really cheap!

WOMAN: Toddlers with tiny toy shovels, that must have been sooo cute.

MAN: If you really want to keep him we better tie him up.

BOBBY: No please, please, oh God please, don't! I'll do anything!

(MAN and WOMAN look at each other.)

MAN: You're the cook – it's your call.

WOMAN: *(thinks a moment)* Oh ok. What about a joke.

BOBBY: A joke?

WOMAN: Yeah, tell us a joke. Something really funny. Whadaya got?

BOBBY: Yes ma'am, I can do that. Funny. Very, very funny. Hang on, just let me think a minute...

WOMAN: Lay it on us Bobby boy.

BOBBY: Uh...uh...ok, ok. Why did the mushroom go to the party? Because he was a fun guy. You know fungi? Like fungus.

(MAN pats BOBBY on the back.)

MAN: Don't try to explain it buddy, that just makes it worse.

WOMAN: Ooh – I have one. What happens when you give a politician Viagra? *(beat)* He gets taller.

(MAN and WOMAN crack up.)

MAN: See Bobby, it's the timing. It's always about the timing. *(beat)* I've got one! Why don't cannibals eat clowns?

(WOMAN rolls her eyes and mouths the punch line.)

Because they taste funny! *(laughs heartily)*

WOMAN: Can you do anything else?

BOBBY: Anything else?

WOMAN: You know, talent. Can you dance?

BOBBY: Well, I...not really.

WOMAN: Sharpen up the knives honey!

BOBBY: No, no wait, wait! *(starts doing an awkward soft shoe dance)*

WOMAN: How about pole dancing?

MAN: I can't watch this...

BOBBY: Pole dancing?

WOMAN: You're a politician and you're trying to act like you don't know what pole dancing is?

MAN: She's got you there buddy.

BOBBY: But...I don't have a pole.

WOMAN; You can pretend! Isn't that what you politicians are good at?

(BOBBY starts gyrating.)

MAN: I am losing my appetite.

WOMAN: Well I am having a very good time.

BOBBY: Can I go now?

MAN: Hey! Can you do mime? Like you're inside a box and you can't get out?

(BOBBY starts acting like a mime.)

WOMAN: Ooh! Mime like you're a baby goat in a box! Those adorable little Internet goats that wear pajamas.

(BOBBY jumps around like a goat in a box.)

WOMAN: The goats are a lot cuter.

MAN: I don't know...maybe if he had jammies on.

BOBBY: Now can I go? Please.

WOMAN: Oh no Bobby. Right now I'm 70/30 crockpot. Let's see you put it all together. Give us your best – I'm talking *American Idol* - pole dancing baby goat mime.

MAN: Honey, you shouldn't play with your food.

BOBBY: Ok! Ok!

(BOBBY does his best to pole dance, mime and jump around like a goat. Gasps for breath.)

Can I go, can I go?

MAN: He gets my sympathy vote for that performance.

WOMAN: So if we let you go, how do we know you won't tell anyone about us?

BOBBY: I will never breathe a word I swear.

WOMAN: Politicians never lie.

BOBBY: No! Almost never...very rarely...only once in a while - if we have to.

WOMAN: Uh huh.

BOBBY: Ok, maybe a little more often that. But I would never lie to you ma'am. Never. Never ever.

WOMAN: *(thinks it over)* You are lucky we just ate. Go on, git.

(BOBBY shouts over his shoulder as he runs offstage.)

BOBBY: I hope I can still count on your vote!

(MAN and WOMAN stand looking satisfied, smiling for a few moments.)

MAN: *(big sigh)* I do love election season.

(blackout)

(end play)

DOWNGRADE

by Eliana Pipes

Eliana Pipes is a playwright, actor and filmmaker. She's the 2019 recipient of the Academy Gold Fellowship for Women and the 2019 Leah Ryan Fund Prize for Emerging Women Writers. She received a BA in English from Columbia Dream Hou$e (Ars Nova ANT Fest, San Diego Rep New Latinx Plays Festival, Two River Theater Crossing Borders Festival, O'Neill Theater Conference Finalist); *Cowboy and the Moon* (National New Play Network MFA Workshop); *Stand and Wait* (Gaffney National Playwriting Prize Winner, Bay Area Playwright's Festival Finalist); *Stiletto Envy* (Samuel French Off-Off Broadway Festival, The Fire this Time Festival). More at **elianapipes.com**

Downgrade was sponsored by **The Huntington Theatre Company** (with Michael Maso/Managing Director, and Peter DuBois/Artistic Director), Boston's leading professional theatre and one of the region's premier cultural assets since its founding in 1982. Recipient of the 2013 Regional Theatre Tony Award, the Huntington brings together superb local and national talent and produces a mix of groundbreaking new works and classics made current to create award-winning productions. The Huntington runs nationally renowned programs in education and new play development and serves the local theatre community through its operation of the Calderwood Pavilion at the BCA. The Huntington has long been an anchor cultural institution of Huntington Avenue, the Avenue of the Arts, and will remain so on a permanent basis with plans to convert our current theatre into a first-rate, modern venue with expanded services to audiences, artists, and the community. Under the direction of Artistic Director Peter DuBois and Managing Director Michael Maso, the Huntington cultivates, celebrates, and champions theatre as an art form. **huntingtontheatre.org**

Downgrade was presented on May 6, 2020, with the following creative team:

Directed by Caley Chase
JAMIE: Rachel Cognata
CEE: Anna Bortnick

The text of Downgrade *is not available for publication in this volume.*

Synopsis: Jamie has a very close relationship with Cee—she's* bubbly, she's captivating, and she's also her cellphone. When Jamie decides to go off the grid for good, Cee fights for her life in a spirited tug of war that illuminates the complex and sometimes painful role that technology plays in our lives. (*Either character can be played by an actor of any gender; please change pronouns freely.)

THE WHEELBARROW

by Ron Radice

Since 2007, **Ron Radice** has had plays performed in 17 states. *The Climbing* was a two-time semi-finalist twice at the National Playwrights Conference at the Eugene O'Neill Theater Center. *To The Top* ran at the Alleyway Theater. *Waiting for the Eire Lackawanna* was accepted in the 2017 LaBute Festival. *Maybe It Won't Happen* was accepted for a reading at the William Inge Festival in 2018. He has recently completed his first novel. He received a first place award for his play from Writer's Digest in 2019. **Contact: rradice@aol.com**

The Wheelbarrow was sponsored by **imaginary beasts** (Matthew Woods, Artistic Director), an incubator for adventurous theatre making. We provide our members a unique chance to explore and develop theatre in an ongoing studio environment. Devoted to pushing the boundaries of how theatre is made and who can make it, we bring together traditional and non-traditional performance artists to produce work for an eclectic public. imaginary beasts is proud to be in residence at the Charlestown Working Theater. To find out more, like us on Facebook, follow us on Twitter (**@imaginarybeast**), or sign up for our mailing list at **www.imaginarybeasts.org**

The Wheelbarrow was presented on May 16, 2020, with the following creative team:

Directed by Matthew Woods
Producer: Laura Detwiler
Shadow Puppetry: Rebecca Lehrhoff
ALBERT: Bob Mussett,
BERNICE: Kiki Samko
CHRISTINE: Amy Meyer

CHARACTERS:

ALBERT—the father

BERNICE—the father's mother

CHRISTINE—the father's daughter

(A forest setting. Today, somewhere in southern USA. At rise, ALBERT is slowly wheeling BERNICE, his elderly mother, in a wooden farm wheelbarrow. CHRISTINE, his daughter, walks with him. They stop.)

ALBERT: *(to BERNICE)* OK, I think we're here. This should be a good place to stop. *(pause)* Besides I'm tired wheeling you around all this day. *(pause)* This spot should do just fine, I think. This'll be your surprise place, Mama. Like I promised you.

BERNICE: *(shouting)* What? What'd you say, Albert?

ALBERT: *(shouting back)* I said surprise!

BERNICE: What?

ALBERT: *(pause)* I said, this should be a good place for your surprise, Mama.

BERNICE: *(shouting)* What?

ALBERT: We'll stop here. Not sure it's the best spot, but we're stopping here anyway. I'm getting tired and it's getting late. *(starts to leave)* I want to look around to make sure this is a good enough place. That we aren't on someone's property. Christine, you watch your grandmother while I'm off. Don't go letting her trying to wander off while I'm away.

(He exits.)

BERNICE: Good riddance. Pain in the ass. Thinks I don't know what his surprise is. *(looking toward CHRISTINE)* What do you think it is? *(CHRISTINE does not answer, looks away.)* So you're in on this, are you? *(pause)* Going to stay mute? Wish he *did.* Always was a pain in the ass. He'll die a pain in the ass. And no one will care a damn when he's gone. *(pause)* You have an opinion on your father? *(pause)* No. You're just like him if you ask me. *(pause)* Dumb. Dumb and mute you are. Playing mute with me ain't going to help you. *(trying to get out of the wheelbarrow)* I need your help. Christine. Come here.

(pause as CHRISTINE hesitates)

I got to go tinkle. *(CHRISTINE still hesitates.)* I don't have all day, damn you. I gotta go in a hurry now. Sittin' in that damn wheelbarrow all the day. *(CHRISTINE moves toward BERNICE but with obvious hesitation.)* Come on. Hurry up! I don't have much time before something happens. *(CHRISTINE comes over and helps BERNICE out of the wheelbarrow.)* Still not talking? *(pause)* Hell with you too then. *(pause)* I'll find my own spot behind the trees. *(starts to walk off)* When he comes back, tell him I went back home. That'll get his ass in motion. Tell him that he'll find me at the house. *(sardonic laugh, as CHRISTINE looks startled)* Ha, got you. Dumb like your father.

(She exits.)

CHRISTINE: Don't go wandering too far. Pa said I shouldn't be letting you wander. *(pause)* Hurry back, Grandma.

(CHRISTINE watches as BERNICE walks off. Goes to wheelbarrow. Looks at it. Tries wheeling it around. Sits in it. ALBERT enters.)

ALBERT: Where is she? Where's she gone to? I asked you to watch her. Why'd you let her wander off. You know how she is. You see what she does back home.

CHRISTINE: Had to go tinkle she said.

ALBERT: I don't want to have to be chasing after her.

CHRISTINE: She'll be back. Couldn't go too far.

ALBERT: Well, this place looks like it will do as good as any other. Especially with dark coming soon.

CHRISTINE: You didn't bring much food.

ALBERT: This is not a picnic.

CHRISTINE: I'm hungry.

ALBERT: There's some food in the bag. Get what you want. We'll need to go back home soon. We don't have a lot of time. *(pause)* Where is she?

(BERNICE re-enters.)

BERNICE: Missing me were you? The life of the party. *(laughs in mockery)*

ALBERT: Mama, we need to talk.

BERNICE: *(watching CHRISTINE eat)* I'm hungry.

ALBERT: Christine, give her something before she starts whining.

(CHRISTINE hands BERNICE a piece of bread.)

BERNICE: Why shouldn't I whine with a fool like you? If I didn't ask you, I'd never get anything. *(pause)* A piece of bread? I want some cheese. Some salami.

CHRISTINE: There's only bread, Grandma.

BERNICE: Bread? I want something else. Hell, of a picnic.

ALBERT: That's what I want to talk about.

BERNICE: I want something good to eat. You hear me? Something good. Not this lousy bread. *(throws bread to the ground)* Birds won't even eat it, I'll betcha.

ALBERT: Stop it, Mama. Stop your complaining. *(pause)* I've made a decision.

BERNICE: I don't want to hear about any of your dumb decisions. You don't know how to make decisions. You wouldn't know a decision if it hit you in the face—which is what I ought to do to you. I want something to eat that's better than this bread!

ALBERT: That's all there is.

(pause)

BERNICE: Maybe, we should go back then.

ALBERT: We will be. *(pause)* Christine and I will be going back to the house. *(pause)* But you're staying here.

BERNICE: What are you talking about? More of your nonsense?

ALBERT: I'm leaving you here.

BERNICE: For what?

(pause)

ALBERT: We can't afford to keep you anymore.

BERNICE: Keep me?! It's my farm you're living on. I'm keeping you, you dumb ass. Been keeping you all these years, you lazy good for nothing. It's a wonder we haven't lost the farm the way you work it.

ALBERT: Well, you needn't be worrying about that anymore.

BERNICE: I'm not just going to sit here. You know that.

ALBERT: You'll do whatever you do, as you always have. But you'll be staying here. I'm not taking you back home with us.

BERNICE: I couldn't walk all the way back. Not with my legs. You know that?

ALBERT: I know. That's why we come this far out.

BERNICE: You'd be leaving me here to die.

ALBERT: Yes.

(pause)

BERNICE: I'm getting cold.

ALBERT: I brought you a blanket.

(He gets the blanket from the wheelbarrow and gives it to BERNICE.*)*

BERNICE: Well, aren't you the sweet and considerate son.

ALBERT: Christine, say your good byes to your grandmother. We'll need to be getting off before dark sets in.

CHRISTINE: *(said matter-of-factly, without horror)* I didn't know you were going to do it like this. She'll die here.

ALBERT: She'll be dying soon anyway.

CHRISTINE: But why here?

ALBERT: It'll be faster.

BERNICE: Go! Go on and get out of here, the two of you. I don't need you—either of you. Don't want you—don't need you. Leave me be. Damn the two of you.

ALBERT: Goodbye, Mama.

BERNICE: Good riddance.

ALBERT: *(to CHRISTINE)* Come on, let's be going.

CHRISTINE: We can't just be going like this, father.

ALBERT: I understand your feelings, and that you'd rather we didn't, but I've made my decision.

CHRISTINE: Papa!

ALBERT: Let's get a move on now, Christine.

CHRISTINE: You're forgetting something.

ALBERT: I told you, I don't want to discuss this. Let's go!

CHRISTINE: The wheelbarrow, father.

ALBERT: I'll not be needing it anymore.

(long pause)

CHRISTINE: But, father, I'll be needing it someday.

(curtain)

MISPLACED

by Cassie M. Seinuk

Cassie M. Seinuk is a Jewish Cuban playwright and stage manager with a BA from Brandeis University and an MFA in Writing for Stage and Screen at Lesley University. *From the Deep* won The Pestalozzi New Play Prize, the Latinx Playwrights Award at the Kennedy Center ACTF, was a recipient of the Boston University Jewish Culture Endowment, and appeared on The Kilroy's Honorable Mention List (2015). *Eyes Shut. Door Open.* won the 2016 OnStage Critics Award for Outstanding New Work and received a grant from the Bob Jolly Charitable Trust. *Dream House* was developed at New Rep. and The Nora, was a semi-finalist for the 2016 National Playwrights Conference at The O'Neill, and was a finalist for the 2017 Massachusetts Cultural Council Artist Fellowship. *Una Me Da Leche*, a trilingual play, was a 2017 semi-finalist for The O'Neill NPC and was presented at the BCA's She Said… Festival in 2019. Seinuk won the 2015 Gary Garrison Ten Minute Play Award at the Kennedy Center in 2015 for her play *Occupy Hallmark*. Seinuk is a member of The Dramatists Guild and Actors' Equity Association. Seinuk serves on the faculty at Boston Conservatory at Berklee. **Contact: Cassiemseinuk.com**

Misplaced was sponsored by **Wellesley Repertory Theatre** (Marta Rainer, Artistic Director), a year-round, award-winning professional theatre company in residence since 1998 on the Wellesley College campus. Founded as a summer theatre by Nora Hussey -- a formidable storyteller and community-builder recognized for her lifetime of achievement on both a local and national level -- Wellesley Rep productions have especially celebrated stories by and about complex and compelling women. Working in harmony with the Wellesley College Theatre student program (which annually introduces 300 students to all facets of theatrical craft and creative autonomy) an average of twelve shows per year are created in Wellesley's theatre spaces. Presenting a diverse and varied program, all theatre at Wellesley intends to challenge its participants, enlighten and enrich its audiences, and be a supportive community presence in the Metro West area. **www.wellesleyrep.org**

Misplaced was presented on April 23, 2020, with the following creative team:

Directed by Nora Hussey
JANE: Ariela Nazar-Rosen
ABE: Michael Underhill

CHARACTERS:

JANE, 30s F, she is dressed like she tried to put herself together, but right now she is very not put together. It takes effort. She has perhaps done something radically with her hair very very recently.

ABE, 30s M, he is dressed like a barista at a coffee shop that is all about being artisanal, local, and with a clean vibe. He used to be a bad boy, and I mean a real bad boy, and he still holds relics of that in his look at demeanor.

(A coffeeshop. It's trendy. Lights on a barista, ABE, male, thirties, used to be a bad boy, has mellowed out with age, but still holds remnants of his old self.

Standing and leaning into the other chair is JANE, also in her thirties, she is dressed like she tried to put herself together, but right now she is very not put together. It takes effort. They are mid conversation.)

ABE: It's fucking strange.

JANE: You're right, it is.

ABE: I mean, I'm just supposed to like...what?

JANE: I honestly don't—

ABE: Have small talk?

JANE: No. That's not—

ABE: You come to my work and expect—

JANE: I don't know what I expected. This is dumb. You are right. I'll just go.

(She starts to go.)

ABE: How did you find me, anyway?

JANE: I— It wasn't easy.

ABE: I'm intentionally unfindable. / I tried to be—

JANE: I mean, yeah, you don't want to know how many versions of your name I like searched for on Facebook, / Instagram, Google... LinkedIn.

ABE: I'm not on social media.

JANE: Intentionally, you said.

ABE: Yeah. I intentionally don't want, people from growing up, all those phony lemmings we went to school with to know I exist,

JANE: I get that.

ABE: —and I especially don't want middle school ex-girlfriends, if you can even call it that, to, when it was a two week "relationship" in the sixth grade—

JANE: It was more like a month, if you count the fact that I thought we were still together until I got the note from Elana.

ABE: Are we seriously arguing the stamina of a middle school—

JANE: I was on my way out. I can keep going, and you'll never know how I found you.

ABE: Well, then you'll never know whatever it is brought you here.

JANE: Yeah, you're right. I'll never know. But I will post your whereabouts on Facebook and then you'll have every kid you ever body checked, cheated off of, or egged in here saying hello. *(She starts to go again.)*

ABE: No no, I'm sorry.

JANE: No, you're not sorry.

ABE: I'm not. Fair. But I can't have those guys finding me. And I wanna know how you did. So that I know which rat to send a flaming bag of shit to.

JANE: Mature.

ABE: Guilty.

JANE: I'll tell you.

ABE: Awesome. And can you sit down? You are making me nervous hovering like that.

(She hesitates, she doesn't sit just yet.)

JANE: Sitting means I'm staying. Sitting means we are talking.

ABE: Yes. Let's talk. So... What do you want to talk about?

JANE: ...

ABE: ...

JANE: I had a miscarriage.

(She sits. Long pause.)

ABE: Oh. O/K...?

JANE: I had a miscarriage three weeks ago, today.

ABE: I'm... / sorry?

JANE: I had a miscarriage three weeks ago today, I was sixteen weeks pregnant, that's about four months, and it was...a shock.

ABE: Shit.

JANE: It was what they call a missed miscarriage. That means that I had no signs. I went in there thinking it would be the same old same old.

ABE: That's... I mean...

JANE: It's all so very very raw and new and—

ABE: I am sorry, honestly, that you have to deal with that, but what...and

I want to say this delicately, what does that have to do with me?

JANE: It doesn't have anything to do with you.

ABE: Look, I'm sorry, but also my break is almost over, and maybe, a therapist might be a better person to talk to... then someone you really barely know.

JANE: I have a therapist. She can't help with this.

ABE: And I can?

JANE: I need to know why you broke up with me.

ABE: In the sixth grade.

JANE: Yes, the first week of the sixth grade.

ABE: That was 20 plus years ago.

JANE: 22 years ago. Yes.

ABE: Is this a joke or something?

JANE: I don't know, do you often hear people jokingly tell you they had a mis/carriage.

ABE: Can you stop saying that word? It's like a real attention grabber. Worse than curse words.

JANE: Miscarriage?

ABE: Yeah. That.

JANE: HELLO! Hipsters of Brooklyn! With your CBD cortados and nitro cold brew, listen up. I want you all to know that I, Jane Ranali, had a miscarriaggggggggge!

ABE: Fuck, are you crazy?

JANE: No! I am just absolutely sick of people reacting to the word miscarriage like I've said...like...the N word.

ABE: Hey! That's not a fair comparison!

JANE: When people hear miscarriage a hush descends on the room. No one knows what to say. And everyone feels awkward.

ABE: Yes. Yes, but that is not like—

JANE: Or should I say "my baby died" would that be easier for people to hear?

ABE: No. I... It's just not...like a thing people share.

JANE: It should be.

ABE: Look, I have zero experience with this. I'm nowhere near having kids like maybe never, so, I'm probably not the person you should be—

JANE: Why did you break up with me?

ABE: Look, maybe we should meet up later, not at my place of / work—

JANE: Was it how I looked? I was awkward back then—

ABE: [and now] —I mean, I don't remember.

JANE: You don't remember?

ABE: It wasn't a big deal to me.

JANE: It was a big deal to me.

ABE: I am gathering that.

JANE: Was it 'cause I was nerdy?

ABE: I don't know.

JANE: All our elementary school classes merged and now all of the sudden there was a clear hierarchy? The cool and the not.

ABE: I mean, I'm sure that played into it, but...I don't remember.

JANE: That answer is not going to work for me.

ABE: God, man, I don't know what to tell you. I barely remember high school let alone middle school, and with the amount of weed I smok<u>ed</u>—

JANE: Who was your first girlfriend?

ABE: Kimmy Taub.

JANE: When was your first kiss.

ABE: In the bus yard, with Kimmy, I think she was wearing a red hat.

JANE: See?

ABE: No!

JANE: What was your first breakup?

ABE: Uh, I think before camp that summer, Kimmy was going to Chipanaw and I was going to Seneca. So we wanted to keep our options open. We thought we were really mature.

JANE: Did she cry?

ABE: It was her idea.

JANE: Did you?

ABE: I don't remember.

JANE: Do you want me to shout the M word again, at full volume.

ABE: Yeah, maybe I cried, a little, to myself, in my room, in the dark.

JANE: Don't pretend you didn't have real emotions about it, you are the same guy who cherry-bombed the Mr. Greene's mailbox because of a bad test score!

ABE: Allegedly. And it was for calling me short, not a test score.

JANE: And smashed all the windows of your dad's car during the divorce.

ABE: Wow. Word got around.

JANE: Yeah, and my brief boyfriend was the one who did all that stuff, so it's stuff I made a point of knowing.

ABE: Shit.

JANE: Yeah. I liked you.

ABE: OK. When she broke up with me...I may have locked my little brother in a closet to feel...powerful or something. Yeah, I remember that. But I don't remember why I broke up with you, or like the thought process there.

JANE: But you do remember. Just like I remember my first boyfriend, you, and the note you sent me in the dining hall asking me to sit next to you on movie night. I remember our first kiss, behind that low tree with the purple leaves and possibly some poison ivy behind tennis courts. I was worried about my breath even though we both had closed mouths. I remember the teddy bear you got me from Hershey Park, I think my mom finally tossed all those old stuffed animals...and I really really remember, like it happened yesterday, I remember when you had Elana Kahny give me your breakup note in the bus lot. There were leaves everywhere, and it was windy. And when I asked her why, she shrugged and said you were getting back with Kimmy. I remember crying my eyes out on the back of the school bus. I remember falling into my mom's lap almost immediately and swearing I'd never have another boyfriend that I was unlikeable. I remember saying prayers before bed, like Dear God please make Abe take me back! I remember over time the pain fading. I remember new crushes forming. I remember thinking you were a hotheaded stoner who I was lucky not to know. And when I totally moved on it didn't just magically erase the pain I felt. The pain of my first heartbreak. You have to know that that was the first time my heart broke. And when it broke it shattered. Whatever love or like is at that time seems so much bigger, more important, tremendous than it ever was, but it was a feeling, a feeling I had. It stayed with me. And I'll always wonder why? What did I do? What did I do wrong? What could I have done differently to not have felt that break.

ABE: I'm sorry... I don't know what to say. We were eleven.

JANE: And the thing is, the thing I think I've connected in all of this is that...my miscarriage feels somehow...the same?

ABE: How?

JANE: You were my first love and my first heartbreak. There would be many many more after that and, yes, they would lead me to my husband, and my life now, and so they all had a point. It took time, a lot of time, but I saw it. But this...I can't see the point in this. This heartbreak that I am feeling now, loss of a child, loss of a future I imagined for her, for me with her. It somehow feels so similar, so connected to...you.

ABE: Shit.

JANE: Yeah, shit. I will never know why she died. And there can be many reasons what could have been and why, but I'll never know. And you exist, you are here in the world, and you can answer a similar question for me, from a similar time. Why?

ABE: No, I can't.

JANE: Why not?

ABE: Because there was no real reason. *(beat)* Look, I'm really sorry for your loss, and I'm sorry to disappoint you. But these things aren't the same. And I don't think knowing why I dumped you will make you feel any better about your...

JANE: Miscarriage.

ABE: Yeah,…miscarriage. Nothing makes sense. Shit just happens.

JANE: Yeah. It does.

ABE: And now I guess, you just gotta sit with it.

JANE: Yeah...

ABE: But at least, I'll sit here too.

(JANE looks at him, for the first time really making a connection with who this person is now and not the person he was then.)

JANE: Elana still has your phone number. She's the one who found you for me. So, ready that flaming bag of shit.

(He laughs. She smiles. Beat. Lights.)

(end of play)

DINOSAUR WOMAN

by Marisa Smith

Marisa Smith's full-length plays include *Venus Rising* (Northern Stage, VT), *Sex and Other Disturbances* (Edgerton winner/Portland Stage Company), *Saving Kitty* (Eliot Norton Award for Jennifer Coolidge Best Actress, Clauder winner), *Mad Love* (O'Neill semi-finalist, Clauder winner/Kilroys List). Radio Play: *The Defenestrator*, produced by Wondery. Marisa's many 10-minute plays have been produced in the Boston Theater Marathon, Barrington Stage, New Jersey Repertory, and in many other theaters around the country and include Heideman finalist *Total Expression*. Film: *Second Wind*, dir. Andrew Silver. Musical: "Americanization" of *Fat Friends* by Kay Mellor, music by Nick Lloyd Webber. **Contact: www.marisasmithplaywright.com**

Dinosaur Woman was sponsored by **Sleeping Weazel**, which produces bold, experimental multimedia theatre and performance with social justice ideals. Now in its eighth year in Boston, the company has premiered sixteen productions of original works — at the former Factory Theatre, Boston Center for the Arts, Boston Playwrights' Theatre, for Outside the Box Boston, and in ArtsEmerson's Next Thing Festival. Sleeping Weazel is a two-time recipient of the Elliot Norton Award (Outstanding Production, Small Theatre) for *The Audacity: Women Speak* in 2019 and James Scruggs' *3/Fifths' Trapped in a Traveling Minstrel Show* in 2018. **www.sleepingweazel.com**

Dinosaur Woman was presented on April 4, 2020, with the following creative team:

Directed by Jessica Ernst
CLARISSA: Veronica Anastasio Wiseman

(CLARISSA, a very well-dressed woman of a certain age, rushes into a beautifully appointed powder room and shuts the door firmly behind her. She's holding a cocktail, leans up against the closed door and takes a deep breath.)

CLARISSA: Thank you, thank you God, for making Stanley Benson have to go to the men's room at that moment. I couldn't make small talk with him for another second. And thank you God for making the Harrison's so filthy rich that even though this monstrosity of a fake Frank Lloyd Wright is *so* wrong, at least it has ten bathrooms, thank you, thank you.

And why was Stanley incredibly nice to me, so complimentary? Was he really drunk?

(CLARISSA drinks her drink.)

Well, he didn't seem *that* drunk. Is he separated? I guess it doesn't really matter at this point. I don't think Stuart would care or even notice if I had an affair.

(She smooths out her dress and touches her necklace.)

I do like this dress. I think it looks okay. Stanley seemed to really like it. What's wrong with me? Why can't I accept a compliment? I was positively mean to the poor man and all he said was that I looked lovely in my "party dress." He actually said, "party dress." But I should have been gracious, he really meant what he said and I just swatted him and his nice words away. I'm such a haughty bitch aren't I? I don't need anyone. I am a happy island of one. Miss Self Sufficient.

(CLARISSA sinks down into a little, round, backless vanity chair.)

Oh… I don't know if I want to be in this world anymore. It seems so ridiculous to me all of a sudden. Everything seems insane and crazy or maybe I'm insane and crazy. I'm starting to hear things I've never heard before. Last night my nine- year old niece, Harper, ordered lavender sorbet and said, "Can I have two biscotti dipped in espresso and please hold the mascarpone infused with maple syrup?" Those are the words that came out of her mouth. This kid has never had a fluffernutter. I asked her. She said no Aunt Clarissa, what's a fluffernutter? It's *criminal.*

I mean, seriously, what's better about modern life, what? What's better now than it was thirty, forty years ago—besides drugs? Yes, *pharmaceuticals* are better. Ambien, Lorazapam…Xanax for emergencies. Anywho, drugs aside, I can tell you SO many things about modern life that are worse.

Air travel. Hands down—a disaster. No room to move—the stewardesses, excuse me, *flight attendants,* aren't glamorous anymore, sometimes they're positively *fat* and can barely squeeze through the aisle, it's very distressing. And you can't complain about the food because THERE IS NO FOOD. I'm sure it's better in first class but Stuart refuses to go first-class even though we could afford it. On that point I agree with him. Which is practically the only thing we agree about any more.

Multitasking. I hate it. I have one friend, Margaret, who's constantly *multitasking* when she talks to you on the phone—I always hear this horrendous clanging and banging when she's emptying her dishwasher or she'll go into a dead zone and lose me because she's hiking up some mountain or running in the woods with her athletic gaggle of girl friends. They're always biking and hiking and swimming and playing tennis, it all sounds so exhausting to me. Women used to go out to lunch and swap recipes and have a spa day. Now Margaret's into *hot* yoga and she wants to try *goat* yoga, which sounds obscene, I have no idea what it is and I don't want to know. Like I really want a goat on my back.

Romance. Where's the romance these days? Where's mystery and flirtation? Flirtation is practically a crime—I read in *The Atlantic* that some college kids had to get a *signed* permission form before they could kiss the object of their desire. You need a contract?

And where are love notes? The joy of getting a letter from your beloved—

does that exist anymore? I mean, seriously, is a text with a bunch of little emojis as good as a thin blue folded air mail letter, so lightweight you can barely feel it between your fingers, so delicate that you have to open it slowly, tenderly, being extra careful not to rip it? Does the post office even make those letters anymore? Can you collect emails and tie them with a ribbon and hide them under your bed for decades and re-read them when you're ninety? No! I have a wicker basket in the basement full of love notes from old boyfriends that Stuart has no idea about. And he never will.

I was twenty-seven when Stuart and I got married. He was solid, a lawyer, I thought he was nice. He was nice in the beginning but he's not nice now.

Occasionally he reaches for me in bed and I acquiesce—it seems like that's the lesser of two evils, better than rejecting him and having to discuss it, which would be so painful and embarrassing for both of us. I view it as a medicinal thing now, he needs release, and if I have enough vodka beforehand, I get a release too. His body hasn't changed all that much since we were married, he's scrupulous about his squash and tennis. Although I'm fascinated by how, over the years, his testicles have literally *dropped,* they hang so low now, and they're sort of like a pendulum. It's like that song we used to sing in camp: *Do your ears hang low, do they wobble to and fro, can you tie them in a knot, can you tie them in a bow?*

Sometimes while I'm waiting for him to come, *dying* for him to come, I sing that song in my head and I remember camp. The beautiful clean lake, the sound of the loons, the blazing bonfire every Friday night, the piney smell of the woods, the icy cold water in the morning at swim class. I keep saying I'm going to go back for an Alumni weekend but I'm afraid I'll cry too much.

I miss *good* sex. When you read about sex now in magazines it's all about getting off. Sex isn't a sport or a meal. Sex is mysterious, it's magical. The most erotic moment I ever experienced was once many, many moons ago in an ancient Irish bar on Third Avenue. It was a very long, long look between me and a man I could not have, a man I yearned for and it struck me to the bone. Lovely.

(pause)

I have to be more positive. There are better things. Like….*Gelato.* Yes. Gelato is right up there with drugs. There was no gelato when I grew up, just *Howard Johnson's* I think. And I haven't even thought about all the things that have stayed the same over the years. Meatballs. Dogs. The ocean. *Anna Karenina!* And trees! We still have trees. I used to climb trees all the time; we had maple trees in our neighborhood that were perfect for climbing. Wow. When did I stop looking at trees in terms of whether they were good for climbing or not? Jeez. That's what I should do. Climb a tree and eat some gelato.

Maybe Stanley would like to do that with me; he seems like a game, enthusiastic kind of guy. He's probably a history buff who likes opera. And

I bet he cooks, he looks like a man who cooks, who makes a great *spaghetti alla vongole.* Maybe he's not *needy;* maybe he's just *open.* I've always secretly scoffed at men who weren't cold and distant, who didn't seem like they needed anyone. Why? Because I liked the challenge? Was it an ego thing—that only *I* could breech their wall? Why did I marry Stuart anyway?

Maybe I should give a Stanley a try. Why not? Stuart doesn't care.

And maybe I should learn to take a compliment. Let people be kind to me. Let them *in* for God's sake. There's an idea. Why not? What horrible thing could happen?

I feel a little better. I have to smoke a cigarette.

(CLARISSA reaches into her purse, reaches for the cigarette and lights up.)

It's good for my mental health. It's relaxing.

(CLARISSA takes a long drag on the cigarette.)

I think I can go back in the party now—I'll talk to Stanley and tell him I'm glad he likes my "party dress. I'll ask him…what *Netflix* shows do you like, and do you like *spaghetti alla vongole*?

He's sort of adorable, Stanley. He's… cozy. He's probably a little furry and has a soft belly but I bet he's kind. At this point I think I need *kind.* A kind man. And I need to be kind. It's not too late for kindness. Hummm…and I wonder about *his* testicles. Have they reached the pendulum stage or are they still cute little kiwis?

(CLARISSA laughs and then sings.)

Do your ears hang low, do they wobble to and fro, can you tie them in a knot, can you tie them in a bow? Can you throw them over your shoulder like a Continental soldier, do you ears hang low?

(end of play)

THE HANDLE

by Scott Sullivan

Scott Sullivan is a writer and actor from South Hamilton, MA. His full-length play *An American Mosaic* was a finalist for Utah Shakespeare Festival's 2016 New American Playwright's Project and the winner of the 2016 Firehouse Center's New Works Festival's Peter Honegger Prize. His play *The Handle* was part of Boston Playwrights' Theatre's Boston Theater Marathon XXII: Special Zoom Edition. His play *Jennie's Turn* is currently a finalist in this year's A Light in Dark Places Play Festival in Los Angeles, CA. **Contact: scott@sullivantutoring.com**

The Handle was sponsored by **The Actors Studio of Newburyport.** Serving the North of Boston region for 28 years, The Actors Studio is a fifty-seat, black box theater. Our production schedule includes original plays and well- known, contemporary and classic plays. We have a dynamic development program for new plays and we offer a variety of classes including Cold Reading, Musical Theater, On Camera, Scene Study, and Improv. In 2014 and 2017 TASN won the BONS Award as the best small live venue on the North Shore. **www.newburyportacting.org**

The Handle was presented on April 18, 2020 with the following creative team:

Directed by Sherry Bonder
ANTON: Peter Leonard Solis
DANNY: Guthrie Scrimgeour

CHARACTERS:

DANNY: Danny O'Connor, 17, from South Boston

ANTON: Anton Jackson, 23, from East Boston

(Davis Square. Somerville, Massachusetts. An outdoor basketball court on a late weekend afternoon. There is a long metal bench with two duffel bags. There is an unseen basketball court some yards away with guys playing pickup basketball. A hum of rims clanging and guys hollering can be heard, which dies down. DANNY and ANTON enter after just finishing a game.)

DANNY: *(coming off the court, basketball in hand)* That's one ugly shot, man. *(a growing smile)* But ya don't miss.

ANTON: *(as they fist-bump)* Thanks, bro.

DANNY: You're deadly from three.

ANTON: And *you've* got a handle.

DANNY: Thanks. *(grins)* Those guys thought they had us.

ANTON: You see the look on their faces.

DANNY: It's like we took their milk money or somethin'.

ANTON: *(sits)* I love playin' these random courts.

DANNY: Yeah, man. Haven't seen ya here before.

ANTON: First time. What do they say—everyone plays in Somerville once, right?

DANNY: *(grins)* Somethin' like that.

(DANNY starts to dribble the basketball, showing off his handle. He dribbles low and impressively, perhaps like Harlem Globetrotter Curly Neal.)

ANTON: That's what I'm talkin' about! *(He stands.)* Just startin' to teach my son how to play. Maybe one day he'll have your handle.

DANNY: *(He smiles, throws ANTON the basketball.)* As long as he can shoot like his old man.

ANTON: Nah. I'm gonna teach him the proper way. *(mimics with the ball)* Find the seams. Elbow in. All that.

DANNY: That game winner you hit—damn, it was from the hip! How'd ya learn to shoot like that?

ANTON: Just always have. *(two beats)* You from here?

DANNY: Nah. South Boston.

ANTON: *(intrigued somehow)* You're from Southie, huh?

DANNY: What about you?

ANTON: Oh, ya know, all around.

(ANTON puts down the basketball, sits on the bench, and starts to take off his sneakers.)

DANNY: *(indicating ANTON's sneakers)* Those your secret weapons?

ANTON: Oh. These. Nah. Just an old pair.

DANNY: Let me look at 'em. *(visibly struck)* They're 17's, bro.

ANTON: I don't know what that means.

DANNY: Jordan 17's. Originals.

ANTON: *(putting on his other shoes)* Air Jordans have a number?

DANNY: Yeah, the 1's came out in '85 and they've been numberin' 'em ever since. *(fixated on the Jordans)* You remember what these cost when they came out? *(ANTON gives no indication.)* ... Unheard of at the time. They came in like a black steel case. They were designed from jazz music.

ANTON: You sure know a lot about sneakers.

DANNY: Just the Jordans 17's.

ANTON: *(uncomfortable)* … Well, it's been real.

DANNY: Where'd ya get 'em anyhow?

ANTON: Huh?

DANNY: Just curious.

ANTON: Oh, uh—some rack somewhere.

DANNY: You got 'em used?

ANTON: Nah. New.

DANNY: *(two beats)* My dad had a pair.

ANTON: Is that right?

DANNY: Same color, same style…. Ten and a half?

ANTON: Yeah, I think.

DANNY: I never got your name.

ANTON: Anton. Anton Jackson.

DANNY: Danny O'Connor. My dad was Jerry O'Conner. … That ring a bell?

ANTON: Nah—I mean, …should it?

DANNY: One night about seven years ago he was playin' ball in Southie at Moakley Park…and someone stole his sneakers.

ANTON: Ya ever find out…who took 'em?

DANNY: Rumor has it…it was some guy named Damon or Damian. But they never found him…. You're Anton, right?

ANTON: Yeah, man. Anton.

DANNY: …Ya sure?

ANTON: Listen, bro, you've got it twisted if ya think I somehow—

DANNY: I'm just makin' sure your name's really Anton.

ANTON: This is ridiculous.

DANNY: So listen—that *handle* I have—it's because I've been playin' ball

all over Boston, seven years runnin'. I've never seen anybody with those sneakers.

ANTON: There's gotta be a ton of guys with these sneakers.

DANNY: Not in that color and size.

ANTON: What— … you wanna see an I.D.?

DANNY: You got one on ya?

(ANTON smirks. He goes to his bag, takes out an I.D. and hands it to DANNY, who examines it for a moment. DANNY hands the I.D. back to ANTON.)

You must think I'm nuts. *(DANNY sits. Three beats.)* Somethin' was torn from me that day. …Somethin' ya can't replace.

ANTON: Wait, so you're sayin' he was…?

DANNY: Murdered for his sneakers.

ANTON: Jesus.

DANNY: It wasn't easy growing up without him. A kid needs a father, ya know.

ANTON: Mine left when I was three.

DANNY: Damn.

ANTON: I was forced to become the man of the family at an early age. It was just me, my mom and my two little sisters. I guess I wasn't ready.

DANNY: We think we have a handle on things, ya know. A father dyin' …a father leavin' …we can't control any of it.

ANTON: I've always wondered how things might have been different if he had been around.

(The noise of rims clanging and guys hollering can be heard anew. DANNY, in particular, hears the words of a father teaching his son how to shoot: "Elbow in, son. Elbow in. Find the seams.")

DANNY: That was weird, huh? *(two beats)* What'd ya mean different?

ANTON: Huh?

DANNY: You said different. You said you wondered how things might have been different if he had been around.

ANTON: Just— … everything. *(gathering his bag, two beats)* Sorry about your pops.

(ANTON starts to exit.)

DANNY: You sure those aren't his sneakers?

ANTON: Look, Danny, I told ya I'm not the guy you're looking for—

DANNY: I know I'm probably jumpin' the gun but— ...That night he was killed, I was there.

ANTON: You...were there?

DANNY: I was ten. I wasn't supposed to be out that late, but I snuck out. Moakley Park has this hill from where ya can watch.... He was playin' with two other guys. ... Out of the blue one of the guys just sucker-punched him. My dad's head hit the pavement and he was knocked unconscious. They took his sneakers and ran. *(two beats)* I just wish I could have done somethin'.

ANTON: *(fatherly)* You were ten.

DANNY: Yeah but still— ... *(recalling something vaguely)* Ya know, one of the guys...not the one who hit him, but the other one...he could really shoot it.

ANTON: ...Oh yeah?

DANNY: He was deadly from three. He had this weird shot. *(something coming back)* He shot from the hip.

ANTON: ...There are a lot of guys who shoot from the hip. *(starting to exit)* Later, man.

DANNY: *(Four beats. ANTON has almost exited.)* I was sittin' on that hill!

ANTON: *(He stops in his tracks, not turning back yet. Four beats)* You were wearin' a Celtics cap. Green and white, with the leprechaun.

DANNY: You son of a bitch.

ANTON: *(turns)* And you ran towards him. I'll never forget it—

DANNY: *(grabbing the basketball, whipping it at ANTON)* YOU SON OF A BITCH!

ANTON: Take it easy!

DANNY: Are you fuckin' kiddin' me?! I've spent seven years waitin' for this. I swore to myself I'd find the guy who—

ANTON: Just take it easy—

DANNY: Like you did with my father?

ANTON: I didn't throw the punch. That was Damian Miller…and he's dead now. *(DANNY goes to his bag with purpose.)* Look, we didn't mean to— …We just wanted the Jordans… We were just two sixteen-year old kids from East Boston without a clue— *(suddenly apprehensive, seeing DANNY's crazed look)* What are ya gonna do…turn me in?

DANNY: Turn ya in? *(crazed smile, taking a knife from his bag)* Turn ya in?? Are you kiddin' me?

ANTON: No, no, no.

DANNY: I promised myself.

ANTON: I have a family—

DANNY: So did he.

ANTON: My son!

DANNY: He'll have to live without a father just like I did.

ANTON: I'm not runnin' this time, Danny, but don't do this—

DANNY: *(grabbing ANTON by the shirt)* You deserve this, you understand?! Payback for what you did to my father! Payback for—

ANTON: *(blurts it)* I was at the wake!

DANNY: *(letting go of ANTON's shirt)* … What are ya talkin' about?

ANTON: When I heard he had died I knew I had to go. …I remember kneelin' at his coffin and sayin' an *Our Father.*

DANNY: *(coming to terms)* You were there.

ANTON: That moment right there is when I vowed to change.

DANNY: It means somethin' you bein' there, but it doesn't bring him back. Doesn't make up for all the years without him.

ANTON: *(something new registering)* And now you're just tryin' to do what ya couldn't do before.

DANNY: Retribution plain and simple. …I gotta do this, ya understand me?

> *(DANNY lowers ANTON to his knees. DANNY puts the knife close to ANTON's throat. ANTON closes his eyes.)*

You understand me?!

> *(The noise from the courts is heard anew. DANNY hears the words "Elbow in, son. Elbow in. Find the seams." It is unclear whether this is real or imagined.)*

Damn it! *(looking up towards the sky)* I still gotta do this, don't I?? *(at the end of his tether)* DON'T I??? *(three beats, then to ANTON)* HOW OLD???

ANTON: What?

DANNY: Your son! How old's your son?

ANTON: Why are you askin' me—??

DANNY: I SAID HOW OLD???

ANTON: He's three!

(DANNY slowly takes the knife away. He pushes ANTON away from him. Four beats.)

I'm sorry, Danny. … Truly sorry.

(ANTON takes his bag and almost exits. ANTON comes back and puts the Jordans on the bench, without DANNY seeing. ANTON exits. DANNY turns and sees the Jordans. DANNY clutches the Jordans.)

(end of play)

ROOM 221

by Michael Towers

A special thank you to Mr. Bill Bowen and Mr. Joel Gray

Michael Towers is the Artistic Director of Westford Academy Theater Arts and the Summer School for the Performing Arts. In his 20-year career as a theater educator, Michael has been blessed with the opportunity to play the roles of husband, father, director, actor and playwright. *Room 221* is the ninth installment in a ten-play collection entitled *Secondary Ed* which examines the dynamic relationships between teachers and their students at the secondary level. Michael is sincerely grateful to Kate Snodgrass, Boston Playwrights' Theatre, his wife Melissa, and his son Patrick for supporting the continued exploration of his craft. **Contact: forgetheaterco@gmail.com**

Room 221 was sponsored by **Forge Theatre Company**, which borrows its name from the heart of the historic Village where it was born: Forge Village in Westford, MA. At 'the Forge', our stage is the anvil where new plays are wrought in readings, rehearsals, and workshop productions. Our actors, directors, and designers collaborate with the playwright to build trust in each other and to inspire risk in our collective art. Together, we shape thought-provoking theater that invites forward moving conversation and forges a community whose foundation is strong but malleable.

Room 221 was presented on May 15, 2020, with the following creative team:

Directed by Michael Towers
Assistant Director: Kyla Schultz
Stage Manager: Emily Blagg
Original Music Composition: Alex Franklin
MR. BECKER: Robert D. Murphy
KYLE: Conor Bellone
LIZZIE: Elle Whitehead
STUDENT A: Thomas Sanders
STUDENT B: Lucy Xiao
STUDENT C: Caroline Burke
STUDENT D: Olivia Dunn
STUDENT E: Dustin Waterhouse
STUDENT F: Sami Killian
STUDENT G: Jaramie Cataldo
STUDENT H: Eva Plankey
STUDENT J: Alex Ross

CHARACTERS:

MR. BECKER: An older gentleman. There is some distance between he and his students, but only in age.

KYLE

LIZZIE

STUDENT A

STUDENT B

STUDENT C

STUDENT D

STUDENT E

STUDENT F

STUDENT G

STUDENT H

STUDENT J

Students are scripted without names to allow for flexibility in casting in terms of number of students and gender. The students and stage directions refer to a Kathleen but she is not assigned to a specific role. She could be any of the characters who don't specifically speak of her. Student J offers to 'do the push up thing' and given the subsequent dialogue, he can be assumed to be Jeremy.

(Room 221—a Science classroom on the second floor. Student desks. A bay of large windows. A teacher's desk at the head of the classroom. On it: An apple. A wooden yard-stick. A steel rod. A small stack of large elastics.

STUDENTS surround and mask an activity in a space where desks have been moved and the area has been cleared. They stand or squat several rows deep on the floor. Some sit or stand on their desktops or desk chairs to gain a better vantage of the action. The students are exuberant: they chant, laugh and cheer- both in anticipation and disbelief. STUDENTS that are more "removed" than others video the action with their phones and/or take pictures.

The masked activity is a push-up contest between the teacher, MR. BECKER and a student, KYLE. The students are pulling hard for KYLE: it is as if the outcome mattered. All of the students count as KYLE completes each push up. There is perhaps some varying opinions as to what constitutes a completed push up. One student may caution another against cheating. The students are very engaged and very excited. One student, KATHLEEN, serves as the lone counter for MR. BECKER. The action and banter is non-stop.

It doesn't matter what the target number of pushups is. Nor does it matter how many pushups the contestants have completed when the lights come up. But it does matter that both contestants are nearing their objective and they are both tiring.

Much to the chagrin of his students, MR. BECKER wins. KATHLEEN announces a number denoting that it has been achieved. The moans and groans continue through MR. BECKER's subsequent dialogue as he prepares himself once again for instruction. He puts his tie back on or his sweater or his glasses or all of the above.)

MR. BECKER: Let's make this space look like a classroom. Please.

(The STUDENTS reluctantly move the desks back to their proper alignment but as they do, they harass KYLE (who may still be on the floor) and petition MR. BECKER for a "re-do." MR. BECKER enjoys their pathetic attempts. There is a mutual fondness between he and his students. Though the groaning may suggest otherwise, ensure that that this appreciation and respect exists - both ways).

Thank you for your participation Mr. Dolan…and company. The Exam will be tomorrow.

(STUDENTS groan.)

As advertised.

STUDENT A: You suck Kyle.

MR. BECKER: *(addressing STUDENT A)* Unless you'd like it to be today.

STUDENT A: You don't suck Kyle.

MR. BECKER: The good news is:

STUDENT B: You were kidding about the exam.

MR. BECKER: There is a consolation prize.

STUDENT C: Only Kyle has to take it?

MR. BECKER: Second Place…

STUDENT D: Has to bring Dunks.

MR. BECKER: Has to lead the Review.

STUDENT B: What?

STUDENT D: No.

STUDENT A: No.

STUDENT D: Please no.

STUDENT F: Can we pick someone else?

STUDENT B: Seriously.

STUDENT C: What about Kathleen?

STUDENT B: Yes!

STUDENT A: She actually gets this stuff.

(STUDENT C starts a "Kathleen-Kathleen" chant. The other STUDENTS join.)

STUDENT B: Seriously.

STUDENT A: No offense Kyle.

KYLE: None taken.

STUDENT C: If you want us to actually learn something//Kathleen should do it.

MR. BECKER: You chose Kyle as your delegate.

STUDENT B: To do push-ups!

STUDENT A: Can we unchoose him?

STUDENT B: Not Boyle's Law…

MR. BECKER: *(to KYLE)* Apparently your classmates don't share my confidence.

STUDENT G: Boyle's Law is not on the Exam.

STUDENT A: I vote Kathleen.

STUDENT B: Whatever.

STUDENT G: That's Chemistry.

STUDENT C: I volunteer as tribute!

STUDENT B: It was a joke.

STUDENT E: Becker's Physics meets *Hunger Games.*

STUDENT G: Maybe that's why you're failing.

STUDENT H: *(responding to* Hunger Games*)* Pretty much.

STUDENT J: Can I do the push up thing?

STUDENT A: Yes! Let Jeremy do the push up thing!

MR. BECKER: Mr. Dolan?

STUDENT B: Tell us about Frank Purdue again.

KYLE: Are you asking me?

STUDENT L (LIZZY): No! How you met your wife!

> *(The STUDENTS chant: How you met your wife. How you met your wife. How you met your wife. Laughter and commotion. Again, the STUDENTS petition for another chance or a postponement of the exam. Through all of the above and most of what follows,* MR. BECKER *never loses focus on* KYLE.

He never entertains the options. It is almost as if this entire exercise was for KYLE, an opportunity for the student to prove something to himself. KYLE should grow with confidence and clarity as the review continues. MR. BECKER offers KYLE a piece of chalk with which to lead the review.)

MR. BECKER: Young's Modulus of Elasticy.

KYLE: Can I phone a friend?

MR. BECKER: *(a feigned retreat, to the class)* Notebooks away.

(The STUDENTS protest loudly. To MR. BECKER. To KYLE. To KATHLEEN. To anyone who will listen.)

Take out a piece of paper. Name date and section in the upper right-hand corner. Question number one:

KYLE: *(a proclamation over the cacophony)* All materials are elastic.

(The STUDENTS seize the opportunity and immediately quiet down. n tempo and tone, MR. BECKER presses KYLE to perform throughout the following.)

MR. BECKER: Your own words.

KYLE: Stuff stretches.

MR. BECKER: Explain.

KYLE: If I took this rubber band and did this to it, it would…do this…

MR. BECKER: Because?

KYLE: That's what rubbers bands do.

MR. BECKER: So what.

KYLE: So what?

MR. BECKER: So what.

KYLE: If I took this ruler and did the same thing…

MR. BECKER: Same thing?

KYLE: Applied force.

MR. BECKER: To a wooden ruler.

KYLE: It would still stretch.

MR. BECKER: And the steel rod?

KYLE: Same thing.

MR. BECKER: How so?

KYLE: All materials are elastic.

MR. BECKER: So you say.

KYLE: So Young says.

MR. BECKER: Prove it.

KYLE: Young's principal//explores

MR. BECKER: Modulus.

KYLE: Modulus.

MR. BECKER: Measures.

KYLE: How much stress a material can endure.

MR. BECKER: Under?

KYLE: Force…es.

MR. BECKER: Name them.

KYLE: Compression.

MR. BECKER: One.

KYLE: Tension.

MR. BECKER: And:

KYLE: Shear.

MR. BECKER: What about stress?

(STUDENT D offers a momentary underscore but his classmates don't bite.)

STUDENT D: If you want to know what stress is:

MR. BECKER: Definition:

STUDENT D: Try filling out fifteen college applications.

KYLE: Materials must react//under…

MR. BECKER: Must?

STUDENT D: My brother spelled his name wrong.

KYLE: Yes.

MR. BECKER: Show me.

(MR. BECKER picks up the steel rod.)

KYLE: With that?

MR. BECKER: On the board.

(KYLE draws three impressive diagrams on the board. An illustration for: Compression, Tension and Shear.)

Your classmates should have more faith in you.

(A beat: KYLE is accomplished.)

KYLE: Pressure equals Force over Area.

(A muffled popping sound emanating from somewhere outside of the building garners MR. BECKER's attention. His focus is divided as he drifts to the window.)

MR. BECKER: So what.

(KYLE draws the respective formulas on the board as he introduces them below. Popping sound. MR. BECKER searches out the window for the source. The STUDENTS don't recognize the change in MR. BECKER's focus or rhythm, but KYLE is sensitive to it.)

KYLE: Young's Modulus measures//

MR. BECKER: Formula:

(again, the popping sound)

KYLE: Stress over strain.

(Popping sound. KYLE is becoming unnerved but he continues to draw on the board without a directive or a response from MR. BECKER.)

Force over area. And…strain… Mr. Becker? Do you want me to go on? It's the change of length over original length.

STUDENT G: That's what she said!

KYLE: Mr. Becker? *(still drawing a diagram on the board)*

(MR. BECKER walks into the hallway - he is noticeably disturbed. He quickly returns and closes the door behind him, locking it.)

The comparative break point informs the Elastic Modulus Number.

STUDENT A: Can Jeremy please do the push up thing?

MR. BECKER: There's a shooter in the building.

STUDENT B: What?

STUDENT A: Are you joking?

MR. BECKER: Push your desks against the door.

(The STUDENTS who know MR. BECKER *well sense that the urgency is real and respond immediately and quickly move the desks against the door. Others freeze in disbelief. Others object. KYLE locks eyes with* MR. BECKER *amongst the flurry and realizes that his fear is genuine. KYLE jumps into action.)*

LIZZY: Is this a drill?

MR. BECKER: Stack them//...

(popping sound, closer)

LIZZY: Mr. Becker?

(popping, closer, more frequent)

MR. BECKER: As high as you can.

(popping, more frequent)

LIZZY: Please tell me this a drill.

(The first student to respond determines that the classroom door opens "out" and the barricade may be ineffective - a fact that MR. BECKER *knew.)*

KYLE: The door opens out!

(*more popping)*

MR. BECKER: Take your belts off.

(More popping. MR. BECKER *binds the belts to the door and to the barricade in an attempt to prevent it from opening out. KYLE assists him on the "front line." The gunshots are only now very real and undeniable: they are coming from the first floor directly beneath Room 221. Sounds of doors being compromised. Screams. Automatic shots fired. These sounds continue until the end of the play. One classroom at a time. The students of Room 221 respond to every stimulus. They scream, moan, whimper.)*

Get away from the door! Get down and stay down.

(The students sprawl on the floor and crawl so that their backs are against the walls. For a moment, the shots are silenced. MR. BECKER *motions for his students to quiet down and stop moving. He listens and crosses to the windows. The silence is haunting. After a moment,* MR. BECKER *faces his class.)*

(with urgency, but great clarity) There's only one and he can't be everywhere - you understand? You have to get outside and run...

STUDENT A: How are we supposed to do that?!

MR. BECKER: Get to the trees beyond the baseball field.

STUDENT A: We just blocked the only way out!

MR. BECKER: Through the window.

STUDENT A: What?!

MR. BECKER: Don't think-do it now.

(MR. BECKER continues his directives as he assists the students through the window. Some respond and move. Others cower and whimper-reluctant to move. He looks each student in the eyes-offering the encouragement that he can. He constantly checks the area below, beyond, and within, with every sense available to him.)

It's twenty feet to the ground. Bend your knees and roll as soon as you touch get up and run towards the trees as fast as you can you understand? Don't stop. Just run. No matter what you see or what you hear don't stop until you're in the trees. Don't stop until you're in the trees!

(The sound of shots again. The shooter is very close. He is on this floor. Sounds of doors being rattled and breached. Screams. Automatic fire. KYLE remains, crouched with LIZZY. She is disconsolate.)

KYLE: *(overlapping with below)* We have to go Lizzy-we have to go. I'm scared too. You can. Look at me. You can. I'm telling you-you can.

LIZZY: *(overlapping with above)* I can't do it. I'm scared. I can't do it. I can't I can't I can't I can't I can't I can't I can't.

(MR. BECKER addresses LIZZY. He gets onto the ground and looks directly into her face:)

MR. BECKER: You may break a leg if you jump but if you stay, you will die—you understand?

(The shooter is across the hall.)

You can live a long time with a broken leg.

(LIZZY shakes her head.)

MR. BECKER: *(to KYLE)* You have to go.

KYLE: What about//…?

MR. BECKER: We'll be right behind you.

KYLE: I'm not leaving you.

MR. BECKER: Goddammit Kyle go!

(KYLE reaches for LIZZY.)

KYLE: Lizzy please…

(LIZZY doesn't move.)

Mr. Becker…

MR. BECKER: Don't stop until you're in the trees.

(KYLE reluctantly jumps out the window.)

LIZZY: Mr. Becker? Can you help me?

(MR. BECKER squats with her. LIZZY moans. MR. BECKER soothes her as he speaks quietly.)

MR. BECKER: The first time I laid eyes on my wife she was sitting at the end of this horse-shoe shaped bar…

(The classroom door rattles. MR. BECKER rises, picks up the steel rod and positions himself to strike the attacker with the rod when he enters the room. A moment of silence.)

(blackout)

LO-FI

by Caity-Shea Violette

Caity-Shea Violette is a national award-winning and internationally produced playwright. Her plays include *Target Behavior* (Kennedy Center's National Partners of the American Theatre Playwriting Excellence Award Winner, The Lark's Shakespeare's Sister Playwriting Fellowship Semifinalist), *Reap the Grove* (O'Neill National Playwrights Conference Semifinalist, Tennessee Williams/New Orleans Literary Festival Finalist), *Credible* (Blue Ink Playwriting Award Semifinalist), *Slow Jam* (Kennedy Center's Gary Garrison National Ten-Minute Play Award Winner), *The Stand* (Susan Glaspell Playwriting Festival National Award Winner), and others. She is a member of Dramatists Guild of America. Caity-Shea earned her BFA in Theatre from University of Minnesota, Duluth and is a graduate of St. Paul Conservatory for Performing Artists. She is currently pursuing her MFA in Playwriting at Boston University. More information about her work is available at **www.caitysheaviolette.com**.

Lo-Fi was sponsored by the **Boston College Department of Theatre**. The faculty, staff, and students of Boston College Theatre are committed to theatre education that combines study with practice, and scholarship with art. We seek to foster creativity, critical thinking, excellence, and professionalism through the integration of courses, productions, workshops, and other activities. We pursue an understanding of theatre not only as a means of artistic expression and a form of entertainment but as a window onto history, a vehicle for social change, and a method of inquiry into all things human. Our 2020-2021 season will include *Sweat* by Lynn Nottage, *Twelfth Night, Proof* by David Auburn, *Idawalley* by Maggie Kearnan, *The History of Colors* by Charly Evon Simpson, *Monty Python's Spamalot*, Book and Lyrics: Eric Idle, Music: John Du Prez. For more information go to **www.bc.edu/theatre/**

Lo-Fi was presented on May 2, 2020, with the following creative team:

Directed by Patricia Riggin
JAMIE: Noelle Scarlett
CHARLIE: David Makransky
V.O. MAN and SOUND: George Cooke
STAGE DIRECTIONS: Alexandra Lewis

The text of Lo-Fi *is not available for publication in this volume.*

Synopsis: Following their sex therapist's advice, Jamie* and Charlie try desperately to set the mood and practice staying mentally present during physical connection in light of previous trauma. (*Either character can be played by an actor of any gender; please change pronouns freely.)

THE VAMPYR

by James Wilkinson

James Wilkinson is a graduate of Trinity College (Hartford). He is co-artistic director of the Boston-based Exiled Theatre and has directed several productions for the company including *Ashes to Ashes*, *hang*, and *She Looks Good in Black*. As a playwright, he wrote Exiled's productions, *Strange Days: five tales concerning dark paths, odd mercies and birthday cake*, and *Nurse Play*. *Nurse Play* was nominated for a 2018 Independent Reviewers of New England (IRNE) Award for Best New Play. His short plays have been featured in the Boston Theater Marathon (2013, 2020), Salem Theatre Company's Moments of Play, and Roxbury Repertory Theatre's Six Playwrights in Search of a Stage. More information about his work as a playwright can be found on his New Play Exchange profile. Between plays, James works as a rogue theatre critic and founded Bostonstagenotes.com. His reviews also appear on Theatermirror.net and Edge Media Network. **Contact: newplayexchange.org/users/6665/james-wilkinson** and **typewritten45@yahoo.com**

The Vampyr was sponsored by **Commonwealth Shakespeare Company**. CSC is dedicated to artistic excellence, accessibility, and education. We present plays of the highest artistic caliber that celebrate ideas and language to create dialogue around compelling issues of our time. We eliminate barriers – physical, economic, and cultural – to bring live theater to audiences throughout Greater Boston. We cultivate in young artists the value of community engagement, and collaborate with educators to bring literature to life in the classroom. **www.commshakes.org**

The Vampyr was presented on April 21, 2020, with the following creative team:

> Directed by Victoria Townsend
> JOLENE: Jasper Bliss
> CLARICE: Karen Shantz
> MAN/TRAVELER: Josh Telepman

CHARACTERS:

JOLENE: A woman. A maid in the hotel, in uniform.

CLARICE: A woman. Front desk concierge.

GUEST: A guest at the hotel. Feel free to change pronouns as needed.

TRAVELER: A man. A guest at the hotel. If you like, you can double cast with GUEST, just be sure to change the appearance enough to make it clear that these are two different people.

(The front desk at a foreign hotel. There should be a door or entryway to a back office. Late at night after it's gone quiet in the hotel. Maybe around 1 or 2 in the morning. JOLENE stands to the side of the desk. GUEST enters. Perhaps in a bathrobe.)

GUEST: Ma'am? Sorry, there weren't enough towels in our room when we arrived. Any chance we can get a few extra sent up? *(no answer from JOLENE)* Ma'am? *(no answer from JOLENE)* Ma'am? Towels?

JOLENE: *Monsieur, je m'en balance de vos serviettes.*

GUEST: I…uh…Don't speak French.

(CLARICE enters. She sees GUEST.)

CLARICE: Ah! Sir, is there anything I can help you with?

GUEST: Uh…Towels?

CLARICE: Jolene, would you be so good as to get this gentleman some towels?

JOLENE: Off shift.

CLARICE: Jolene.

JOLENE: I'm off shift, Clarice.

(Battle of wills. CLARICE relents.)

CLARICE: *(to GUEST)* Sir, I will have some towels sent right up. What is your room number?

MAN: 408.

CLARICE: They'll be there shortly. *(MAN leaves. To JOLENE.)* You're off shift?

JOLENE: For a couple hours now.

CLARICE: But still in uniform?

JOLENE: If I got out of uniform, it wouldn't look like I belong at the hotel.

CLARICE: Go home Jolene.

JOLENE: Are you working the front desk?

CLARICE: Go home Jolene.

JOLENE: Since when do you work the front desk?

CLARICE: Change in management. Go home Jolene.

JOLENE: They trust you to work the front desk?

CLARICE: Take it up with management. Go home Jolene.

JOLENE: I guess that it is only the night shift…still… *(pause)* I'm staying here tonight.

CLARICE: Are you working first thing in the morning?

JOLENE: I don't want to leave. It's nice when the hotel goes quiet after dark. No one moving in the halls. Except me.

(CLARICE pulls out a key and puts it on the counter.)

CLARICE: Third floor, room twenty-five. It's empty. You can sleep there.

JOLENE: Not tired.

(JOLENE knocks the key to the floor. CLARICE picks it up and puts it back on the counter. JOLENE knocks the key to the floor. CLARICE picks it up and puts it back on the counter.)

CLARICE: You're a child.

JOLENE: There's a vampire up on the fourth floor.

CLARICE: Take the damn key, Jolene.

JOLENE: There's a vampire up on the fourth floor. We crossed paths while I was upstairs. No one else was around. He had a man pinned against the wall who was making a noise. They thought they were alone. The vampire's mouth was on the man's neck and he was sucking. Hard. He had an erection. I think both of them did but I don't think they saw me watching.

(Pause. JOLENE giggles.)

CLARICE: Did you finish attending to the rooms?

JOLENE: Do you not believe me?

CLARICE: Who's the maid on call tonight? Ruth? I'll be checking with her—

JOLENE: *(overlapping)* You're so damn temporal, Clarice.

CLARICE: And if you haven't left every room in a pristine state—

JOLENE: They're so relentlessly needy. Aren't they? The guests. That's all they do all day. They want and need. They want and need. It's enough to make you sick.

CLARICE: If you have an idea on how to run a hotel without guests, take it up with management.

JOLENE: At the end of the hall on each floor, do you know what's there? Of course you don't. No one does because no one notices it. There's a chair no one ever sits in. They serve no function as chairs.

They're decorative, like wallpaper. *(pause)* I sat in one. For two hours and watched the guests go by. No one paid any attention. They carried on like I wasn't there.

CLARICE: You spent two hours on shift doing nothing?

JOLENE: You're skittering past the point, Clarice.

CLARICE: God damn it, I knew that you slacked off—

JOLENE: I don't think the guests, stuck in their cycles of want, realize how close I get to them. Everything they leave, they leave for me. The coffee cups left on the side table. The sheets bunched at the foot of the bed. The bloody tissues stuffed into the toilet. The pools of semen collected in the tub. I know what they're doing. They're daring me to get involved. *(pause)* You've forgotten your towels.

CLARICE: Shit! *(dials telephone)* We're not done with this.

JOLENE: There are days I wish I could be like you.

CLARICE: *(There is no answer on the other line. She tries another number.)* Competent?

JOLENE: You're so happy to get that man his towels.

CLARICE: *(no answer on the other line)* Damn it. Am I the only one working tonight?

JOLENE: Maybe the vampire got her.

CLARICE: *(dry)* Either that or the werewolf on six. What's the number for the housekeeping cell?

JOLENE: I'm off shift.

> *(CLARICE gives a frustrated sigh and goes to a back office.*
>
> *TRAVELER enters in a large coat and carrying a suitcase. He goes to the desk and rings the bell. He looks at JOLENE. She stares back at him. She stares him down. He shifts his weight nervously.)*

Hi, you.

> *(TRAVELER takes out a room key on a tag, throws it on the desk and exits as fast as he can. When he tosses the key, it lands on the floor. JOLENE picks the key up. It is covered with a red liquid that stains JOLENE's hands. She pockets it and goes back to where she was standing. CLARICE reenters.)*

CLARICE: Did someone just come through here?

JOLENE: No.

CLARICE: I thought I heard the bell. (*JOLENE rings the bells twice.*) You are a child! *(CLARICE dials a phone number. Someone picks up on the other line.)* Ruth! There you are…Can you please bring a few extra towels to room 408?...I don't know. Three?

JOLENE: The vampire was on the fourth floor.

CLARICE: *(to JOLENE)* That's a risk I'm willing to have Ruth take. *(to phone)* Yes…No…408…That's right. Thank you, Ruth. Oh, and one more thing. After, do a check of all the unoccupied rooms and let me know if each isn't perfectly made to order…Thank you.

(CLARICE hangs up.)

JOLENE: Temporalist…The rooms are clean.

CLARICE: They better be clean.

JOLENE: They're clean.

CLARICE: Top to bottom.

JOLENE: Top to bottom. *(pause)* Well…as much as I could be expected to do. *(pause)* I left a bed.

CLARICE: Just the one bed?

JOLENE: There was a man on it.

CLARICE: You left the bed?

JOLENE: I can't clean through a man.

CLARICE: You could ask him to get off the bed.

JOLENE: He was handcuffed to the bedframe. *(pause)* It may not have been his fault. Someone may have nicked the "Do Not Disturb" sign. When he saw me, he had a look in his eyes that said I wasn't supposed to see him naked and handcuffed. He probably would have yelled at me to get out, but his mouth was gagged with underwear. He had the saddest penis I've ever seen. It just sort of…flopped…you know how they do. *(pause)* I cleaned the room. I left the bed.

CLARICE: And the bed's contents?

JOLENE: He looked so ashamed when I entered. Then it changed. To fear. When he saw that I was going to vacuum the rug, scrub the bathroom, wiped down the furniture and then leave…I saw it in his eyes. He was so afraid. Of me. Me. Why do you think that was?

CLARICE: What room was he in?

JOLENE: They can do whatever they damn well please. I'd never get involved.

CLARICE: What can I send him? What do we have? Fruit basket?

JOLENE: Why?

CLARICE: Why—? To apologize for your—

JOLENE: For my what? He's not going to bring it up.

CLARICE: Jolene, what's the room number? We at least need to make sure he isn't still—

JOLENE: I watched a woman go into the room afterwards. He's either uncuffed or been smothered with a pillow.

CLARICE: And if it's the latter?

JOLENE: Ugh…They're going to leave it for me to clean aren't they?

CLARICE: JOLENE, THE GOD DAMN ROOM NUMBER!

(pause)

JOLENE: You're really upset about this. Clarice, you can't fall into their traps.

CLARICE: In the morning, when management gets here—

JOLENE: They want you to get involved, but you can't let them—

CLARICE: —And they get wind of your tales about vampires—

JOLENE: The vampire was real!

CLARICE: *(overlapping with following line)* Jolene, I don't care how long you've been here, I will march right into management and demand your fucking pink slip. If I have to scream until I am blue in the face I will not be leaving that office until you are out the door.

JOLENE: *(overlapping with previous line)* I don't understand why you're doubting it. I saw him. I saw them both. It was a vampire in the hotel. Almost like it is in the movies. Why should I lose my job just because you're having a failure of imagination?

(pause)

What's so hard to believe? I saw the two men in the hall—

CLARICE: And one bit the other on the neck?

JOLENE: No. I don't think his teeth were sharp enough.

CLARICE: Pretty sad fucking vampire who can't bite.

JOLENE: He had a little knife.

CLARICE: I mean, what does this vampire do? Gum his victims to death?

JOLENE: Stop it.

CLARICE: He'll starve to death before he gets anywhere.

JOLENE: I told you he had a little knife.

CLARICE: What, a bread knife to butter his victims?

(JOLENE throws the key she picked up from TRAVELER at CLARICE.)

Ow!

JOLENE: The vampire threw the man up against the wall. In his hand he had a little knife. He took that knife and made two stabs at the man's neck. Like this. *(demonstrates two stabbing motions on her own neck [or maybe CLARICE's])* The blood poured out. The vampire drank. I was in the chair at the end of the hallway so he didn't see me. Didn't notice that I was watching.

(CLARICE picks up the key and notices the blood.)

CLARICE: Where did this come from?

JOLENE: The man was going to cry out but the vampire got him in the neck one more time with his little knife. He drank from the hole and the man didn't say much more.

CLARICE: Jolene, where did this come from?

JOLENE: Then the vampire pulled him into one of the rooms and the hall was empty. Like it was any other day. But I know what I saw. I saw a vampire in the hotel.

CLARICE: You—You—Jolene, You didn't do anything?

JOLENE: What's there to do? I had already cleaned the room he was pulled into. I wasn't going to go back in there.

(Somewhere in the hotel, there is a scream.)

There's nothing personal about this. I just don't get involved.

(fade to black)

(end of play)

WITH INTENT

by Stephen Wrobleski

Actually based on a true story

Stephen Wrobleski (Wro) is a writer, director, and actor who has worked all over the New England area in professional and regional theatres. As a director, the bulk of his time has been spent at Wellesley High School where he was the drama teacher for 16 years and won the state championship in the Massachusetts Educational Theater Guild Festival (METG) three times. In 2017 he won the Moss Hart Memorial Award for the devised play *Now In Color*, a story about race at Wellesley High School and the world at large. A passionate filmmaker, Wro has made several short films. Favorites include *Valediction*, which won Best Actress and third place in the Providence 48 Hour Film Project and was a finalist in the FiLMiC pro competition; *On Par*, which won Best of Boston and Best Actress at Boston's 48 Hour Film Project; and *Citizen's Band*, which was accepted to multiple festivals and won Best Sci-Fi for the New England Online Film Festival. He has been a finalist in the NYC Midnight Short Screenplay competition and has written several screenplays and plays, including *TAZORBACK*, *Turmoil*, *Fan Girls' Night Out*, *Aquarium Play*, and the TV series *St. George and the Dragon*. **Contact: wrobleskis@gmail.com**

With Intent was sponsored by **Fresh Ink Theatre**, which provides an avenue for the development of new work on the Boston small theatre scene in a collaborative playwright-centered manner. The company was born in the summer of 2011 and debuted at the Factory Theatre the following December with the nearly sold-out run of Priscilla Dreams the Answer by Walt McGough. Fresh Ink's unique submission model and development process have led to successful runs of plays by local playwrights including Kira Rockwell, MJ Halberstadt, Ginger Lazarus, Walt McGough, Patrick Gabridge, and many more. Fresh Ink also created the Ink Spot Festival of staged readings as another avenue to showcase new work in process, as well as the annual Mad Dash 24-hour play festival, which brings together theatre artists from across Boston to create eight new plays in a single day. Now entering its tenth season, learn more at **www.freshinktheatre.org** for details about the upcoming season.

With Intent was presented on April 29, 2020, with the following creative team:

Directed by Francis Xavier Norton
SARA: Sarah Gadzowicz
PHIL: Bob Mussett
GRANT: Drew Cleveland
MONIQUE: Regine Vital

CHARACTERS:

SARA: An intelligent woman falling in love with Phil.

PHIL: A semi-intelligent man falling in love with Sara.

MONIQUE: Best friend to Sara.

GRANT: Best friend to Phil.

(The action takes place in two separate conversations on each side of the stage. At times we flashback with SARA and PHIL. There is even a moment where all the worlds combine. Two conversations are overlapping each other in different locations on the stage. One between a romantic couple, SARA and PHIL and at different times SARA will talk to her friend MONIQUE and PHIL will talk to his friend GRANT.

The conversation starts with SARA and PHIL talking to their friends, MONIQUE and GRANT, in separate locations. When the lights change, the conversation switches to a flashback where SARA and PHIL are talking to each other, without the presence of their friends.)

SARA: CAN I SHARE SOMETHING?

PHIL: CAN I GET YOUR OPINION?

MONIQUE: Is the relationship going well?

GRANT: I thought she was special.

SARA: It is—was—we had a fight.

PHIL: She is. We had an argument.

MONIQUE: That's all?

GRANT: People argue all the time.

SARA: Not like this.

PHIL: Not like this.

(Lights change.)

SARA: I had to respond to my mother.

PHIL: Were you not listening?

SARA: Really?

PHIL: What did I say, then?

SARA: I'm not taking part in this.

PHIL: If it mattered to you, you would know what I said.

SARA: My feelings are not predicated on whether or not I subsume your every word.

PHIL: Don't say words I only barely understand by context.

SARA: Work on your vocabulary.

PHIL: I could care less about freakin' vocabulary, snob.

SARA: I see. You *couldn't* care less about grammar, too.

(Lights change.)

MONIQUE: He said that to you?

GRANT: She said that to you?

SARA: Yes.

PHIL: Yes.

GRANT: Nothing new here.

MONIQUE: This is pretty common.

GRANT: You get mad at her.

MONIQUE: You get mad at him.

GRANT: It's normal.

MONIQUE: It's normal.

SARA: That's not everything.

MONIQUE: Nice grammar smack down.

GRANT: You didn't know it's "couldn't care" instead of "could care"?

PHIL: Whose side are you on?

MONIQUE: Is he always so defensive?

SARA: He can be a jackass.

(Lights change.)

PHIL: I don't think wanting you to pay attention to me should be an issue.

SARA: It shouldn't be an issue if I don't hear every single word you say.

(pause)

PHIL: Have we had this fight before?

SARA: It feels that way.

PHIL: I don't think it's good to fight like this.

SARA: Are you trying to say that you're done?

PHIL: I didn't say that.

SARA: —Then why did you put it like that—

PHIL: I said that it's not good to fight like this.

SARA: That's what you implied.

(Lights change.)

GRANT: That's not what you said.

PHIL: Exactly.

(Lights change.)

No, I didn't.

SARA: You're impossible to talk to when you get defensive.

PHIL: I'm not defensive.

(Lights change.)

MONIQUE: He sounds defensive.

(Lights change.)

PHIL: You tell anyone that they're defensive, anything they say sounds defensive.

(Lights change.)

MONIQUE: He's being a child.

(Lights change.)

SARA: You're being a child.

PHIL: Don't treat me like a child.

SARA: Could we stick to the matter at hand?

PHIL: You called me defensive.

SARA: You're being defensive.

PHIL: Then you called me a child!

SARA: Stop acting like a child!

PHIL: I'm not a child!

SARA: This has nothing to do with what we're fighting about. It's not important—

PHIL: —it's important to me!

(SARA lets out a long fart without breaking eye contact.)

(Lights change.)

MONIQUE: You did what now?

(Sara shrugs.)

GRANT: Huh?

PHIL: I know.

MONIQUE: That's weird.

SARA: Yeah.

GRANT: She didn't break eye contact?

MONIQUE: You didn't break eye contact?

PHIL: No.

SARA: No.

GRANT: Did you leave?

PHIL: I couldn't: I was transfixed.

MONIQUE: Did you break it off?

SARA: I didn't. He surprised me.

GRANT: Transfixed? She farted at you, with full eye contact.

MONIQUE: You farted with intent.

SARA: I did.

(Lights up on all. For a moment, the worlds blends so now they can all talk to each other.)

GRANT: That's a lot of pressure, right?

MONIQUE: *(to GRANT)* That's some next level shit. *(MONIQUE and GRANT are laughing with each other.)*

GRANT: *(to MONIQUE)* Good one. Ummmm, it really put a strain on the relationship.

MONIQUE: *(to GRANT)* I think you mean stain.

(MONIQUE and GRANT crack up. PHIL starts to laugh. SARA glares at him and he stops.)

SARA: I didn't poop myself. Can we get on with this?

MONIQUE: Fine.

(MONIQUE and GRANT have a laugh wind-down.)

They've skidded to halt. — *(She giggles.)*

SARA: Monique!

MONIQUE: Sorry. *(chuckle)* Sorry. *(serious)*

(Lights change.)

GRANT: Why did you stay?

PHIL: I don't know how to say it.

(Lights change.)

You called me defensive.

SARA: You're being defensive.

PHIL: Then you called me a child!

SARA: Stop acting like a child!

PHIL: I'm not a child!

SARA: This has nothing to do with what we're fighting about. It's not important—

PHIL: —it's important to me!

(FART)

(Lights change.)

There's something about her.

(Lights change.)

SARA: This has nothing to do with what we're fighting about. It's not important—

PHIL: —it's important to me!

(FART)

(Lights change.)

I realized I'd fallen in love.

(Lights change.)

(FART)

(Lights change.)

SARA: I think he's in it.

MONIQUE: If he didn't leave, he's in it.

GRANT: What happened after the...

MONIQUE: The fart.

(Lights change.)

(PHIL and SARA look at each other. They stare at each other.)

PHIL: I'm sorry.

SARA: I'm sorry, too.

(They come together in the center of the stage and hold hands.)

(the end)